101 MARVELLOUS MOVIES YOU MAY HAVE MISSED

David Stratton AM is an award-winning film critic, film historian and lecturer, television personality and producer. He has served as President of the International Critics Jury for the Cannes and Venice Film Festivals, and was for 28 years co-host with Margaret Pomeranz of SBS's *The Movie Show* and ABC's *At the Movies*. A former critic for international film industry magazine *Variety*, he currently writes for *The Australian*.

Other books by David Stratton

I Peed on Fellini: Recollections of a life in film
The Avocado Plantation: Boom and bust in the Australian film industry
The Last New Wave: The Australian film revival

101 MARVELLOUS MOVIES

YOU MAY HAVE MISSED

DAVID STRATTON

ALLEN&UNWIN
SYDNEY · MELBOURNE · AUCKLAND · LONDON

First published in 2018

Copyright © David Stratton 2018

Allen & Unwin
83 Alexander Street
Crows Nest NSW 2065
Australia
Phone: (61 2) 8425 0100
Email: info@allenandunwin.com
Web: www.allenandunwin.com

A catalogue record for this
book is available from the
NATIONAL
LIBRARY   National Library of Australia
OF AUSTRALIA

ISBN 978 1 76063 212 0

Internal design by Bookhouse, Sydney
Set in 11/14.6 pt Minion Pro by Bookhouse, Sydney
Printed and bound in Australia by Griffin Press

10 9 8 7 6 5 4 3 2 1

Contents

Introduction

How does a good movie become forgotten, overlooked or neglected? There are, not surprisingly, many reasons.

Often it's because the film in question failed at the box office on its original release and thereafter fell into that gaping limbo where movies perceived to be unsuccessful wind up. So why does a good movie fail in the first place?

The word 'good' is, of course, highly subjective. Some of the 101 films included in this book received poor or mixed reviews on their initial release, and that alone may be the reason for their later obscurity.

A film's lack of success can also be a matter of timing. It may open at just the wrong moment, perhaps because some entirely unconnected event resulted in audiences staying away. This was the case with some films scheduled to open in September 2001, one of which (*Buffalo Soldiers*) is included here.

There are more mundane reasons. Almost every week four or five feature films open, sometimes more. Reviewers can't always cover them all, and film-goers—unless they're extremely dedicated—can usually manage to see only one of them. The method by which films are released these days—on multiple cinema screens—means that if a film is not a success over the opening weekend it may have disappeared by the following Thursday.

This is particularly true of Australian films, which can be overlooked because they're often handled by small distributors without access to the generous promotion and advertising budgets available to the larger companies. Nineteen 'pure' Australian films are listed in the following pages, plus three co-productions, made in collaboration with other countries.

When I accepted the challenge to compile this book I made the entirely arbitrary decision to include no film made before 1980. This was because the field would have been just too vast if I had reached way back into the cinema's distant past to find neglected gems. I also decided to include only films made in the English language, although there is one exception to this—Angelina Jolie's debut as director, *In the Land of Blood and Honey* (2011).

Some of the films listed in the book are very small productions. I've included the first low-budget features of important directors like Alexander Payne and Christopher Nolan, because comparatively few people have seen them. On the other hand, there are also films made by some very famous directors, among them David Lynch, Ang Lee and Sidney Lumet. And, somewhat surprisingly, perhaps, there are forgotten films that star very famous and popular actors, including Cate Blanchett, Dustin Hoffman, Sean Connery, Clint Eastwood, Meryl Streep, Paul Newman, Robert Redford, Robert De Niro, Al Pacino, Annette Bening, Jack Nicholson and Denzel Washington.

A few of the films I've included were never released in cinemas in Australia and some others never even made it to video. During my research for this book, I managed to view all but one of them again, though a few were hard to find. In one instance the film director was kind enough to direct me to a video link, and in another the producer was able to lend me a rare, out-of-print, DVD. I hope that if readers become interested in some of these titles and try to seek them out they'll be successful—there are so many ways to locate a hard-to-find movie these days. In order to give you a headstart, the publisher has included a list of the ways you may be able to access these movies at the back of the book.

You'll find all kinds of films included in *101 Marvellous Movies*: comedies, westerns, musicals, thrillers, romances. For me one of the most interesting genres is that of the political film, and it became clear, while working on the book, that this is the genre that is probably most difficult to market in the cinema. Audiences, it seems, aren't very keen to go to the cinema to see political films and, given that reality, it's interesting that so many are still being produced.

I hope this book serves as a reminder of films you might have seen long ago and would like to see again, or, even better, that it introduces you to films you may want to discover for the first time.

I don't claim that the 101 films listed here are masterpieces, but they are all films that are well worth seeing for one reason or another. Certainly they don't deserve the obscurity into which most of them have fallen. And they're the tip of the iceberg—there are many more neglected movies waiting to be re-discovered. I wish you joy as you discover these, and many more, marvellous movies.

Dates and times

There is often confusion regarding the dates and running times of films.

Information sites such as IMDB or Wikipedia will assign to a film the date of its first release. My method is to go to the film itself and use the copyright date that appears on the film. For example, although it was released in 1986, *At Close Range* carries the date 1985 on the film itself, and this is the year under which it's listed here.

Running times can vary widely according to which version of the film is seen. My twenty years as a *Variety* reviewer schooled me in the practice of timing every movie and not relying on outside sources. The running times listed here have all been timed by me, with a stopwatch, starting at the opening image and ending at the conclusion of the credits. Some variations may occur when a film is played on a PAL region DVD.

Generally speaking, I've attempted to list the main production companies of the films rather than the names of the distributors, which may vary from country to country, or funding bodies not directly involved in the production.

I offer apologies in advance for any errors the reader might discover.

Affliction

(USA, 1997)

Largo Entertainment. DIRECTOR/SCRIPT: Paul Schrader. ACTORS: Nick Nolte, James Coburn, Sissy Spacek, Willem Dafoe, Mary Beth Hurt, Jim True, Marian Seldes, Holmes Osborne, Brigid Tierney, Sean McCann. 110 MINS.

The township of Lawford, Upstate New Hampshire. Wade Whitehouse (Nick Nolte), the community's only policeman, is separated from his wife, Lillian (Mary Beth Hurt), who has custody of their teenaged daughter, Jill (Brigid Tierney). On Halloween night, Lillian allows Wade time with Jill, but being in the company of her father and his friends makes Jill uncomfortable and she calls her mother to fetch her. Next day Wade's friend Jack (Jim True) takes a wealthy outsider, Evan Twombley (Sean McCann), on a deer hunt; Twombley is shot dead in what it is assumed was an accident. Wade, who is in love with Margie Fogg (Sissy Spacek), visits his parents but discovers that his mother has frozen to death because his father, Glen (James Coburn), hasn't had the heating system fixed. Obsessed with obtaining custody of Jill, and convinced by his younger brother, Rolfe (Willem Dafoe), that Jack has murdered Twombley and that organised crime is somehow involved, Wade becomes increasingly irrational and violent.

Affliction is an adaptation of a semi-autobiographical novel by Russell Banks, who also wrote *The Sweet Hereafter* (which was turned into an excellent film). It's a stark movie, made bleaker because of its wintry setting in a snowbound, isolated community. The central theme is the way violence afflicts everyone who comes in touch with it. In grainy, jittery flashbacks we see that Glen Whitehouse—a role for which James Coburn won a Best Supporting Actor Oscar—is a brute of a man who drunkenly assaults his wife and sons. In adult life, Rolfe has managed to escape and is a teacher at a university in another state: it's he who occasionally narrates the film, and at the very beginning tells us that it's 'the story of my older brother's criminal behaviour and disappearance', so we know from the start to expect the worst.

Wade lives in fear of following in his father's drunken, ignorant, violent footsteps. His marriage has collapsed, he has no relationship with his daughter, and he is on testy terms with most of the people in the community, the exception being the sweet Margie and even she, eventually, gives up on him. Ironically it's his rational and articulate brother who sows the seeds of suspicion in Wade by giving him the idea that Twombley may have actually been murdered. And it's Wade's typically tough and uncompromising approach towards the suspects, including his businessman boss, Gordon LaRiviere (Holmes Osborne), that leads to his downfall.

Director Paul Schrader also grew up in an isolated and restrictive environment, but escaped from it thanks to his love of cinema. He came to attention as a screenwriter—*Taxi Driver* was one of his first successes—and has since directed a large number of films of varying quality but always of interest. *Affliction* is one of his finest achievements, a movie that evokes the Scandinavian family dramas of Ibsen and Strindberg in a harsh, violent American setting; and Nick Nolte gives arguably his finest performance as the inarticulate, hopeless and ultimately pathetic Wade.

By its very nature, a drama as bleak and uncompromising as this one would struggle to find an audience in the multiplexes, so it was no real surprise that, despite its award recognition, the film quickly disappeared, and seems since to have been almost entirely forgotten.

After Dark, My Sweet

(USA, 1990)

Avenue Pictures. **DIRECTOR:** James Foley. **SCRIPT:** Robert Redlin, James Foley, from the book by Jim Thompson. **ACTORS:** Jason Patric, Rachel Ward, Bruce Dern, George Dickerson, James Cotton, Corey Carrier, Rocky Giordani. **110 MINS.**

The American Southwest. Kevin Collins (Jason Patric) quit the boxing ring after killing a man and spent some time in a mental institution. Now he's hitchhiking rather aimlessly through America ('I wonder where I'll be tomorrow?' he muses in voice-over narration). The day after he speaks these words he goes for a drink in a bar in a small Californian desert town, where he meets Fay Anderson (Rachel Ward), an alluring widow who, without much hesitation, tells him 'I'm taking you home with me.' She treats him like a child ('Come on now, there's a good boy') and introduces him to 'Uncle' Bud (Bruce Dern), a former cop. But at first she rejects his sexual advances, instead offering him a job as a gardener/handyman, with accommodation supplied. Fay and 'Uncle' Bud discuss with Collins the proposed kidnapping of Charlie Vanderventer (James Cotton), the schoolboy son of a local millionaire, and Bud claims that his contacts within the police department will alert him to the progress of the police investigation after the child is taken. Fay, who is becoming fond of 'Collie', as she calls Collins, has concerns that he may be in over his head. The kidnapping goes ahead, but initially Collie kidnaps the wrong child. Eventually he succeeds in snatching Charlie and brings the boy, who suffers from diabetes, back to Fay's house.

The books of pulp fiction writer Jim Thompson (1906–77) were regularly brought to the screen by both American and French directors; *The Killer Inside Me*, *The Getaway*, *The Grifters* and several others made tasty thrillers, and Thompson also collaborated on the screenplays of the Stanley Kubrick films *The Killing* and *Paths of Glory*. James Foley's film of Thompson's *After Dark, My Sweet* sticks pretty closely in outline to the book, though the end result is quite a long way from the sort of thing we expect from classic film noir. Using the Scope screen and filming on location in bright sunlight, Foley creates a character-driven suspense film without the usual trappings of the minor thriller genre. Indeed the title is a misnomer—not a single scene takes place after dark.

Otherwise, there's a classic set-up: a flawed good guy on the run from his past; a femme fatale who goes around in shorts, has a predatory eye for the main chance and who says of her late husband 'He's gone to hell!'; an obviously crooked ex-cop; and a kidnap plot that, predictably, doesn't go according to plan, bringing in its wake death and disaster. Yet Foley's deliberately languid handling of this material subverts the genre at every turn. It's 80 minutes before Collie and Fay finally have sex together—in a steamy, extended sequence—and the climax comes with abrupt suddenness, to be followed by a strangely desolate epilogue.

Patric is effective in the lead, playing a character everyone, but him, considers to be stupid and therefore just the patsy needed for their elaborate plot. But it's Rachel Ward, in one of the best of the handful of starring roles she was given in Hollywood films of the 80s and early 90s, who lights up the screen as the unpredictable Fay. Bruce Dern brings quiet menace to the part of 'Uncle' Bud, the instigator of the foolhardy plot.

Made by a small production company, the film attracted little attention at the box office after its premiere at the Montreal World Film Festival.

3

Agora

(SPAIN, 2009)

Mod Producciones. DIRECTOR: Alejandro Amenábar. SCRIPT: Alejandro Amenábar, Mateo Gil. ACTORS: Rachel Weisz, Max Minghella, Oscar Isaac, Ashraf Barhom, Rupert Evans, Michael Lonsdale, Homayoun Ershadi, Sammy Samir, Richard Durden. 141 MINS.

Alexandria, Egypt, AD 391. Egypt is still part of the Roman Empire, but Rome's power is waning. Hypatia (Rachel Weisz) teaches philosophy to students in the city's great Library; among her devoted followers are Davus (Max Minghella), a slave, and Orestes (Oscar Isaac), both of whom are obviously attracted to her. But Hypatia makes it clear she has no time or inclination for a relationship and rejects the advances of Orestes in a humiliatingly public fashion. Evangelical Christians, led by Bishop Cyril (Sammy Samir), are becoming increasingly provocative; the Alexandrians challenge these radicals but are overwhelmed by an unexpectedly large force, and the Library is sacked. Roman officials strike a truce, but four years later the Romans themselves have converted to Christianity and now the Christians find themselves in conflict with the Jews. Bishop Cyril insists that Alexandria be purged of non-Christians, and this includes Hypatia.

In some ways a throwback to the sort of Roman-era epics of the late 50s and early 60s (spectacles like *Ben-Hur* and *Spartacus*), this handsomely produced, English-language Spanish film was made in Malta on huge sets that recreated ancient Alexandria and its famous Library. Unusually for this sort of film, the Christians are not the good guys—in fact, as led by the fanatical Bishop Cyril (ironically played by an Egyptian-born actor), they are as brutally intolerant and ideological as today's Taliban. And this is presumably the position of Alejandro Amenábar, whose previous films included *The Others* and *The Sea Inside*. When fanatical Christians attack and

4

desecrate the Library, a great centre of knowledge and learning, it's a crime similar to the destruction of the Buddhas of Bamiyan by the Taliban—or the bombing of the National Library of Sarajevo.

I know of no other film that features the character of Hypatia, who must, indeed, have been a most remarkable woman, an astronomer as well as a philosopher and teacher. Stunningly well played by Weisz, this is a character of steely commitment and devout morality who finds herself almost alone in facing the enemies of knowledge and education. Scenes in which Hypatia and her elderly father, Theon (Michael Lonsdale), discuss the things that matter to them are most beautifully done.

Agora—the title refers to the marketplace in the centre of the city—is an immensely ambitious film, and a very beautiful one. In a way its theme explores the very origins of today's Middle East conflicts, and does so with lucidity and power.

Unfortunately, it failed to find an audience, perhaps because it was made without the support of a major distributor, but more likely because of the essentially downbeat subject matter. Films in which the 'good guys' lose as comprehensively as they do here are difficult to market as entertainment, and *Agora* was seen neither as a 'serious' film for the world's art-houses nor as a mainstream action spectacle. All credit goes to Amenábar for his ambition, and the skill with which he's realised this very impressive film which, one hopes, will become better regarded and better known with the passage of time.

An immensely ambitious film,
and a very beautiful one

Apartment Zero

(UK, 1988)

Summit Co. **DIRECTOR/SCRIPT**: Martin Donovan. **ACTORS**: Colin Firth, Hart Bochner, Dora Bryan, Liz Smith, Fabrizio Bentivoglio, Cipe Lincovsky, Juan Vitali, Mirella D'Angelo, James Telfer, Francesca d'Aloja, Miguel Ligero, Elvia Andreoli, Luis Romero. 124 MINS.

Buenos Aires, 1988. Adrian LeDuc (Colin Firth), though born and bred in Argentina, dresses—in suit and tie—and acts like a particularly fastidious Englishman. His mother (Elvia Andreoli) is dying in hospital. Adrian runs a repertory cinema, but audiences are declining (just two women show up for a screening of Orson Welles' *Touch of Evil*; 'Videos are killing me,' he complains) and he needs money. He decides to rent out a room in his large apartment, which is filled with photographs of movie stars, and eventually settles on Jack Carney (Hart Bochner), an American who claims to work for an international computer company. Jack, who in Adrian's view has something of James Dean about him, ingratiates himself with the other residents of the apartment building, including a pair of elderly Englishwomen (Dora Bryan, Liz Smith); Vanessa, a transgender woman (James Telfer); Carlos (Fabrizio Bentivoglio), a ladies' man; and Laura (Mirella D'Angelo), a neglected wife. A serial killer is terrorising the district, having killed twelve victims so far. Adrian, who is attracted to Jack, eventually discovers that he was formerly a mercenary, brought to Argentina at the time of the military junta to take part in the killing of those opposed to the regime. Could it be that he's *still* killing?

Martin Donovan, who was born in Buenos Aires, has directed and written a small handful of films of which *Apartment Zero* is the most distinguished. Unfolding just six years after the Falklands War between Britain and Argentina, it carries resonances not only of that conflict (when Adrian tries to hail a taxi the driver, assuming he's British, takes off yelling 'Malvinas!' at him), but also of the bitter period of the 'disappeared', when opponents of the military junta vanished, presumably murdered. Donovan creates a sinister atmosphere somewhere between Hitchcock and David Lynch as the outwardly charming Jack befriends every inhabitant of the gracious old apartment building, while the anti-social Adrian keeps his distance. (He says of an acquaintance: 'He didn't know who Geraldine Page [a famous American actress] was. I couldn't talk to him after that.') The film is pervaded with a very black sense of humour as, for example, in a scene that evokes Hitchcock's *Frenzy*, Jack is forced to break some bones in order to fit a corpse into a small trunk—or in a typical film-buff conversation: 'Did you see *Blue Velvet*?' 'No, but I saw *National Velvet*.'

Firth plays the inhibited, starchy quasi-Englishman to perfection, while Canadian actor Bochner is so effective as the ingratiating but creepy Jack that you wonder why he hasn't had a more prominent career. And it's great to see Dora Bryan and Liz Smith as the chatty English spinsters who have somehow established themselves in a comfortable ménage so far from home.

The combination of politics, suspense and humour, plus the fact that Colin Firth wasn't as big a name as he would later become (his Mr Darcy was another seven years away), resulted in a film very few people saw at the time, and it doesn't have much of a reputation. It's certainly overlong, and drags a bit in the middle. But its intriguing blend of genres and moods, and the eerie atmosphere it creates, make it ripe for rediscovery.

5

At Close Range

(USA, 1985)

Hemdale. DIRECTOR: James Foley. SCRIPT: Nicholas Kazan. ACTORS: Sean Penn, Christopher Walken, Mary Stuart Masterson, Christopher Penn, Crispin Glover, Candy Clark, Millie Perkins, R.D. Call, David Strathairn, Kiefer Sutherland, J.C. Quinn, Eileen Ryan. 111 MINS.

Rural Pennsylvania, 1978. Brad Whitewood Jr (Sean Penn) lives with his younger brother Tommy (Christopher Penn), his mother (Millie Perkins) and grandmother (Eileen Ryan) in a dilapidated farmhouse. He hangs out with his mates in town and is attracted to sixteen-year-old Terry (Mary Stuart Masterson). One day Brad's father, Brad Sr (Christopher Walken), who had abandoned the family years earlier, shows up unexpectedly. Brad Jr is drawn to his father, even when he discovers he is the leader of a ruthless gang of thieves. Brad Sr shows his son how to launder money, but is angered when Brad Jr introduces Terry to members of the gang. Brad Sr discovers from an informer that the FBI is moving in on him; he has the informer killed and then sets about eliminating anyone who might be able to give evidence against him, including members of his own family.

Made five years before *After Dark, My Sweet* (see #2), James Foley's second feature is based on the true story of the 'Johnston Gang', who had recruited teenagers to help take part in robberies in rural Pennsylvania and who had cold-bloodedly executed younger gang members in an attempt to preserve security. The screenplay, by Nicholas Kazan—son of the eminent film and stage director Elia Kazan—concentrates on the relationship between the ruthless father and his impressionable sons, especially the older son. Early scenes establish Brad Jr as a reckless but basically decent kid who stands up for his mates when he perceives one of them is being ripped off. But once Brad Sr, menacingly played by Christopher

Walken, re-enters the boy's life, things change. The older man's surface charm belies an utterly ruthless disposition, but it takes some time for his son to appreciate this fact—and, when he does, it's too late.

Brad Jr's principal relationships are with his brother, Tommy, played by Sean Penn's younger brother, Christopher, and with Terry, the sweet, innocent teenager with whom he falls in love. 'Don't say anything against the family' warns Brad Sr early in the film, but when his son becomes alienated from him—horrified by the ruthlessness with which his father deals with potential informers—both Brad Jr and Terry find themselves in mortal danger. As the film builds towards its climax it becomes almost unbearably tense, a tribute to the brilliantly controlled direction and the very strong performances. Notable too is the fine location photography by Juan Ruiz Anchía. The film's one major miscalculation is the song 'Live to Tell', performed by Madonna (Sean Penn's wife at the time) over the end credits, jarringly shattering the mood established in the film's final scenes.

At Close Range premiered at the 1986 Berlin Film Festival, where it was well received—but it proved to be almost too intense for audiences to handle. The film was scheduled to open in Australia soon after the establishment of *The Movie Show* on SBS television that year. The distributor declined to arrange the usual advance press screening, but having seen the film in Berlin I was eager to cover it on the program—despite that, a screening for Margaret Pomeranz was refused. Lacking almost anything in the way of promotion or distributor support, the film disappeared after a few days.

6

An Awfully Big Adventure

(UK, 1994)

Portman Productions. DIRECTOR: Mike Newell. SCRIPT: Charles Wood, from a novel by Beryl Bainbridge. ACTORS: Hugh Grant, Alan Rickman, Georgina Cates, Alun Armstrong, Rita Tushingham, Peter Firth, Prunella Scales, Alan Cox, Edward Petherbridge, Nicola Pagett, Carol Drinkwater, Pat Laffan. 112 MINS.

Liverpool, 1947. Fifteen-year-old Stella Bradshaw (Georgina Cates) lives with her Uncle Vernon (Alun Armstrong) and Aunt Lily (Rita Tushingham). She never knew her parents, but from time to time phones her mother, who apparently lives in London, and pours out her heart to her. Stella is stagestruck and persuades her uncle and aunt to allow her to audition at the Playhouse, the local repertory theatre where the General Manager is Meredith Potter (Hugh Grant). Besotted with Meredith, Stella is too naive to realise that he's gay. When the well-established actor P.L. O'Hara (Alan Rickman) joins the company to play Captain Hook in a production of *Peter Pan*, Stella is a prime target for the womanising actor.

Beryl Bainbridge's book takes its title from a line in J.M. Barrie's *Peter Pan*, and its incisive portrait of life backstage in a repertory theatre in a provincial city during the post-war period has been lovingly brought to the screen by Mike Newell, who was coming off the international success of his previous film, *Four Weddings and a Funeral*. Newell deftly explores the lives of these hard-working thespians, the backstage gossip, the secret relationships, the betrayals and disappointments. All this is seen through the extremely unworldly eyes of its young protagonist, who is most beautifully portrayed by Georgina Cates, a talented actor whose career so far hasn't lived up to the promise of this early role. Not yet sixteen, Stella is welcomed at first as a dogsbody by Potter and his stage manager, Bunny (Peter Firth), but is completely unable to comprehend the undercurrents of jealousy and tension among her fellow thespians. Stella's innocence is so complete that it comes as quite a shock when she's almost off-handedly seduced by the wearily decadent O'Hara (Alan Rickman); 'I'm beginning to get the hang of this,' she observes, brightly, during their second liaison. As the jaded roué, Rickman perfectly conveys the supercilious boredom of a relatively celebrated man who is quite accustomed to having his way with young women and who will think nothing more of their relationship the next day. In one of his finest roles, Hugh Grant's gay actor–manager is also totally convincing.

The film takes a little while to establish its mood, and there are a few minor confusions as marginal characters are rather haphazardly introduced. Nor do the characters of Stella's uncle and aunt completely convince. But the strengths of the film far outweigh its weaknesses.

Unwisely, the distributors promoted the film as being the latest from the director and star of *Four Weddings and a Funeral*, an accurate but very misleading assertion. *An Awfully Big Adventure*—even the title promises a different kind of movie—is a very dark film indeed, dealing as it does with a form of paedophilia and, as it turns out, incest. As a result the film, which apart from one or two establishing shots of the Liverpool waterfront was shot entirely in Dublin, fared poorly at the box office and quickly disappeared, so that the exceptional performances from most members of the cast have been pretty much forgotten.

An incisive portrait of life backstage in a repertory theatre in a provincial city

7

Bad Blood

(NEW ZEALAND/UK, 1981)

Southern Pictures–NZ Film Commission. DIRECTOR: Mike Newell. SCRIPT: Andrew Brown. ACTORS: Jack Thompson, Carol Burns, Denis Lill, Donna Akersten, Martyn Sanderson, Marshall Napier, Cliff Wood, David Copeland, Ken Blackburn, Pat Evison. 109 MINS.

Koiterangi, South Island, New Zealand, 1941. In this small farming community inland from Greymouth and dwarfed by snow-capped, mist-shrouded mountains, Stan Graham (Jack Thompson) and his wife Dot (Carol Burns) live with their two children in the small wooden house Stan built, located opposite the local school. The Grahams are outsiders in this cloistered part of the country, and conflict arises when Stan refuses an order issued by the wartime government to hand over his guns to the police. After milk from the Grahams' cows is rejected as unfit for consumption, matters come to a head; Stan threatens a neighbour with his gun. Police arrive to investigate, and Stan shoots three of them, later also killing a civilian who attempts to help the wounded officers. Stan flees, but returns to the house at night and kills three volunteer members of the Home Guard stationed there. He is badly wounded, but hides out in the bush while a large-scale manhunt, involving the army, begins.

This tragic true story, brought to the screen by New Zealand writer/producer Andrew Brown and British director Mike Newell, stars Jack Thompson in arguably his finest screen performance as the unstable Stan Graham. Pugnacious, aggressive and not very bright, Stan—egged on by his equally unstable wife, Dot (a great performance from Carol Burns)—escalates his feud with his neighbours from violent arguments to lethal force. Newell stages the steady progression of Stan's anti-social behaviour with skill, and there's considerable suspense once the shooting starts.

What makes this tragedy even more affecting is the presence of the Graham children, who witness the murders committed by their father in the confined space of their little house. 'My Dad shot all the cops,' proclaims Stan's small son, with what sounds like admiration. While Stan himself is a rather pathetic, simple character, Dot is more complex. A former barmaid, she feels she has always been rejected by the locals and harbours a deep grudge against them. 'They got what was coming to them,' she mutters to herself after the deaths of the policemen.

The film is also impressive in its depiction of this small community: the scattered houses, the dirt road, the little local store, the church, the dance hall where people of all ages gather on Saturday nights (a social event despised by the anti-social Grahams). Once the police have been killed, confusion reigns as the untrained, undisciplined volunteers gather cheerfully at first, as though it were all part of an extravagant game, and then anxiously when they grasp they may have to face a killer who, they now realise, won't hesitate to kill again.

There's also a dry sense of humour to *Bad Blood*, epitomised in a scene in which one of Stan's few defenders repeats a quote attributed to Goebbels: 'Tell Stan to hold the South Island and I'll send another bugger to take the North.'

One of the film's outstanding elements is the photography by Australian Gary Hansen, whose images evoke this rainy, misty, rather grey part of the world so powerfully that you can almost feel the damp. The future director of *Once Were Warriors*, Lee Tamahori, is credited with operating the sound boom on the film.

Perhaps the film's box-office failure, and consequent slide into obscurity, has something to do with the very intensity, power and intelligence with which the filmmakers have brought this tragic story to the screen.

8

Bad Influence

(USA, 1990)

Epic Productions. DIRECTOR: Curtis Hanson. SCRIPT: David Koepp. ACTORS: Rob Lowe, James Spader, Lisa Zane, Tony Maggio, Marcia Cross, Christian Clemenson, Kathleen Wilhoite. 100 MINS.

Los Angeles. Michael Boll (James Spader), a data-processing executive at a finance company, is eager to be promoted to Senior Analyst, but his rival, Patterson (Tony Maggio), is secretly sabotaging him and has removed the vital Section 47, on which Michael has been working, from the computer system. Breaking a lunch date with his controlling fiancée, Ruth (Marcia Cross), Michael gets into an argument with a man in a bar and is helped by a stranger. The stranger, Alex (Rob Lowe)—who we previously saw walking out on his naked girlfriend and throwing souvenirs of their time together into a garbage truck—befriends Michael and soon discovers that he's not happy about his impending marriage and is anxious about securing the promotion. Alex introduces Michael to the sultry Claire (Lisa Zane) and secretly films them having sex together on Michael's own video camera; he then arranges to have the video screened to guests at a party to celebrate the engagement of Michael and Ruth. He gets Michael drunk one night and they rob a couple of retail stores at gunpoint. Next day Patterson withdraws from the Senior Analyst contest after being badly beaten up. Realising that Alex was behind all these events, Michael sends him away—but Alex retaliates violently.

Bad Influence was directed by Curtis Hanson, a skilled filmmaker with a wide knowledge of and love for cinema history. The influences here come from Alfred Hitchcock, and especially *Strangers on a Train*, another film in which a weak man is manipulated by a wily and devious stranger with murder as the end result. Michael lives in an apartment converted from an old warehouse and has filled the place with stuff he rarely uses, including the video camera that will be used against him, and a bag of golf clubs—one of which proves a handy weapon later on for the maniacal Alex. Michael is 'a drip' (the description given to him by a bar-room bully), and all too easily falls under the spell of Alex, a handsome, charming, manipulative psychopath. Alex is adept at lying, effortlessly gatecrashes parties to which he is not invited, and all too easily homes in on Michael's many weaknesses. His motive seems to be nothing more than sadistic enjoyment; he loves getting under the skin of Michael and changing his 'friend's' life, but his utter ruthlessness is his undoing. In the end, Michael's greatest ally proves to be his older brother, Pismo (Christian Clemenson), whom he had previously despised because he had served a short prison term for drug dealing and because he was always borrowing money.

In casting the film, Hanson takes full advantage of Rob Lowe's real-life bad boy image, and the fact that James Spader had recently been seen in the edgy *sex, lies, and videotape*. And the director displays his film-buff credentials when he has Jean-Luc Godard's *Alphaville* screening on the wall of a room where a party is taking place. Hitchcockian quotes abound.

Despite good reviews, the film was only a moderate success in 1990 and has been little seen since. Hanson went on to make two more impressive thrillers (*The Hand That Rocks the Cradle* and *The River Wild*) as well as his 1997 breakthrough, *L.A. Confidential*.

9

Beyond Rangoon

(USA, 1995)

Castle Rock Entertainment. DIRECTOR: John Boorman. SCRIPT: Alex Lasker, Bill Rubenstein. ACTORS: Patricia Arquette, U Aung Ko, Frances McDormand, Spalding Gray. 99 MINS.

Burma (Myanmar), 1988. Laura (Patricia Arquette), recovering from the murders of her husband and small son by a home invader, is travelling in Asia with her sister, Andy (Frances McDormand). One night, on a stopover in Rangoon, she witnesses Aung San Suu Kyi making a speech to her supporters despite being threatened by armed soldiers. Next day, while packing for a flight to Bangkok, Laura discovers her passport is missing and is forced to stay behind to obtain a replacement at the American Embassy. While awaiting her next flight, she hires U Aung Ko (played by himself), a former teacher, to guide her out of the city into the countryside. But the military begins a crackdown on dissidents, martial law is declared, and Laura finds herself fleeing for her life.

The aim of British director John Boorman in making this film was to alert American audiences to the activities of the military dictatorship in Burma, or Myanmar, and the courageous role being played at the time by Aung San Suu Kyi. Boorman's decision to dramatise the situation with a thriller in which a 'typical' American gets caught up in the violence is, arguably, a positive one. Boorman no doubt realised that Western cinema audiences could not be expected to empathise with anonymous Burmese being treated brutally by a military dictatorship, but at least they could perhaps be persuaded to care about the plight of an American woman. Beautifully photographed by Australian John Seale, the film— shot in Malaysia—certainly shows the Burmese military in a very bad light as they ruthlessly slaughter anyone who shows any sign of dissent.

The nightmare situation in which Laura finds herself is somewhat alleviated by the friendship she forms with U Aung Ko, a gentle former Buddhist monk whose career as a teacher was brought to an abrupt end when he tried to help a dissident student.

The downside of the film is that Laura's behaviour seems extremely foolhardy. A sensible woman in her position, knowing that Burma is a country of unrest and finding herself alone after her sister and the other members of her tour leave without her, would surely stay close to her hotel or the American Embassy. To embark on what she knows from the start is a problematic journey into the hinterland, even in the company of such a reassuring character as U Aung Ko, is not very sensible. But of course unless she behaves in this way there's no movie, and as a result no vividly staged scenes of military atrocities and breathtaking escapes.

On balance *Beyond Rangoon* survives these drawbacks, and certainly its heart is in the right place. Boorman, whose career produced commercial highs like *Deliverance* (1972) as well as a number of less successful films, is an accomplished filmmaker, and he handles the gripping sequence in which Laura ventures into an abandoned village seeking medicine for the wounded U Aung Ko with nail-biting tension.

The film's end titles bring us back to its original intentions. We're reminded that 'thousands' of Burmese citizens have been massacred because of their rejection of the military dictatorship, and that 'torture and repression are being carried out to this day'. The film ends with a photograph of Aung San Suu Kyi and a reminder that she was awarded the Nobel Peace Prize in 1991, which is rather ironic in light of more recent events.

Perhaps because cinema audiences shy away from this kind of political message, the film—after premiering at Cannes—performed poorly at the international box office.

10

Beyond the Sea

(UK / GERMANY, 2004)

Archer Street Productions–Quality International–Trigger Productions. DIRECTOR: Kevin Spacey. SCRIPT: Kevin Spacey, Lewis Colick. ACTORS: Kevin Spacey, Kate Bosworth, John Goodman, Bob Hoskins, Brenda Blethyn, Greta Scacchi, Caroline Aaron, Peter Cincotti, William Ullrich. 118 MINS.

Hollywood in the early 1970s. On a studio sound stage, singer and occasional actor Bobby Darin (Kevin Spacey) is starring in a film about his life, but his perfectionism is infuriating members of the crew. The child actor cast as Young Bobby (William Ullrich), who claims to know the real Bobby better than anyone, suggests they begin at the beginning, in the Bronx where the future Bobby Darin, then a sickly child named Walden Robert Cassotto, lived with his devoted mother, Polly (Brenda Blethyn), his sister, Nina (Caroline Aaron), and her husband, Charlie (Bob Hoskins). Though a doctor tells Polly that the boy 'will be lucky to see his 15th birthday', Bobby finds inspiration through music and, taking the name 'Darin'—after he sees a malfunctioning electric sign for a Chinese restaurant in which the 'Man' of 'Mandarin' was unlit—heads uptown. He finds work in clubs, signs a record deal and has a hit with 'Splish Splash', a song aimed at young teens. His cover recording of 'Mack the Knife' is a big hit and soon he's rivalling the ageing Frank Sinatra. After acting in a couple of films he's cast in *Come September*, which is filmed in Italy; his co-stars are Rock Hudson and Sandra Dee (Kate Bosworth), and soon he's romancing, and then marrying Dee, despite the fierce opposition of Mary (Greta Scacchi), her formidable mother. The couple have a son, but their work commitments entail long separations and Dee begins drinking too much. Darin is nominated for a Best Supporting Actor Oscar for *Captain Newman M.D.* (with Gregory Peck and Tony Curtis), but misses out to veteran Melvyn Douglas. His sister Nina reveals that she is his real mother, not Polly. Bobby becomes a political activist, but is shattered when Bobby Kennedy is assassinated. Darin dies in 1973 after heart surgery.

Kevin Spacey had been determined to film a biopic of Bobby Darin for a long time before he finally managed to raise money in England and Germany to film in Europe. Though too old for the role (Spacey was 45 when the film was made, and Darin was only 37 when he died, but this discrepancy is acknowledged— quite wittily—early in the film), Spacey nails the character with complete confidence, singing all his own songs, Darin-style. It's a magnificent performance. His staging is first class, too, with Darin's story told via an intricate, not always linear, structure. The choreography (by Rob Ashford) is vigorous and bewitching, and the skill with which Spacey glides into and out of the musical sequences sometimes rivals even that of Gene Kelly.

The screenplay, co-written by the actor–director, is deft and often amusing—when Mary, played in wonderfully bitchy style by Greta Scacchi, realises that her inexperienced daughter plans to marry Darin, she responds with: 'I wish you'd concentrated more on Rock Hudson.' During his relatively brief career Darin wrote 163 songs and made 486 recordings, and Spacey is clearly a major fan—but he plays the character warts and all; his Bobby has a nasty temper and is prone to smashing thing up when he doesn't get his own way.

The film's box-office failure in 2004 was perhaps due to the fact that Bobby Darin was hardly a household name among younger cinema-goers at the time, and that Spacey himself was never a major movie star. Though the reviews were positive, the film flopped overseas and was a direct-to-video release in Australia. *Beyond the Sea* was the second of only two films Spacey has directed to date (the first, *Albino Alligator*, is even more obscure)—and, in light of his spectacular fall from grace, it's doubtful he'll make another, or that this clever and beautifully made biopic will ever find fresh supporters.

11

Billy Lynn's Long Halftime Walk

(USA/UK/CHINA, 2016)

TriStar–The Ink Factory–LStar Capital. DIRECTOR: Ang Lee. SCRIPT: Jean-Christophe Castelli, from the novel by Ben Fountain. ACTORS: Joe Alwyn, Kristen Stewart, Chris Tucker, Garrett Hedlund, Makenzie Leigh, Vin Diesel, Steve Martin, Tim Blake Nelson, Bruce McKinnon, Deirdre Lovejoy, Brian 'Astro' Bradley, Arturo Castro, Ismael Cruz Cordova, Barney Harris. 113 MINS.

Texas, 2004. US Army hero Billy Lynn (Joe Alwyn), and other members of the Bravo Squad, are winding up a tour of the US to win public support for the ongoing war in Iraq. At the Dealey Plaza Hotel complex in Dallas, not far from Billy's home town of Stovall, the men are expected to take part in the half-time celebrations during a Thanksgiving Day football match featuring the hometown team, Dallas Cowboys. During the day Billy recalls his time in Iraq and his friendship with Sergeant Shroom (Vin Diesel), who was mortally wounded during a confrontation with insurgents. In trying to save him, Billy had fought hand-to-hand combat with one of the Arabs and had killed the man. He also recalls his recent visit home and the concern of his sister, Kathryn (Kristen Stewart), who urged him not to return to Iraq. In Dallas, he catches the eye of pretty cheerleader Faison (Makenzie Leigh), an avowed Christian who nevertheless is not averse to a quick sexual encounter. Norm Oglesby (Steve Martin), owner of the Cowboys, offers to finance a film about the exploits of the Bravo Squad, but the recompense he proposes for the men is so meagre they turn him down. The soldiers get into a fight with backstage staff at the stadium. Sergeant Dime (Garrett Hedlund) persuades Billy to join his mates and return to the war, despite the objections of his sister Kathryn.

Much of the commentary about Ang Lee's devastating anti-war film originally focused on technical aspects of the production. The film was photographed in an innovative new system, using 4K 3D at

120 frames per second. This required special projection equipment, which was used in only a handful of venues in America; in Australia it wasn't even shown in 3D. The pioneering techniques used by the immensely talented Ang Lee (*Brokeback Mountain*, *Life of Pi*) are certainly interesting, but tend to distract from the film itself.

Nineteen-year-old Billy, who has been lauded as a hero for stabbing an Arab insurgent to death in Iraq, is not only suffering from post-traumatic stress syndrome, but is living an American nightmare. At an awkward family dinner, where his father (Bruce McKinnon), presumably a veteran of the war in Vietnam, is confined to a wheelchair and has nothing to say to his son, while Billy's mother (Deirdre Lovejoy) mouths platitudes about the war, only his beloved sister is really concerned about him, as well she might be. We learn her boyfriend had left her after he was responsible for a car crash in which she was badly injured, and that Billy had beaten him up—and that only by enlisting for the war had he escaped a prison sentence for assault. The hideousness of the 'show' being staged in Dallas—ironically very close to the site of President Kennedy's assassination—with its scantily clad cheerleaders and its obscenely wealthy businessmen in attendance, contrasts with the poverty of 'ordinary' Americans, like the waiter who confides in Billy that he plans to enlist himself because 'what else is there?'; 'We're a nation of children' says the doomed Shroom, a practising Buddhist, and the phony patriotism and confected glitter on display at the stadium certainly seems to confirm that.

The actors are all superb: Joe Alwyn makes Billy a genuinely touching character, while Steve Martin gives a remarkable performance as the odious Oglesby.

Films dealing with the Iraq War have—with the exception of *The Hurt Locker*—been poison at the box office, and this extraordinary condemnation of all that's false and rotten in America was no exception. Outside the US it might have become a cult success, but the distributors showed little interest in promoting it.

The Birth of a Nation

(USA/CANADA, 2016)

Fox Searchlight-Mandalay Pictures-Bron Studios. DIRECTOR/SCRIPT: Nate Parker. ACTORS: Nate Parker, Armie Hammer, Penelope Ann Miller, Jackie Earle Haley, Aja Naomi King, Mark Boone Jr, Colman Domingo, Aunjanue Ellis, Dwight Henry. 114 MINS.

Southampton County, Virginia, in the early 1830s. Nat Turner (Nate Parker), the child of slaves, is told that it is his destiny to become a great man. Elizabeth Turner (Penelope Ann Miller), the wife of plantation owner Samuel Turner (Armie Hammer), teaches the boy to read the Bible. As Nat grows to manhood, Samuel Turner—who is impoverished and fears he will lose the plantation—discovers that he can earn money by taking Nat to neighbouring plantations where he reads the Bible to the slaves who work there. Nat observes that some slaves are treated better than others and witnesses some appalling cruelties. Nat marries Cherry (Aja Naomi King) and they have a son; but when Cherry is raped by slave-catchers he has no legal way of avenging this injustice. Nat gathers his friends around him and they begin an ill-fated rebellion against their white masters.

The true story of Nat Turner's slave rebellion, with its echoes of *Spartacus*, another slave rebellion from an earlier era, had been filmed before, both for the cinema and television, but this version, written and directed by its lead actor (his directorial debut) is the most detailed and graphic reminder of the scourge of slavery in the period prior to the American Civil War. The film screened to great acclaim at the Sundance Film Festival in January 2016, receiving a standing ovation and winning the Grand Jury Prize and the Audience Award. A bidding war for international distribution rights ensued, with Fox Searchlight Pictures emerging as the winner. But before the film was released in cinemas, stories began to circulate about an alleged rape committed by the director at Penn

State University in 1999. As a result, Fox Searchlight appeared to get cold feet, especially when negative reviews started appearing; in the end the film's US box-office was disappointing, and the film was a direct-to-DVD release in Australia.

The film thus raises all those thorny questions surrounding proven and alleged sex offenders—how can we separate the work of art from the behaviour of the artist? Despite the accusations made against Nate Parker, his film surely deserved better treatment. The story of Nat Turner was, indeed, a tragic one: the revolution failed, as it was doomed to do, with great loss of life, and Turner himself was hanged. But Parker, like the British (black) director Steve McQueen, who made the successful *12 Years a Slave* three years earlier, was clearly focused on shedding light for contemporary audiences on the horrors of the past—and this he does graphically and with considerable success.

It could be argued that Parker was unwise to purloin the title of D.W. Griffith's contentious, pioneering masterwork, filmed almost 100 years earlier, for his own film, and some used this hubris as a stick with which to beat him. Others have pointed out that Nat Turner's actions brought about the deaths of many innocent people of his own race. But the fact remains that the horrors he experienced, the humiliations he endured, and the violence perpetrated by whites against blacks in the antebellum South led to his actions, misguided as they might have been, and Parker's film vividly and powerfully brings the whole sorry story to life.

. . . . a detailed and graphic reminder
of the scourge of slavery

Blessed

(AUSTRALIA, 2009)

Head Gear Films. DIRECTOR: Ana Kokkinos. SCRIPT: Andrew Bovell, Melissa Reeves, Patricia Cornelius, Christos Tsiolkas, based on their play *Who's Afraid of the Working Class?* (co-written by Irene Vela). ACTORS: Frances O'Connor, Miranda Otto, Deborra-Lee Furness, Victoria Haralabidou, Monica Maughan, William McInnes, Wayne Blair, Tasma Walton, Sophie Lowe, Anastasia Baboussouras, Harrison Gilbertson, Eamon Farren, Eva Lazzaro, Reef Ireland, Kellie Jones, Amanda Ma. 117 MINS.

Melbourne. Fifteen-year-old Katrina (Sophie Lowe) and her friend Trisha (Anastasia Baboussouras) cut classes, smoke, drink liquor and are arrested for shoplifting. Bianca (Miranda Otto), Katrina's mother, is a gambling addict. Trisha's mum, Gina (Victoria Haralabidou), worries that her son, Roo, might be the unidentified victim of drowning she is hearing about in radio broadcasts, but actually Roo is alive and well, though he has been paid to appear in a porn movie. Orton (Reef Ireland) runs away from home with his younger sister, Stacey (Eva Lazzaro); their mother Rhonda (Frances O'Connor) becomes aware that the presence in her home of her lovers has been upsetting her children. Daniel (Harrison Gilbertson) breaks into the home of Laurel (Monica Maughan) and accidentally kills her; his mother, Tanya (Deborra-Lee Furness), works as a nurse and has a cool relationship with her husband (William McInnes), who gives Bianca cash he stole from his wife, who blamed Daniel for the theft.

This achingly moving film, the best to date of several fine features directed by Greek-Australian Ana Kokkinos, is divided into two parts: 'The Children' and 'The Mothers'. In the first part we follow a group of kids over a few hours; in the second we follow their mothers over the same period, and sometimes the scenes overlap but are seen from a different perspective. The crisscrossing of the different stories is beautifully worked out in the confident and assured direction.

The film is harsh, confronting, honest and powerful. It's a scream of anger against parents who neglect their children, yet at the same time the screenplay—based on a play, *Who's Afraid of the Working Class?*—is filled with sympathy for the situations in which these women find themselves. Tanya and Gina are good, caring women who find they just can't control their kids. Bianca is foolish and weak, and even the very pregnant Rhonda, with her reliance on seemingly unreliable men, is not entirely to blame for what happens to her children; likewise Laurel, who hid something very important from the Aboriginal boy she adopted and who is now a grown man (Wayne Blair), has issues with her children. Kokkinos and her four writers present a scenario that, while it is a sad reflection of contemporary society, acknowledges that there are no easy answers.

The performances of the fine ensemble cast are flawless, and it's invidious to single out one of the actors, but I'll never forget the scene in which Frances O'Connor's Rhonda is confronted with the stark reality of what's happened to her children.

This is strong stuff indeed—too strong for audiences, unfortunately, and the film, one of the finest ever made in Australia, was a box-office disappointment. Thank goodness films as important and artistically successful as *Blessed* have been made in this country, and hopefully there'll always be a place for movies as relevant and fearless as this one.

Bobby

(USA, 2006)

Weinstein Company–Bold Films. DIRECTOR/SCRIPT: Emilio Estevez. ACTORS: Harry Belafonte, Nick Cannon, Emilio Estevez, Laurence Fishburne, Heather Graham, Anthony Hopkins, Helen Hunt, Shia LaBeouf, Lindsay Lohan, William H. Macy, Svetlana Metkina, Demi Moore, Freddy Rodriguez, Martin Sheen, Christian Slater, Sharon Stone, Mary Elizabeth Winstead, Elijah Wood. 123 MINS.

The Ambassador Hotel, Los Angeles, 5 June 1968. A cross-section of staff and guests await the reception that evening for Democratic Presidential nominee Robert F. Kennedy. The hotel's former doorman, John Casey (Anthony Hopkins), chats with Nelson (Harry Belafonte) about famous guests who have stayed at the hotel in the past. Paul Ebbers (William H. Macy), the present manager, who is having an affair with a telephonist named Angela (Heather Graham), knows that his wife, Miriam (Sharon Stone), the hotel manicurist, is suspicious. Ebbers fires Daryl Timmons (Christian Slater), the catering manager, for his open racism. In the kitchen several of the staff are illegal immigrants from across the border; Jose Rojas (Freddy Rodriguez), who is too young to vote, and chef Edward Robinson (Laurence Fishburne) discuss RFK's support of minorities. A couple of the candidate's aides experiment with LSD. Virginia Fallon (Demi Moore), an alcoholic singer, argues with her manager, Tim (Emilio Estevez), while Diane (Lindsay Lohan) has agreed to marry William (Elijah Wood) to prevent him being conscripted to fight in Vietnam. Jack (Martin Sheen, the director's father) and his wife Samantha (Helen Hunt) are invited guests at the party that never takes place after Kennedy is assassinated in the hotel.

As a director Emilio Estevez has had a decidedly chequered career, but *Bobby* is a standout achievement, a passionate, heartfelt reminder of what was promised and what was lost on that fateful night in 1968. Structured like a combination of *Grand Hotel* and *Nashville*, the film is rich in character and detail. Kennedy himself appears only in newsreel footage as he makes campaign speeches throughout the day. Like *Nashville*, the film offers a cross-section of American characters who will be in one way or another affected by the tragic events about to unfold. The climax, in which Estevez employs re-created footage intercut with actual material, is devastating, especially as we hear, over the scenes of chaos and horror, the calm voice of Kennedy making his final speech. The emotional power conveyed here is overwhelming.

An exceptional ensemble cast does significantly good work, with Demi Moore giving one of her best performances as the troubled Virginia. An interesting sub-plot features Svetlana Metkina as Lenka, a journalist from the Czechoslovakian newspaper *Rudé Právo*, who is desperate to obtain an interview with the candidate, pointing out to his reluctant minders that her country is promoting 'socialism with a human face'—a concept that, just two months later, would be crushed by Russian tanks.

Despite the strong cast, *Bobby* was unable to attract much of an audience, confirming yet again that films with political themes are not destined for box-office success. Of course, given that the bleak ending was never in doubt, it's also possible that people stayed away for fear of being depressed. They missed a terrific movie.

15

Broken

(UK, 2012)

Cuba Pictures. DIRECTOR: Rufus Norris. SCRIPT: Mark O'Rowe, from the novel by Daniel Clay. ACTORS: Tim Roth, Cillian Murphy, Eloise Laurence, Rory Kinnear, Robert Emms, Zana Marjanovic, Clare Burt, Bill Milner, Denis Lawson, Charlie Booty, Lily James, Lukas Fernandes-Pendse, Faye Daveney, Martha Bryant, Rosalie Kosky-Hensman. 91 MINS.

A cul-de-sac in the London suburbs. Archie (Tim Roth), a lawyer deserted by his wife, lives with his two children and a live-in helper, Kasia (Zana Marjanovic), who is having a relationship with their neighbour Mike (Cillian Murphy), a schoolteacher. Archie's eleven-year-old daughter, nicknamed Skunk (Eloise Laurence), is a diabetic and nervous about starting high school. Skunk witnesses a neighbour, widower Bob Oswald (Rory Kinnear), father of three rebellious daughters, attacking Rick Buckley (Robert Emms), who has learning difficulties. Sunrise (Martha Bryant), the youngest of the Oswald daughters, who is the same age as Skunk, falsely accuses Rick of rape, an accusation that leads to more violence. Meanwhile Kasia, finding that Mike is unwilling to commit himself to her, begins a relationship with Archie, upsetting Skunk, who consoles herself with Jed (Bill Milner), a sympathetic youth.

Broken, the first film made by the well-regarded British stage director, Rufus Norris, is based on a critically acclaimed novel by Daniel Clay. Seen as a microcosm of Britain in 2012, it's a powerful and unsettling drama in which delicately balanced young lives are ruined by bigotry, selfishness, thoughtlessness and sheer stupidity. The foul-mouthed and quick-tempered Oswald, very convincingly portrayed by Kinnear, is, in this confined environment, a walking disaster. His three wayward daughters, as prone to gutter language and bigotry as their father, take after him; they are quick to make unfounded accusations against the weaker and less powerful members of the community, while Oswald is even quicker to exact his own sort of violent justice, no matter how flimsy, or non-existent, might be the evidence offered by his girls. The grim presence of the Oswalds in the cul-de-sac affects everyone else who lives there. Poor Rick, because of his disabilities, is an easy target, but so too is the innocent but troubled Skunk.

Daniel Clay's novel was, he claimed at the time of publication, influenced by Harper Lee's *To Kill a Mockingbird*, and while the relationship between Skunk and her lawyer father doesn't very closely parallel that of Scout and her lawyer dad in Lee's great book, you can see ways in which there are connections. If you see *Broken* in this light, the character of Rick would equate with that of Boo Radley.

For a first feature, *Broken* is extremely impressive. Norris succeeds admirably in dissecting these characters, depicting through looks and gestures the damage that can so easily be done to the vulnerable weak by the thoughtless strong. Eloise Laurence gives a particularly fine performance as the troubled yet tenacious Skunk.

It's true that there is one too many coincidence, and that Norris' device of depicting some scenes out of chronological sequence leads on occasion to minor confusions, but these are relatively unimportant quibbles when the overall film is so powerful and troubling, and when such a bitterly authentic image of contemporary London society is so convincingly depicted.

The film was a very modest success in the UK, and rather less so in Australia.

A microcosm of Britain in 2012, *Broken* is a powerful and unsettling drama

A Bronx Tale

(USA, 1993)

Savoy Pictures-Tribeca Productions. DIRECTOR: Robert De Niro. SCRIPT: Chazz Palminteri, based on his play. ACTORS: Robert De Niro, Chazz Palminteri, Lillo Brancato, Francis Capra, Taral Hicks, Kathrine Narducci, Joe Pesci. 121 MINS.

The Bronx, 1960. Nine-year-old Calogero (Francis Capra) worships his bus driver father, Lorenzo (Robert De Niro), but hangs out at the notorious Chez Bippy bar where strongman Sonny (Chazz Palminteri) rules the roost over assorted gamblers and petty crooks with names like Jimmy Whispers, Eddie Mush and JoJo the Whale. Calogero is a witness when Sonny guns down a man who was hitting another man with a baseball bat over an apparent argument about a parking space. Quizzed by the police, Calogero refuses to identify Sonny, who thereafter takes the boy under his wing, to the dismay of his father. In 1968, Calogero, now using the name C (Lillo Brancato), sees his contemporaries begin to take action against African-Americans who are starting to move into the neighbourhood. C is attracted to Jane (Taral Hicks), a black girl, and Sonny lends him his car to take her on a date. But the actions of his racist friends lead to violence and death.

Dedicated to Robert De Niro Sr and to songwriter Sammy Cahn, the first of only two films to date directed by Robert De Niro (the other, *The Good Shepherd*, was made in 2006), the film explores the same kind of milieu and themes as those made famous by Martin Scorsese. De Niro's film, however, is far less violent than most Scorsese films, and the story of a boy and the two men who shape his character unfolds in quite a minor key. This is not so much a film about 'goodfellas' as it is about the racial tensions that occurred in this part of New York during the 1960s. It's also a pleasantly nostalgic look at Bronx life. The early scenes, as the wide-eyed nine-year-old observes the various colourful characters who inhabit the local bar, are beautifully handled, and the conflicting philosophies expressed by the youth's hard-working and honest father on the one hand and the charismatic petty gangster, with his expensive suits and fancy cars, on the other, are persuasively presented. Lorenzo warns his son that 'people don't love Sonny—they fear him'; when C later asks his mentor if it's better to be loved or feared, Sonny tells him 'fear lasts longer than love'. Sonny's principal philosophy is that 'nobody cares'; 'The only thing that matters,' he advises C, 'is if it's good for *you*.'

Scenes of the romance with Jane, the pretty African-American girl, who is far more forward than the shy C, are directed with intimate warmth. And interestingly Sonny, whatever his failings, is no racist: unlike the other Italo-Americans who inhabit this corner of the Bronx, it doesn't bother him at all when C confides in him about his attraction for Jane.

In the end, C decides that what he learnt from these two very different father figures was that 'the saddest thing in life is wasted talent'. Certainly De Niro demonstrated, with his directorial debut, that he had talent in this area, though he's barely used it since. Handsomely photographed by Reynaldo Villalobos, the film is further distinguished by a great collection of popular songs of the period, from Dean Martin to The Beatles, from Frank Sinatra to Jimi Hendrix. The casting is outstanding: Brancato looks uncannily like the young De Niro, so that he totally convinces as the man's son.

Perhaps the film failed at the box office because it didn't deliver on the perceived promise of a Scorsese-type thriller.

Buffalo Soldiers

(UK/USA/GERMANY, 2001)

Gorilla Entertainment–Odeon Pictures–Medien und Filmgesellschaft. DIRECTOR: Gregor Jordan. SCRIPT: Gregor Jordan, Eric Axel Weiss, Nora Maccoby, from the novel by Robert O'Connor. ACTORS: Joaquin Phoenix, Ed Harris, Scott Glenn, Anna Paquin, Elizabeth McGovern, Dean Stockwell, Gabriel Mann, Leon Robinson, Sheik Mahmud-Bey, Glenn Fitzgerald, Haluk Bilginer. 98 MINS.

Stuttgart, West Germany, 1989. Soldiers serving at the Theodore Roosevelt US Army base are thoroughly bored. Private Ray Elwood (Joaquin Phoenix), battalion secretary to incompetent Colonel Berman (Ed Harris), is involved in wholesale black market schemes. When the tank being driven by a trio of hopelessly stoned soldiers careens through a small town, crushes a VW and demolishes a petrol station, two army truck drivers are also killed; Elwood and his men arrive at the scene, realise the trucks contain huge amounts of weaponry, and steal them. Elwood enters into negotiations with The Turk (Haluk Bilginer) about the purchase of the armaments. However, a newly arrived Top Sergeant, Robert Lee (Scott Glenn), has taken a personal dislike to Elwood, especially after Elwood starts dating his precocious daughter, Robyn (Anna Paquin). Matters escalate when Elwood receives a huge stash of raw heroin from The Turk and the unit becomes involved in military manoeuvres.

After making his film debut with the very successful Sydney-located black comedy *Two Hands* (1999), Australian Gregor Jordan was given the opportunity to direct this ferociously funny adaptation of a book by Robert O'Connor about American soldiers stationed in West Germany. The story that unfolds is part of a long tradition of both dramas and comedies (*From Here to Eternity*, *M*A*S*H*, *Catch-22*, *Sgt. Bilko* and *The Phil Silvers Show* TV series among them) about the boredom faced by soldiers in both peace and war, and how wily entrepreneurs can subvert the system. Elwood, superbly played by Joaquin Phoenix, tells us he likes three things about his posting in Germany: his Mercedes, the lack of a speed limit on the autobahns, and the thriving black market. This is a place where the soldiers have nothing to kill but time, and though war might be hell, peace is simply enervating. Elwood is secretly having an affair with the bored wife (Elizabeth McGovern) of his inept commanding officer (a wonderfully dim-witted Ed Harris), and appears to be relatively 'together' when compared with many of the soldiers on the base, most of whom seem to be permanently stoned—there's a great scene in which a group of men, watching TV reports of the tearing down of the Berlin War, speculate as to the whereabouts of Berlin, and whether their current location is in East or West Germany.

After the explosively hilarious set-piece of the runaway tank and its aftermath, the film develops into a conflict of wills between the wily Elwood and the vengeful Lee, with some renegade Military Police, led by Saad (Sheik Mahmud-Bey), adding further complications.

The film premiered at the Toronto International Film Festival two days before the tragedy of 9/11. Harvey Weinstein's Miramax Films, the designated distributor, decided that this was not the time to release a film that could be seen as attacking the US military. (This was not the only film casualty of those events: images of the Twin Towers were digitally removed from *Zoolander* and the Arnold Schwarzenegger thriller, *Collateral Damage*, was briefly placed on the backburner.) International distributors followed suit and *Buffalo Soldiers* was finally released two years later (in Australia it opened in August 2003), by which time Iraq had been invaded and the international mood had undergone a radical transformation. Sadly this accomplished satire became, as one critic wrote in 2001, 'the wrong film at the wrong time'.

Bullseye

(AUSTRALIA, 1986)

PBL Productions. DIRECTOR: Carl Schultz. SCRIPT: Robert Wales, Bob Ellis. ACTORS: Paul Goddard, Kathryn Walker, John Wood, Paul Chubb, Lynette Curran, Bruce Spence, Kerry Walker, John Meillon, David Slingsby. 93 MINS.

The 1860s, Emu Plains, near Roma, Queensland. A bull bred in England, and claimed to be the most expensive animal ever brought to the colony, arrives at the property managed by Don McKenzie (Paul Chubb). Harry Walford (Paul Goddard), who, apart from the Aboriginal workers, is the lowest paid stockman employed on the property, is in love with Lily Boyd (Kathryn Walker), the McKenzies' maid. When Lily receives word of an inheritance from a recently deceased aunt in Adelaide and departs, Harry decides to rustle a few cattle; he and his mate Bluey McGurk (John Wood) flee the station mustering a thousand stolen cattle and the priceless bull. After a dangerous and arduous journey through the desert they finally arrive in Adelaide and sell the cattle. Lily, who only inherited £5, is working in a brothel run by Mrs Gootch (Kerry Walker); Harry, by chance, becomes her first customer. Harry is arrested and brought to trial; the alcoholic Samuel Merrit (John Meillon) is hired as his defence counsel.

This much-troubled production was inspired by a true story; a stockman named Harry Redford actually stole about 1000 head of cattle and successfully overlanded them from Central Queensland to the stockyards in Adelaide. The decision to transform this factual history from a dramatic outback drama into a rollicking adventure with lots of typical Aussie humour proved beneficial; newcomers Paul Goddard and Kathryn Walker, both appearing in their first films, play their roles straight, while a gallery of talented character actors enjoy themselves in largely comical supporting roles, among them John Wood as Harry's loyal mate, Bruce Spence and David Slingsby as cheerfully untrustworthy characters, Paul Chubb as the station manager, Lynette Curran as his feisty wife who denies him sexual relations until Harry is proved innocent, Kerry Walker as the brothel madam, John Meillon as the alcoholic barrister—even Wharf Revue alumnus Phil Scott as the brothel's singer/pianist.

The film was shot on spectacular locations around Bourke, NSW, by Dean Semler, and visually it's more than a match for some of the great Hollywood westerns. The production design by George Liddle is also outstanding.

How could a film so visually handsome, beautifully directed and for the most part thoroughly entertaining be seen by so few people? The film's problems really started when its production company, PBL—at the time an offshoot of the Nine Network—formed a partnership with a British company, Dumbarton Films, a subsidiary of Video Arts, a company owned by John Cleese. The role of Video Arts was to handle distribution sales not only internationally but also in Australia. On the film's completion, Dumbarton sought distribution from an American major (Paramount had recently released *Crocodile Dundee* with enormous success); but surprisingly every major turned down the film, and then Dumbarton itself ceased trading. By this time the film had been hanging around on the shelf for far too long, and Hoyts, its eventual Australian distributor, gave it a tentative release in Brisbane only, then dumped it before it made it to other states. It seems never to have been released on DVD.

This is particularly regrettable because Schultz, who was born in Hungary and fled the country in 1956 as a teenager during the Soviet invasion, was, until he left to work in America and the UK, one of Australia's best directors. *Bullseye* was made between two of his finest and most popular films, *Careful He Might Hear You* (1983) and *Travelling North* (1986), and it certainly merited better treatment than it received. On any number of levels, including the charming lead performances, it's a thoroughly winning experience.

19

Bulworth

(USA, 1998)

20th Century Fox. DIRECTOR: Warren Beatty. SCRIPT: Warren Beatty, Jeremy Pikser; ACTORS: Warren Beatty, Halle Berry, Don Cheadle, Oliver Platt, Paul Sorvino, Jack Warden, Isaiah Washington, Sean Astin, Christine Baranski, Kimberly Deauna Adams, Richard Sarafian. 108 MINS.

March, 1996. The US primary elections are in full swing. In California, President Clinton has been elected unopposed by the Democrats, while Robert Dole is the Republican choice. With little fanfare or attention, Democratic Senator Jay Billington Bulworth (Warren Beatty) embarks on the final week of his campaign. While his aides hover about him, the clearly exhausted and distracted Bulworth—who hasn't eaten or slept for days—flicks aimlessly through the TV channels during his meetings with lobbyists. One such lobbyist is Graham Crockett (Paul Sorvino), who represents health insurance companies. Bulworth promises he will obstruct a bill to reform healthcare in exchange for a $10 million life insurance policy on himself. He then contacts Vinnie (Richard Sarafian), a gangster, to arrange for his own assassination. Now that he knows he is soon to die he feels liberated and, at a campaign speech in a church in South Central Los Angeles, before a black congregation, he tells the truth: that the Democrats will never do anything significant for the African-American community, because the community can't come up with substantial amounts of cash for political donations—the sort of money provided by the white establishment for politicians like himself. Later, at a party in Hollywood, he denounces film industry leaders, many of them Jews, for 'churning out garbage'. He meets Nina (Halle Berry), an attractive young black woman, and decides to call off the assassination—but Vinnie has died in the meantime and Bulworth has no idea who has been hired to replace the assassin.

Warren Beatty was one of the biggest Hollywood stars of the 60s and 70s, and he used his clout to promote his strongly left-wing political views in films like *Bonnie and Clyde*, *McCabe and Mrs Miller*, *The Parallax View* and *Shampoo*, as well as *Reds*, which he directed. Perhaps the fact that he was such an openly partisan member of the film community explains why, when his star began to fade, his fall from grace was so rapid. *Bulworth* is one of the most outspoken political films ever made anywhere, but the pill is coated with jet-black humour. Attacking both sides of the political establishment equally, the film seems to predict the arrival of a Donald Trump in its depiction of the disdain many politicians have for their constituents, the blatant lies they tell and how easily they get away with it.

It's fascinating to see the film in light of the Trump administration's attempts to dismantle Obamacare. At the centre of *Bulworth* is a debate about the appalling state of America's health services, something about which Beatty is clearly genuinely angry.

The story, conceived by Beatty himself, is hardly original. The idea of a man who decides to hire someone to kill him, and then has second thoughts after meeting an attractive woman, was the basis for a very popular Douglas Fairbanks vehicle (*Flirting with Fate*, 1916), and since then has been reworked several times—most notably in a German comedy, *The Man in Search of His Murderer*, made by Robert Siodmak in 1931.

The film is beautifully made, with A-1 creative contributions from Vittorio Storaro, the cinematographer, Dean Tavoularis, the production designer, and Ennio Morricone, the composer. Beatty himself, who co-scripted with Jeremy Pikser, heads a formidable cast that includes Oliver Platt and Jack Warden as Bulworth's principal aides, Christine Baranski as his uninterested wife, and the delectable Halle Berry as the femme fatale. This is a rare film in that it's shocking in some ways and utterly honest. Needless to say, it was a box-office flop.

Burke & Wills

(AUSTRALIA, 1985)

Hoyts–Edgley Productions. DIRECTOR: Graeme Clifford. SCRIPT: Michael Thomas. ACTORS: Jack Thompson, Nigel Havers, Greta Scacchi, Matthew Fargher, Ralph Cotterill, Drew Forsythe, Chris Haywood, Monroe Reimers, Barry Hill, Roderick Williams, Hugh Keays-Byrne, Arthur Dignam, Ken Goodlet. 140 MINS.

Melbourne, 1860. Robert O'Hara Burke (Jack Thompson), a fiery-tempered Irishman in love with Julia Matthews (Greta Scacchi), a beautiful opera singer, becomes obsessed with the challenge of crossing Australia from south to north and back. A rival expedition is setting out from Adelaide, but Burke pushes ahead with support from various influential politicians and businessmen, among them the devious Ambrose Kyte (Hugh Keays-Byrne). Burke's expedition is joined by British scientist William Wills (Nigel Havers), and eventually they set out with a slow-moving party that consists of nineteen men plus horses and specially imported camels. After some setbacks—including dust storms, encounters with Aboriginals and a crocodile attack—Burke, Wills and John King (Matthew Fargher) reach the Gulf of Carpentaria. Certain now that all Australia will 'beat a path to my door', Burke leads the weary men south again, but increasing delays result in missing a crucial rendezvous by a few hours. The only survivor of the expedition is King, who survives thanks to the help of Aboriginals, and who eventually returns to Melbourne to make a moving public address describing the fate of the Burke and Wills expedition.

Burke & Wills was the brainchild of Graeme Clifford, a most enterprising Australian who left Sydney after abandoning his medical studies to obtain a job in the editing department of the BBC. While travelling through Canada he met American director Robert Altman in Vancouver, and became his assistant on *M*A*S*H* and *McCabe and Mrs Miller*. He then edited Altman's *Images*, and through his friendship with Julie Christie (who had played Mrs Miller), was introduced to Nicolas Roeg and assigned the complex task of editing his masterpiece, *Don't Look Now*. Clifford's first feature as director, *Frances* (1982), was a biography of the 1930s Hollywood movie star Frances Farmer, after which he returned home to Australia with the idea of making an epic film about the doomed explorers. The budget for *Burke & Wills* was $8.9 million, which was very high at the time, and the film was shot almost entirely at the locations the original explorers travelled through.

Russell Boyd's magnificent location photography is just one of the distinctive elements of the film. No doubt influenced by Altman, Clifford's use of overlapping dialogue in the crowd scenes is impressive, his depiction of mid-19th century Melbourne aristocracy is vivid, and the fidelity with which he, his actors and crew follow in the footsteps of the legendary explorers is impressive.

Jack Thompson gives a controlled performance as Burke, Nigel Havers makes a touching figure of Wills, and the strong supporting cast represents a roster of fine Australian talent.

Arguably, though, this would have been a difficult box-office attraction from the start, since the fate of the two 'heroes' was, of course, known to everyone. As Hoyts executive Jonathan Chissick noted a few years later: 'A heroic story, but basically audiences didn't want to see a picture about two guys trekking through the desert and dying.' Matters weren't helped by the near simultaneous release by the rival Greater Union company of a crude parody, *Wills & Burke*.

Burke & Wills fared poorly in Australia, and as a result was a hard sell abroad—it never made it into cinemas in the UK, a territory where, one would have thought, it would have had a ready-made audience.

A disappointed Graeme Clifford subsequently made a couple of undistinguished films in Hollywood, but his 'magnum opus' remains seen and remembered by very few.

Citizen Ruth

(USA, 1996)

Independent Pictures. DIRECTOR: Alexander Payne. SCRIPT: Alexander Payne, Jim Taylor. ACTORS: Laura Dern, Swoosie Kurtz, Kurtwood Smith, Mary Kay Place, Kelly Preston, M.C. Gainey, Kenneth Mars, Burt Reynolds, Tippi Hedren, David Graf, Kathleen Noone, Lance Rome, Jim Kalal, Alicia Witt. 98 MINS.

Omaha, Nebraska. Ruth Stoops (Laura Dern), a single mother of three kids, is addicted to a number of illegal substances and also regularly sniffs glue. When her latest lover (Lance Rome) unceremoniously kicks her out, she smashes the windows of his car and steals a can of brake fluid. A cop discovers her stoned, and she's arrested—for the sixteenth time in a year. During an examination held while she's in custody, it's discovered that she's pregnant. Judge Richter (David Graf) angrily condemns her lifestyle ('You sicken me!') and orders her to get an abortion. After the hearing Ruth is approached by a militant anti-abortion group, led by Norm Stoney (Kurtwood Smith) and his wife, Gail (Mary Kay Place), who offer to help her and invite her to stay at their place, where she behaves badly—as does their sulky teenage daughter, Cheryl (Alicia Witt), with whom Ruth goes out on a night-time binge. The Stoneys take Ruth to a clinic, where she's counselled on keeping the baby. Diane (Swoosie Kurtz), a member of the group, is actually a spy for an equally militant pro-choice faction, and she persuades Ruth to accompany her to an isolated house where she lives with her lover, Rachel (Kelly Preston). There follows a standoff between the two violently opposed groups, the case becomes hot news on national television, and the leaders of both groups fly in to offer Ruth money if she follows their policies. These are Jessica Weiss (Tippi Hedren), who is pro-choice, and Blaine Gibbons (Burt Reynolds) leading the anti-abortionists. Ruth decides to take the cash from the pro-choice group, but doesn't tell them she's suffered a miscarriage.

She escapes from the clinic via a bathroom window and heads off, avoiding the crowds that are haranguing one another.

This rarely seen early feature from the director of *About Schmidt*, *Sideways*, *Nebraska* and *Downsizing* is a no-holds-barred attack on the extremists on both sides of the abortion debate. The extremely bold approach pays off; the film is nothing if not memorable. It opens with a scene in which Ruth is having sex in a squalid room littered with empty bottles, while on the soundtrack we hear Bobby Caldwell's cover version of the Frank Sinatra standard, 'All the Way'. After he's finished, the man literally throws Ruth out of the room, and hurls her TV set—apparently her only possession—after her. From the start, then, Ruth is established as homeless, sexually promiscuous and deeply troubled.

'I was only declared unfit to care for *two* of my children,' she protests to the court, and she's clearly a terrible mother. Director Alexander Payne and actor Laura Dern pull no punches in their portrayal, and yet Ruth becomes a sympathetic character surrounded by extremists who have their own conflicting agendas, and want to use her rather than help her. 'It's *my* body, my choice!' she continually asserts, but none of the banner-carrying ideologues fighting over her take much notice of what *she* wants.

Payne doesn't make it easy for the audience. Even Ruth, whose fall-back position is always to get stoned and to take whatever money is currently on offer, is no conventional heroine, but Dern is magnificent in the role. Also unexpectedly good in a strong cast is Burt Reynolds as the leader of the anti-abortion crusaders.

Payne deliberately sets about satirically tweaking the noses of everyone with an opinion, for or against, concerning this most controversial issue. Any film that sets out deliberately to offend its potential audience is likely to be a commercial challenge.

All of which explains why *Citizen Ruth* is a forgotten and neglected movie.

22

The Clinic

(AUSTRALIA, 1982)

The Film House–Generation Films. DIRECTOR: David Stevens. SCRIPT: Greg Millin. ACTORS: Chris Haywood, Simon Burke, Gerda Nicolson, Rona McLeod, Suzanne Roylance, Veronica Lang, Pat Evison, Max Bruch, Gabrielle Hartley, Jane Clifton, Ned Lander, Mark Little, Betty Bobbitt. 88 MINS.

A Melbourne suburb. The film unfolds over the course of a day at a clinic for sexually transmitted diseases. Dr Eric Linden (Chris Haywood), a laid-back, casually dressed doctor, welcomes Paul Armstrong (Simon Burke), a young intern, to observe his working methods. The patients who arrive for treatment are a very mixed bunch. A young man has just flown home from Asia and wants to be assured that he's clean before going home to his girlfriend. A couple of Chinese patients have a problem with understanding English. A European migrant seeks help because he can only get an erection when he's alone, never when he's with a woman. A distraught young man (Ned Lander) has been fired from his job because his boss discovered he had syphilis. A patient with crabs agrees to pose for photographs for an instruction manual. Paul himself is afraid he has a sexually transmittable disease, but is found to be healthy. There is a bomb threat.

The Clinic is not by any means a traditional comedy. In fact the combination of humour ('Do you come here often?' a female patient is asked in the waiting room) and a serious examination of a significant social problem proved too confronting for many, so that, despite positive reviews and a clever promotional campaign ('A Highly Infectious Comedy') by the film's distributor, the film was not a great success. Made on a low budget, with basically just one location—the elaborate studio set of the clinic with its various examination rooms and reception area—the film's strength is in a screenplay, by Greg Millin, that functions both as an educational warning about the perils of sexual promiscuity, and as a very black comedy in which the most intimate sexual details are discussed.

This was the first feature film directed by David Stevens, who had come to attention as a screenwriter (*Breaker Morant*) and as a television director (*Homicide, A Town Like Alice, Women of the Sun*). He does a very professional job with the controversial material, finding just the right balance between comedy and drama. The revelation that Dr Linden is gay (he receives a phone call from his boyfriend's mother) adds another level to what is already an unusually candid film. Interestingly, AIDS is not mentioned; in 1982 the full impact of the scourge was not yet apparent.

Viewed again today, the film is somewhat diminished by some uneven acting among the minor roles, but the principal performances are excellent. Haywood's immensely likeable doctor is one of his most engaging performances, and Burke, too, is in excellent form. Pat Evison, as one of the clinic's doctors, also gives a mature and moving portrayal.

The following year, Stevens directed *Undercover*, a relatively costly film about the fashion industry in the 1920s that proved a disappointment at the box office. In 1988 he directed *Kansas* in the US, and subsequently wrote the play and screenplay that were the basis for the successful Australian film *The Sum of Us* (1994), which he did not direct. He continued to work in television for several years, and died in 2018.

The Clinic is not by any means a traditional comedy

23

Close My Eyes

(UK, 1990)

FilmFour-Beambright Productions. DIRECTOR/SCRIPT: Stephen Poliakoff. ACTORS: Alan Rickman, Clive Owen, Saskia Reeves, Karl Johnson, Lesley Sharp, Kate Gartside, Karen Knight, Niall Buggy. 104 MINS.

London, 1985. Richard Gillespie (Clive Owen), employed as a planner for London's Docklands, is reunited with his sister, Natalie (Saskia Reeves), after a long absence; the siblings were brought up separately after their parents divorced and have seen one another only occasionally. Over the next few years they become closer. By 1990, Natalie has married Sinclair Bryant (Alan Rickman), a wealthy businessman who lives in a magnificent Thames-side house, while Richard now works for an agency engaged in monitoring the Dockside developments. Richard and Natalie embark on an incestuous affair when she visits his flat one day; later she tells Sinclair that she's spending a weekend in Nuneaton when in fact she's with Richard in London. Sinclair suspects she's being unfaithful. Natalie is determined to break with Richard who, by this time, is completely besotted with her.

Close My Eyes was the second film directed by Stephen Poliakoff, who was previously writer-in-residence at London's National Theatre. One of his recurring concerns as a writer has been climate change and the problems facing the environment, and *Close My Eyes* takes place during an unusually hot London summer when the Docklands area was undergoing massive changes and rebuilding. The intensely sexual relationship between brother and sister is depicted in at times startling detail, with Clive Owen, in his first major screen role, and Saskia Reeves giving bravely uncompromising performances. This is, of course, a relationship that can never end well ('We're doing something illegal,' Natalie warns); but at the same time she insists the relationship isn't 'a real affair', but somehow something else. She seems perfectly happy with Sinclair and troubled about deceiving him, whereas Richard, who has had no shortage of girlfriends in the past, becomes totally, senselessly devoted to his sister and impatient for their next liaison.

This is very much an 'end of the 80s' movie; Richard's boss, Colin (Karl Johnson) is dying of AIDS, and the massive rebuilding taking place in the Docklands area isn't living up to expectations ('It was going to be a great modern city—and look what happened'). Richard's job, which he often neglects, is described as a sort of 'urban Greenpeace', its aim being to monitor the development and to ensure it's in keeping with government policy, but it all seems to be pretty ineffectual. One of the film's strengths is the production design by Luciana Arrighi, who skilfully contrasts the expensive lifestyle of Sinclair and Natalie with Richard's poky little flat and, similarly, the lavishly appointed office building where Sinclair works, with its glass lifts and general air of opulence, with the dingy office where Richard and his colleagues carry out their chores.

Despite generally positive reviews, the film was not a box-office success, possibly because the theme of incest was a turn-off. Even the three excellent central performances were apparently not enough to attract any kind of significant audience.

24

Cradle Will Rock

(USA, 1999)

Touchstone Pictures-Cradle Productions. DIRECTOR/SCRIPT: Tim Robbins. ACTORS: Emily Watson, John Turturro, Angus Macfadyen, Bill Murray, John Cusack, Joan Cusack, Rubén Blades, Cary Elwes, Vanessa Redgrave, Susan Sarandon, Hank Azaria, Philip Baker Hall, Cherry Jones, Bob Balaban, Harris Yulin, Jack Black, Jamey Sheridan, Paul Giamatti, Barnard Hughes, Barbara Sukowa, John Carpenter, Gretchen Mol. 134 MINS.

New York, 1936. The WPA (Works Progress Administration), part of President Roosevelt's policy to counter the effects of the Depression, funds the Federal Theatre Project, which subsidises low-cost theatres and their productions. The policy is being attacked by right-wing politicians, and project head Hallie Flanagan (Cherry Jones) is called to testify before the clearly hostile Dies Committee in Washington. *The Cradle Will Rock*, a 'play with music' by Marc Blitzstein, is in rehearsal at a small Broadway theatre and is being produced by Local 891, a company headed by Orson Welles (Angus Macfadyen) and John Houseman (Cary Elwes). Olive Stanton (Emily Watson), a homeless young woman, is given a role in the play. Hazel Huffman (Joan Cusack), who works for Federal Theatre, testifies to the Committee and claims that Communists are infiltrating the project. Funds to the theatre are cut, and there's a last-minute change of venue before the play opens to considerable success.

On the comparatively rare occasions that art and politics collide, something very combustible occurs; so it was in 1936 when Italy's Fascism and Hitler's efficiency seemed attractive to some on the Right in isolationist America. Self-described as 'a (mostly) true story', this splendidly rich film centres on a period when a progressive US Government, under political pressure, suddenly had second thoughts about the way work for the unemployed was being funded and handled. This was really the beginning of the infamous McCarthy era (though McCarthy himself wouldn't appear on the scene for some years) as Congress began its Un-American Activities enquiries.

Tim Robbins' third film as director (and arguably his best) focuses partly on 22-year-old Orson Welles, but there is a wealth of colourful characters here. Nelson Rockefeller (John Cusack) hires Diego Rivera (Rubén Blades) to paint a huge mural in the foyer of his bank, but destroys the artwork when he sees, among the workers depicted, an image of Lenin. Bill Murray plays Tommy Crickshaw, a fiercely anti-Communist hypnotist. Vanessa Redgrave is Countess La Grange, a very wealthy woman and patron of the arts. Susan Sarandon portrays Margherita Sarfatti, an envoy of Mussolini's Italian Government, who has been charged with selling priceless old paintings to millionaire American collectors, like William Randolph Hearst (John Carpenter—not the director!) to help fund the Fascist cause.

These and a great many more colourful characters are involved in this fascinating chapter of America's Depression history, and Robbins throws them all together with complete confidence. The result is an exuberant film, superbly shot in long fluid takes by cinematographer Jean Yves Escoffier. Cary Elwes' performance as Welles' long-time collaborator, John Houseman, is the only character that doesn't quite ring true.

Robbins had directed *Bob Roberts* (1992) and *Dead Man Walking* (1995), both well regarded, prior to this, his most ambitious project as a director. Despite being a tremendously entertaining tale with a preposterously happy ending—despite an Equity ban on the production, the actors involved voluntarily put on the show for a rousingly successful performance—the film tanked at the box office, and Robbins has only directed one obscure film since.

25

The Crossing Guard

(USA, 1995)

Miramax Films. DIRECTOR/SCRIPT: Sean Penn. ACTORS: Jack Nicholson, David Morse, Anjelica Huston, Robin Wright, Piper Laurie, Richard Bradford, Priscilla Barnes, David Baerwald, Robbie Robertson, John Savage, Leo Penn, Richard Sarafian. 106 MINS.

Los Angeles. John Booth (David Morse) is released from prison after serving five years for a drink-driving accident in which a seven-year-old girl was killed. The dead girl's parents, Freddy Gale (Jack Nicholson) and Mary (Anjelica Huston), separated as a direct result of their bereavement ('You were small and weak. I wanted you big and strong,' Mary tells Freddy), and Mary is now married to Roger (Robbie Robertson). John goes home to live with his parents Helen (Piper Laurie) and Stuart (Richard Bradford). Freddy, who owns a jewellery shop, is lonely and angry; he spends his evenings getting drunk at a strip club and having sex with the girls he meets there. He has decided to kill John, but when he arrives at the caravan where John is living in the driveway of his parents' home, Freddy's gun refuses to fire. Freddy gives John three days before he promises to return and kill him. During that period, John—who was himself almost suicidal—meets Jojo (Robin Wright), an artist, and falls in love. Now he has a reason to live.

The second feature Sean Penn wrote and directed (after *The Indian Runner* in 1991) is a drama about the variety of ways in which grief and guilt affect different people. Freddy and John have both been destroyed by the death of Freddy's little girl. John blames himself and has lost the will to live; Freddy is consumed with thoughts of vengeance. Mary, on the other hand, has rebuilt her life. She attends group therapy sessions that bring her some comfort, and she's happy in her new marriage.

The film also attempts to explore the meaning of 'freedom', that word that meant so much to young people in the 60s and 70s. As John says, 'Freedom is just entertainment.' He can't get over the fact that, as he tells Jojo, the dying girl apologised to him for not looking both ways before she crossed the road.

Penn said at the time of the film's release that the title was symbolic. 'A crossing guard takes people who, through either immaturity or blindness, cannot find their way safely across a street on their own,' he stated. Both John and Freddy fall into this category—and it's no coincidence that Freddy is stopped by the police for drink driving as he's heading for John's home on the fateful third day.

The leads are superb. Nicholson conveys the anger and agony of his character with tremendous skill, and there's a touching moment when, out on the street, he's distracted by a little girl calling for her Daddy. Morse, too, impresses as a basically decent man whose life, and the lives of others, was ruined by one stupid decision that had such fateful consequences. And Huston is heartbreakingly good as the woman who lost her only daughter, and her husband, yet has the capacity to forgive.

Despite the star power of Jack Nicholson, and the strong supporting cast, the film's grim subject matter kept audiences away. Penn has gone on to direct three more features since (see #71), with mostly positive results. He's certainly as interesting a director as he is an actor.

26

The Custodian

(AUSTRALIA, 1993)

JD Productions. DIRECTOR/SCRIPT: John Dingwall. ACTORS: Anthony LaPaglia, Hugo Weaving, Barry Otto, Kelly Dingwall, Essie Davis, Gosia Dobrowolska, Bill Hunter, Christina Totos, Skye Wansey, Tim McKenzie, Norman Kaye, Steven Grives, Bogdan Koca, Joy Smithers, Naomi Watts. 110 MINS.

An unnamed Australian city. Detective-Sergeant James Quinlan (Anthony LaPaglia) is going through a crisis; his marriage to the alcoholic Helen (Joy Smithers) is on the rocks, he's left home and moved into a cheap hotel, and he's sick of the everyday corruption he experiences within the police department. He makes the decision to expose the corrupt cops and principally his partner, Detective Church (Hugo Weaving). Quinlan makes anonymous contact with Reynolds (Kelly Dingwall), an investigative journalist, and Ferguson (Barry Otto), a lawyer with Police Internal Affairs. Reynolds gets the reluctant go-ahead from the TV network for which he works to proceed with a story on police corruption, though he doesn't realise that one of the corrupt cops he's tracking—Quinlan—is his own secret informant. Church gets wind of the fact that Ferguson is on his trail, and tries to intimidate him through his wife, Claire (Skye Wansey), which leads to a violent climax.

There has rarely been a better cast for an Australian feature film than the one assembled by director and screenwriter John Dingwall for his second and final feature as director (*The Custodian* followed the excellent *Phobia*, made in 1988). LaPaglia, the Adelaide-born actor who began appearing in films in America, returned to Australia for his first local role as the honest cop who, in order to root out endemic corruption, is forced to pretend to be corrupt himself. Hugo Weaving as the evil Church and Barry Otto as the tenacious and courageous Ferguson have rarely been better. Dingwall's son, Kelly, is fine as the crusading journalist, and then there are Essie Davis, in her first screen role as Jilly, the owner of a coffee shop who falls in love with Quinlan, Bill Hunter as the chief executive of a TV station, Gosia Dobrowolska as his chief of staff, who lends her support to Reynolds when he most needs it, Norman Kaye as a judge and, in a tiny role, Naomi Watts. All are superb.

Though the city in which these events unfold isn't named, it's clearly Sydney, and Dingwall's literate, tense and intelligent drama dissects the links between cops and criminals with disturbing conviction. He had written scripts for many TV cop shows (*Matlock Police*, *Division 4*, *Homicide*) as well as the screenplays for *Sunday Too Far Away* and *Buddies* (which he also produced), before he made *Phobia*, which he self-funded on a minuscule budget.

In similar ways to William Wyler's police drama *Detective Story* (1951), Dingwall, with *The Custodian*, favours dialogue—smart, sharp, pithy dialogue—over conventional action. Arguably the only criticism that can be levelled against *The Custodian* is that it's shot in a rather televisual style, with an over-reliance on close-ups. But in every other respect it's a remarkably good thriller that has the viewer on the edge of their seat from start to finish.

Dingwall had major difficulties finding distribution for both his feature films and, as a result, both were under-seen and have been seriously neglected. It's high time both of them, but especially the very accessible *The Custodian*, were better known and appreciated.

Dingwall's literate, tense and intelligent drama dissects the links between cops and criminals with disturbing conviction

27

Daniel

(USA, 1983)

World Film Services. **DIRECTOR:** Sidney Lumet. **SCRIPT:** E.L. Doctorow, based on his novel, *The Book of Daniel*. **ACTORS:** Timothy Hutton, Mandy Patinkin, Lindsay Crouse, Amanda Plummer, Edward Asner, Ellen Barkin, Lee Richardson, Joseph Leon, Tovah Feldshuh. **129 MINS.**

New York City, 1938. Paul Isaacson (Mandy Patinkin) meets Rochelle (Lindsay Crouse) at a left-wing rally against Fascism in Europe. They marry and have two children, Daniel and Susan. After the war, Paul is named by his old friend Selig Mindish (Joseph Leon) as the head of a Communist cell involved in stealing atomic secrets. First Paul, then Rochelle, are arrested by the FBI, tried and found guilty. After a number of appeals, both are executed in the electric chair in 1953. In the 1970s, their son Daniel (Timothy Hutton) is married to Phyllis (Ellen Barkin) and they have a child. Susan (Amanda Plummer) is still traumatised by what happened to her parents; after experimenting with sex, drugs and religion she has become involved in radical politics. When Susan slashes her wrists in a suicide attempt, Daniel sets out to try to prove his parents were innocent.

E.L. Doctorow's novel, *The Book of Daniel*, published in 1971, was very loosely based on the execution of Julius and Ethel Rosenberg, and the novelist's own screenplay cuts back and forth between the past—photographed by Andrzej Bartkowiak in burnished orange hues—and the present. The past is a nostalgic, happy place where Paul and Rochelle took their kids to hear Paul Robeson perform at an outdoors concert, and openly supported the Soviets in the war against Nazism. The siblings were close then, but in the grimmer present, with its anti-Vietnam demonstrations and its sense of betrayal, they've moved apart from each other. The Watergate scandal that doomed the Nixon presidency, and which was playing out during the period in which the 1973 events unfold, is never mentioned. Like Daniel, the audience never learns the true facts—were Paul and Rochelle really guilty of espionage, or were they, as their lawyer, Jacob Ascher (Edward Asner), sorrowfully explains, victims of 'the medieval temper of the times'? Did they, in fact, willingly suffer at the direction of the Communist Party, whose American leaders wanted them to become martyrs for the cause—or, perhaps, even because they were needed as scapegoats to protect the real spies? These questions are raised, and the viewer must decide the truth. Mainly, though, the film is concerned with the legacy of the times and, specifically, the legacy of the ruinous Blacklist of the McCarthy period. It's the children who have suffered most, not only Daniel and the tragic Susan but also Linda (Tovah Feldshuh), the daughter of the alleged informer, Mindish, who named names and betrayed his friends, and who, as a reward, got off with a light prison sentence. Perhaps the story's hero is Ascher, who fought a losing battle to defend the Isaacsons, tried to care for their children, and who sacrificed his health as a result.

Sidney Lumet is wonderful with actors and the film is flaw-lessly cast with mostly Jewish actors, a reminder that immigrants from Europe were often on the radical side of American politics. He also uses as counterpoint some magnificent Paul Robeson songs, including—in a powerful sequence intercutting between two funerals some twenty years apart—the haunting 'There's a Man Going 'Round Taking Names'.

Lumet, whose first film was *12 Angry Men* in 1957, made many films during a long career, mostly thrillers but also the occasional comedy. His interest in politics was most apparent in *Daniel* and *Running on Empty* (see #81) and, not surprisingly perhaps, these are two of his less successful films at the box office. *Daniel* was possibly perceived as being too steeped in American left-wing politics (although, as noted, it's pretty even-handed), and the intricate flashback structure confused some. At any rate, it had a brief release and quickly disappeared from view.

The Deep Blue Sea

Deep Blue Sea Productions. DIRECTOR/SCRIPT: Terence Davies, from the play by Terence Rattigan.
ACTORS: Rachel Weisz, Tom Hiddleston, Simon Russell Beale, Barbara Jefford, Ann Mitchell, Jolyon Coy, Karl Johnson, Sarah Kants. 98 MINS.

London, 'about' 1950. Hester Collyer (Rachel Weisz) has left her husband, Sir William (Simon Russell Beale), a judge, for Freddie Page (Tom Hiddleston), an RAF pilot who saw action in the Battle of Britain, but Freddie has abandoned Hester and she has attempted suicide in front of the gas fire in her flat. She is found in time by a concerned neighbour and revived. She remembers meeting Freddie for the first time and the passionate love affair they had shared. She also recalls a painful visit to her mother-in-law, Mrs Collyer (Barbara Jefford). Freddie, meanwhile, returns to the flat and finds Hester's suicide note. The couple meet again, but Freddie is determined to leave England for South America, and there seems to be no future in their relationship.

Terence Rattigan's play, *The Deep Blue Sea*, was first performed in 1952 with Peggy Ashcroft in the role of Hester. The play was filmed, rather unimaginatively, in 1955 by Anatole Litvak, with Vivien Leigh as Hester, Kenneth More as Freddie, Eric Portman as Miller and Emlyn Williams as Sir William, but the film was a commercial failure and is hardly ever screened. Following several stage revivals, Terence Davies' adaptation came to the screen in 2011 to general critical acclaim.

The film is much more Davies than Rattigan. Davies, known for the heart-breaking autobiographical films set in his native Liverpool (*Distant Voices, Still Lives, The Long Day Closes*) has transformed Rattigan's play into his own very personal vision. It's as though the lovers in the celebrated David Lean–Noel Coward romantic drama *Brief Encounter* (1945) had pursued their passion rather than just talk about it and long for it. The film begins with an extraordinary eight-minute sequence—which the director described as a 'prelude'—in which a violin piece by Samuel Barber accompanies a slow camera glide from a bombed-out house up the wall of the house next door, and eventually into the rather shabby room used by Hester and Freddie for their lovemaking, and where Hester has attempted to kill herself. It's a magisterial curtain raiser and is followed by an almost wordless sequence in which the couple meet for the first time and, despite the fact that Hester is married, begin their affair. Back in the present, Hester is saved by Mr Miller (Karl Johnson), a neighbour and former doctor, struck off for—it's hinted—his homosexuality.

Davies' Liverpool films were distinguished by the naturalistic scenes in which members of an extended family and their friends enjoy themselves in the local pub by singing songs that were popular during and after World War II, and there's another pub sing-along here. Also typical of Davies is a wartime flashback in which Hester and Sir William shelter in the Aldwych tube station during an air raid and everyone starts singing 'Cockles and Mussels'. Later we see Hester and Freddie dancing to the Jo Stafford song 'You Belong to Me', a hugely popular tune from 1952.

With its drab, misty, slightly soft-focus look and its colour palette of browns and greys, the film sharply evokes the post-war period in London. A scene in which Hester observes her landlady, Mrs Elton (Ann Mitchell), caring for her sick husband is extraordinarily touching, and there's an amusingly brittle performance from Barbara Jefford as the mother of the judge.

Hester was traditionally played by an older actress, but Weisz is superlative in the role and is given consummate support. But, sadly, a film that opens with an attempted suicide and continues to depict the actions of an unfaithful wife abandoned by her lover proved a very tough sell, and so this beautiful film quickly disappeared.

29

Devil in the Flesh

(AUSTRALIA, 1985)

J.C. Williamson Film Management–World Film Alliance. DIRECTOR/SCRIPT: Scott Murray, from the novel by Raymond Radiguet. ACTORS: Katia Caballero, Keith Smith, John Morris, Jill Forster, Colin Duckworth, Reine Lavoie, Louise Elvin, Odile Le Clezio, Luciano Martucci. 103 MINS.

Rural Victoria, 1943. Paul Hansen (Keith Smith), a shy teenager, lives with his parents John (John Morris) and Jill (Jill Forster). Marthe (Katia Caballero) lives alone nearby; her Italian husband, Ermanno (Luciano Martucci), has been interned as a POW. Paul and Marthe become friends, then lovers. Despite their attempts to keep their relationship secret, the locals begin to gossip and the word gets back to Paul's parents. When the war ends, so does the relationship. Some time later, Paul visits Marthe and Ermanno and meets, for the first time, his baby son.

If ever there was a case of unfortunate timing, Scott Murray's first and only feature film, *Devil in the Flesh*, is a perfect example. Murray, a Francophile, and long-time editor of the now defunct film magazine *Cinema Papers*, based his screenplay on the famous French novel, *Le Diable au corps*, by Raymond Radiguet, and the 1947 Claude Autant-Lara film version that made a star of actor Gérard Philipe. However, at almost exactly the same time that Murray was making his film in and around Castlemaine, Victoria, the celebrated Italian director, Marco Bellocchio, was making *his* version of the book, *Il diavolo in corpo*. Both films screened at Cannes in 1986, the Bellocchio in an official section, and Murray's film in the Marche (Market). The Italian version, with its sensational unsimulated fellatio sequence, completely overshadowed the Australian film.

Which is a great shame because Murray's film, despite the alterations made to Radiguet's book, which was set during World

War I and ended with the adulterous heroine dying in childbirth, is more faithful than Bellocchio to the *spirit* of the source material.

Andrew de Groot's painterly photography is one of the reasons for this. He beautifully captures the small, sleepy town with its bustling centre and elegant houses on the fringes, as well as the surrounding countryside—the vineyards, the dusty unsealed roads, the quiet railway station. Paul's awkward relationship with his parents is neatly depicted, especially in a scene where he and his father discuss loyalty ('Loyalty to a friend may be more important than allegiance to an idea'). Katia Caballero is radiant as Marthe, while in the early scenes Keith Smith is believably awkward as the teenager who becomes involved with an older woman. Their love scenes are quite candidly presented, leading to the transformation of the teenager into a far more confident young man as the film progresses. Not that Paul is completely devoted to Marthe; while she's away he picks up an attractive blonde model (Louise Elvin) and has sex with her—but they have nothing to say to one another afterwards. Paul is believably boorish when a cherished weekend alone with Marthe is interrupted by the unexpected arrival of one of her friends (Odile Le Clezio).

Murray's handling of these scenes make you wish he'd pursued a film-directing career; the last sequence of the film, in which Paul meets his son and the husband of his mistress, is most beautifully handled. Impressive, too, is the music score by French composer Philippe Sarde.

Australian reviews of the film were mixed, and the film struggled to find a local audience. At some stage the title was even changed to *Beyond Innocence*, to no appreciable advantage. The version that eventually screened on television was almost 15 minutes shorter than the original.

Seemingly just about the only country where the film made any kind of impact was India, where it was widely released after a screening at the New Delhi Film Festival.

30

Enemy

(CANADA / SPAIN / FRANCE, 2013)

Roxbury Pictures-Mecanismo Films-Pathé. DIRECTOR: Denis Villeneuve. SCRIPT: Javier Gullón, from the novel by José Saramago. ACTORS: Jake Gyllenhaal, Mélanie Laurent, Sarah Gadon, Isabella Rossellini, Tim Post, Josh Peace, Kedar Brown, Darryl Dinn, Misha Highstead. 91 MINS.

Toronto. Adam (Jake Gyllenhaal), a history professor who lives with his girlfriend, Mary (Mélanie Laurent), is one of a group of men watching the entertainment at a sophisticated sex club. The act ends with a woman preparing to crush a spider under her heel. One of Adam's friends recommends a DVD he thinks will interest Adam; Adam rents it and, while viewing it, is surprised to see, in a small role (that of '3rd Bellhop'), his exact double, actor Anthony Clair (also Gyllenhaal). Intrigued, Adam tracks down Anthony's agent, visits the agency office, and intercepts a letter addressed to the actor. Adam phones Anthony's apartment and the call is answered by Helen (Sarah Gadon), the actor's pregnant wife. Helen meets Adam and is amazed at the close resemblance to Anthony, even including small details like a facial scar. Anthony ends up demanding that the men change places and sleep with the other's woman. The exchange will become permanent.

There have been many films featuring identical twins, often in mystery dramas—*The Dark Mirror*, *A Stolen Life*, *Dead Ringer*, *Dead Ringers*, *The Double* among them—but this Canadian movie from the director who went on to make *Arrival* and *Blade Runner 2049* is one of the most intriguing, in large part because it offers no easy explanations. In fact it becomes something of a challenge to work out which character is Adam and which is Anthony, and that's the point of the movie.

The film is based on a novel, *O Homem Duplicado*, by Portuguese writer José Saramago, and follows the English translation of the original fairly closely. That means that it's not giving much away and that the viewer is asked to decipher the puzzle without a great deal of help from the script. This proves to be an enticing quest, as what starts out as a dry comedy becomes more and more horrific as the Kafkaesque elements of the story rise increasingly to the surface.

On one level this is a mystery story, but it's a mystery without a traditional resolution. On another it's a horror film, with the role of the mysteriously recurring spider—an invention of the film not to be found in the book—also never fully explained. And it's also an erotic movie since, though the sexual scenes are discreetly depicted, they nevertheless carry with them a considerable charge given the questions raised about the identities of the men involved.

Gyllenhaal is adept at enacting the minimal differences between the two almost identical characters, while Isabella Rossellini plays Anthony's mother, bringing with her resonances of David Lynch and *Blue Velvet*.

Unfortunately this teasing, intriguing film seems to have proved simply too challenging for distributors and audiences alike. Villeneuve made it back-to-back with a far more traditional thriller, *Prisoners*, which also starred Gyllenhaal (and Hugh Jackman), and that film tended to steal *Enemy*'s thunder. As a result it failed to achieve a cinema release in many countries, including Australia.

What starts out as a dry comedy becomes more and more horrific

31

Everybody Wins

(USA/UK, 1990)

Orion Pictures–Recorded Picture Co. DIRECTOR: Karel Reisz. SCRIPT: Arthur Miller. ACTORS: Debra Winger, Nick Nolte, Will Patton, Jack Warden, Judith Ivey, Kathleen Wilhoite, Frank Converse, Frank Military, Steven Skybell, Mary Louise Wilson. 97 MINS.

Highbury, Connecticut. In this small New England town, part-time TV journalist Tom O'Toole (Nick Nolte), who has lived with his sister since the death of his wife three years earlier, is approached by Angela Crispini (Debra Winger) who seeks his help in freeing a young man, Felix Daniels (Frank Military) who has, she claims, been wrongly convicted of the stabbing murder of his uncle, Dr Victor Daniels, a prominent local citizen. Though frustrated by Angela's obvious flakiness, Tom agrees to see Felix in prison. Angela then tells him the name of the man she believes to be the real killer: Jerry (Will Patton), the leader of a local gang of bikies and a religious cultist. She claims Jerry tried to give himself up to the police, but that they refused to listen to him. Discovering that his old adversary, State's Attorney Charley Haggerty (Frank Converse) is in charge of the prosecution, Tom becomes heavily involved in Angela's crusade, and they become lovers. But she still won't tell him everything she knows, and he discovers that in the past she has worked as a prostitute. He also discovers that Angela had been Haggerty's mistress and that he was the love of her life. But, sensing a major scandal involving drugs and sex, Tom continues to investigate.

Arthur Miller, one of the 20th century's most important dramatists, wrote a few screenplays during the course of his long career, two of which were originals and not based on material he'd originally written for the theatre: *The Misfits* (1961), a vehicle for his then-wife, Marilyn Monroe, and *Everybody Wins*. Many of Miller's themes crop up in the latter film, which was directed by

Czech-born, British based Karel Reisz, whose screen work includes *Saturday Night and Sunday Morning*, *Isadora* and *The French Lieutenant's Woman*.

'It's like chasing feathers in a tornado,' complains the exasperated Tom at one point, describing the frustrations he experiences in dealing with the volatile Angela. Indeed his role as an investigator—he's a journalist rather than a private eye, but the mechanics remain the same—are constantly thwarted by the unreliability of his client. Tom is a fairly straightforward character, attracted to the case of Felix Daniels not only by the seductiveness of Angela, but also because he senses a cover-up and scandal that will blow the small town wide open and destroy the career of the State's Attorney and some crooked cops.

But Angela is constantly undermining his investigation with new revelations that muddy the waters at every turn. Only gradually does the besotted Tom begin to realise just how deeply involved she really is, and how impossible his situation has become. The later scenes, in which the local Judge (Jack Warden) assumes centre stage, are particularly good. 'Most of the people in jail belong there,' claims the Judge, and his actions indicate just how deeply corruption penetrates society. Even Tom's thoroughly respectable sister (Judith Ivey), a schoolteacher, is willing to give a good grade to an exam paper with atrociously bad spelling because the pupil involved is a sporting star. The use of the old song 'A Hot Time in the Old Town Tonight', played over the film's final scene, underscores the irony.

Though it contains all the elements of a classic private eye movie, *Everybody Wins* probably seemed a bit tame in 1990. Savaged by American critics, the film had a very limited release. It was the last film Karel Reisz directed.

32

Family Business

(USA, 1989)

TriStar-Regency. DIRECTOR: Sidney Lumet. SCRIPT: Vincent Patrick. ACTORS: Sean Connery, Dustin Hoffman, Matthew Broderick, Rosanna DeSoto, Janet Carroll, Victoria Jackson, Bill McCutcheon, Deborah Rush, Marilyn Cooper, James S. Tolkan, Luis Guzman. 109 MINS.

New York. Vito McMullen (Dustin Hoffman), who manages a meat packing business, is the son of a Scottish father, Jessie (Sean Connery) and a Sicilian mother. While celebrating Passover with the family of his Jewish wife, Elaine (Rosanna DeSoto), Vito is surprised and pleased when their son, Adam (Matthew Broderick) puts in an appearance. Adam has just dropped out of college before completing his Master's in molecular biology, and Vito is dismayed when the young man receives a call from his grandfather, who needs cash to bail him out of prison for punching a cop. Jessie has always been an unapologetic minor criminal, something his son resents but his grandson rather admires. Adam proposes that Jessie join him in stealing some valuable chemicals and logs—involving the genetic improvement of farm crops—from a lab, and Vito reluctantly goes along to make sure Adam is safe.

Sidney Lumet (see #27, 72 and 81) frequently made films about families, or groups of closely connected people, involved in crime. His first feature, *12 Angry Men*, paved the way in 1957, and in the following years he made both big successes (*Serpico, Murder on the Orient Express, Dog Day Afternoon, Network*) and also a great many well-regarded but less popular films. *Family Business* is one of his most intriguing efforts. He'd worked with Sean Connery before (on *The Hill* and *The Offence*), and in this film the actor plays a Scot who emigrated into New York's melting pot and then married into a multicultural family but was never able to fit in and was constantly committing minor crimes. His son, Vito, always hated his father's lawlessness, while Adam, his grandson, was equally unhappy with the way *his* father forced him into the straight and narrow.

The heist at the centre of the film is a curious one, given that what's robbed isn't cash or jewellery but chemicals and documents, and that, in any case, it all proves to be a fake—the lab *wants* the chemicals stolen because the scientists who work there have discovered that they don't work, and they want more time to perfect their research.

As with every Lumet film this is primarily an actors' piece, and the trio at the centre of the narrative have rarely been better. Hoffman, particularly, is extremely moving as the exasperated 'nice' guy who resents the attitudes of a father he sees as completely irresponsible and who fears his son will take after the old man. Adam responds to this concern by remarking: 'That's America. Every generation is a little bit better.' Lumet is also interested in the ethnically mixed melange of which the McMullens are a part. The film begins and ends with a funeral attended not only by family members, but also by large numbers of police of Irish background, who sing 'Danny Boy' with gusto; the man behind the scam at the lab is Chinese; and Jessie explains the fact that Vito is so much shorter than he is by the fact that his mother is Sicilian.

With a cast like this you would expect the film to have been a success, but in fact it failed badly at the box office, perhaps because Lumet isn't interested in sticking rigidly to genre. It's *not* a heist movie, though it was billed as such, and it's not exactly a comedy, though there are some great comedic moments. Instead, it's a drama about families, and a particularly interesting and compelling one.

33

Father

(AUSTRALIA, 1990)

Barron Entertainment. DIRECTOR: John Power. SCRIPT: Tony Cavanaugh, Graham Hartley. ACTORS: Max von Sydow, Carol Drinkwater, Julia Blake, Steve Jacobs, Tim Robertson, Simone Robertson, Nicholas Bell. 100 MINS.

Melbourne. German-born Joe Mueller (Max von Sydow) has lived in Australia since the end of the war. A retired widower, he shares a comfortable apartment with his devoted daughter, Anne (Carol Drinkwater), son-in-law Bobby (Steve Jacobs), a Vietnam veteran, and two granddaughters. With no advance warning, a TV current affairs program goes to air featuring an elderly woman, Iya Zetnick (Julia Blake), who accuses Mueller of wartime atrocities. Mueller vigorously denies the charges, but winds up in court. A muck-raking journalist informs Anne that Mrs Zetnik had previously laid similar charges in Britain and that they proved to be unfounded; he also claims that she has a history of mental illness. Mueller is acquitted but the case is not yet over.

The screenplay makes the point that any time a war is fought involving civilians, horrific things can occur. 'It's in all of us,' says Bobby, speaking of his own experiences in Vietnam and atrocities committed against non-combatants. The audience is invited to decide Mueller's guilt or innocence of the terrible war crimes of which he's accused, and Sweden's von Sydow—one of Ingmar Bergman's favourite actors, who enjoyed an international career after his Bergman films—gives such a sympathetic portrayal of the elderly German that it's difficult to believe he really was, in the distant past, a Nazi killer. Though there are one or two improbabilities in the narrative, the film as a whole is thought-provoking and powerful, though it's curious that the TV program makes no attempt to contact Mueller before going to air with the sensational story in which serious accusations are made against him.

The film was to have been directed by Steve Jodrell, but he left during pre-production and was replaced by John Power, here making only his second—and, as it turned out, last—feature after the nostalgic *The Picture Show Man* (1977). Power does a very competent job, and elicits strong performances from his cast, especially Julia Blake as the accuser.

Unfortunately, in one of those remarkable coincidences that occur from time to time, the film was made simultaneously with a high-profile Hollywood movie with an almost identical plot, *Music Box*, by French director Costa-Gavras. A month before *Father* was screened for the Australian press, *Music Box* shared the Golden Bear at the Berlin Film Festival. Both films feature an elderly European who has lived since the war in an English-speaking country—America in the case of the Costa-Gavras film; both men have loving daughters and grandchildren; both are accused of Nazi war crimes; and in both films there's a court case that ends with the accused being declared innocent. The main difference is that in the American film the daughter is a lawyer who literally defends her father. Presumably the producers of *Father* were completely unaware that *Music Box* was in production, but by the time both films were completed it was obvious which one would find international distribution. Despite positive reviews in Australia—Matt White in the *Mirror* claimed it was 'One of the best Australian films I have seen in years. A powerful drama that strikes at the heart of an Australian family', and Paul LePetit in the *Sunday Telegraph* wrote: 'The most powerful and compelling film to be made in Australia for years'—the film struggled at the local box office and has apparently never made it to DVD.

34

The Favour, the Watch and the Very Big Fish

(FRANCE/UK, 1991)

Les Films Ariane–Umbrella Films. DIRECTOR/SCRIPT: Ben Lewin, from a story by Marcel Aymé. ACTORS: Bob Hoskins, Natasha Richardson, Jeff Goldblum, Michel Blanc, Jean-Pierre Cassel, Jacques Villeret, Angela Pleasence. 89 MINS.

Paris. Louis (Bob Hoskins) works as a photographer taking 'devotional pictures' of religious tableaux at the Calvary Studios run by Norbert Norman (Michel Blanc). Zalman (Jean-Pierre Cassel), the actor who was to have portrayed John the Baptist for Louis, has a bad case of the flu and asks a favour of Louis—to stand in for him at a recording session for the dubbing of a porno film. At the studio, Louis discovers that his 'co-star' is an attractive woman named Sybil (Natasha Richardson), and the two hit it off. Sybil tells Louis a story: three years earlier, while working as a waitress in a smart restaurant, she was offered a valuable watch by an obnoxious child if she could make the gloomy-looking pianist (Jeff Goldblum) smile. This led to the start of a frustrated relationship that ended when the pianist was jailed for three years after attacking a rival. He's about to be released from prison and Louis agrees to accompany Sybil to meet him—but she fails to show up.

Australian director Ben Lewin's second film, made in Paris in English, is an expansion of a ten-page short story, 'Rue Saint-Sulpice' (the title of the French version of the film), by Marcel Aymé. It's an exceedingly quirky, whimsical and very droll comedy based on coincidences, instant romances and missed connections. It's a great idea to have the principal characters meet for the first time in a recording studio to supply the soundtrack to a porno film (which we don't see): the expressions we see on Hoskins' face during the recording process speak volumes about his character. The ups and downs of the Louis–Sybil romance are compared with Sybil's relationship with the mournful pianist, and in both relationships there are constant frustrations that have potentially dire consequences. But Lewin, like Robert Altman, revels in the throwaway bits and pieces going on at the edges of the main story. The lovely opening scene, in which a bishop and a nun arrive at the photographic studio in pouring rain and the nun's coif becomes sodden and uncontrollable, continues as the pair encounter the chaotic interior of the *atelier* that is filled with animals, including a goat, taking part in a tableau about Francis of Assisi. The 'very big fish' of the title makes a rather brief appearance when Louis purchases what looks like a large swordfish at a market and takes it home for his sister to prepare—and she puts it through a shredder, serving it up as a grey-black mess.

Very often this kind of pan-European production, spoken in English with a cast composed of actors from several countries, ends up as the sort of non-culturally specific and unconvincing 'Euro-pudding' much derided by critics. This is one occasion where that accusation doesn't stand up; the Paris setting provides the backdrop, but the story—the crazy, cheerfully improbable, weirdly romantic story—could really take place anywhere.

Bob Hoskins is at his best in his role as the hapless Louis; his comedy timing is perfect. Natasha Richardson never looked lovelier or played such an outspoken and cheeky character. Jeff Goldblum revels in a role that has him mistaken for Jesus Christ to the point that he starts to believe it himself—though he discovers that walking on water, in this case the Seine, is not a good idea. The fine French actors who compose the supporting cast are also flawless, especially Michel Blanc as the wily, opportunistic head of the Calvary Studios.

Given the film's enormous qualities, it's all the more surprising that today it's so little known and regarded.

35

Finders Keepers

(USA, 1984)

CBS Theatrical Films. DIRECTOR: Richard Lester. SCRIPT: Terence Marsh, Ronny Graham, Charles Dennis. ACTORS: Michael O'Keefe, Beverly D'Angelo, Louis Gossett Jr, Pamela Stephenson, Ed Lauter, David Wayne, Brian Dennehy, John Schuck, Jim Carrey. 95 MINS.

San Francisco, 1973. Michael (Michael O'Keefe), a minor conman fleeing his creditors, acquires the uniform of an army sergeant and boards a train heading east. Meanwhile heiress Georgiana Latimer (Pamela Stephenson) has faked her kidnapping and, with her lover, Sirola (Ed Lauter), as her accomplice, has stolen millions in cash from her father. The loot is hidden in a coffin loaded onto the same train on which Michael is travelling, and the senile train guard, Stapleton (David Wayne), jumps to the conclusion that Michael is escorting the corpse of a fallen comrade. On the train Michael meets Standish (Beverly D'Angelo), a would-be actress, who tries to help him. Sirola tries in vain to kill Michael, who he believes is after the money in the coffin. Frenetic complications ensue, eventually involving the corrupt mayor (Brian Dennehy) of a small town, who is protecting his gormless nephew Lane Bidlekoff (Jim Carrey in his first major screen role), a draft dodger who is wrongly thought to be the corpse in the coffin. Eventually Sirola kidnaps Standish in an attempt to get Michael—who has discovered the cash—to hand over the loot; but the location he chooses for the handover, an empty house, is being moved to another location on a large truck.

Richard Lester, an American, found fame in Britain when he directed The Beatles in *A Hard Day's Night* and *Help!*; his other successes included the award-winning *The Knack*, *A Funny Thing Happened on the Way to the Forum*, *The Three Musketeers*, *Juggernaut*, *The Bed Sitting Room*, *How I Won the War*, *Robin and Marian* and many others. *Finders Keepers* proved to be his penultimate feature film, and, although it's up there among his best work, it was a dismal commercial failure. This might have been due to the fact that the production company, CBS Theatrical, with its background in network television, was not attuned to the complexities of cinema distribution, or that the leading actor was relatively unknown; or that, even long after the Vietnam War had ended, a comedy centring on the return home of a soldier killed in action—even though there is no body and it's all a fake!—was in poor taste.

Yet *Finders Keepers* is head and shoulders above most Hollywood comedies of the period. 'Who wrote this dialogue? Kafka?' moans one of the characters, and the screenplay skilfully combines one-liners like that one with good old-fashioned slapstick. In an early scene, a clumsy cop (John Schuck) returns home unexpectedly to find his wife sharing a bath with a bemused Michael, but this kind of old-style bedroom farce quickly gives way to elaborate visual gags, such as the hilarious climax that takes place in the house being transported along a highway. David Wayne's befuddled train guard is also a wonderfully colourful character; he never stops talking about his obsession—American presidents—and claims to be able to speak on the phone to the current incumbent, Richard Nixon (he calls him 'Nickersen') any time he wants to—and, indeed, he does. The backdrop to all this is the Watergate scandal, which is unfolding dramatically, as we see from newspaper headlines.

Lester directs at a frantic pace, so there's not a dull moment in this cheerfully improbable series of crazy events and encounters. The one weak character is that of Michael's mentor, Century (Louis Gossett Jr), the man who—as we see in brief but unnecessary flashbacks—adopted him as a child. His character is one of the few false notes in an otherwise expert concoction. O'Keefe is outstanding as the resourceful hero.

36

Following

(UK, 1999)

Next Wave Films. **DIRECTOR/SCRIPT**: Christopher Nolan. **ACTORS**: Jeremy Theobald, Alex Haw, Lucy Russell, John Nolan, Dick Bradsell, Gillian El-Kadi, Jennifer Angel, Nicolas Carlotti, Darren Ormandy, Rebecca James. **70 MINS**.

London. A Young Man (Jeremy Theobald), who might be called Bill—the credits list him only as Young Man—is giving a statement to a policeman. He explains that he is an unpublished writer and his life has been so boring that he's taken to following complete strangers in the street. One day he followed a man named Cobb (Alex Haw), who went into a cafe. Cobb approached the Young Man and told him that he is a thief, and that for him stealing is a game. For example, he will break into an apartment and steal a woman's panties, and later break into another apartment and conceal the underwear in a man's trouser pocket. Later, in a bar, the Young Man meets a Blonde (Lucy Russell); she tells him that the owner of the bar is her former lover and that she's frightened of him. She persuades him to break into the bar's safe and steal incriminating photographs of herself, along with a pile of cash. But things aren't at all what they seem, and the Young Man discovers that the Blonde and Cobb have set him up.

Christopher Nolan's first feature, made when he was 28, was filmed on and off over the course of a year, and shot on black and white 16 mm film that the future director of *Inception* and *Dunkirk* purchased one reel at a time. The total budget is said to have been a minuscule £3000, making it one of the cheapest feature films ever produced. Nolan's influence is clearly the film noir of the 1940s and 1950s, those terse, convoluted black and white thrillers that proved to be the path by which important directors from Anthony Mann to Stanley Kubrick entered the film business. Unfolding with a non-linear structure—a structure employed by Nolan on most of his subsequent films, including *Dunkirk*—the film is an intriguing thriller that contains a number of twists, a femme fatale and an ingenuous protagonist, all the elements of the classic Hollywood thriller. The main clue as to when exactly a specific section of the movie is taking place can be found in the protagonist's appearance; in some scenes he's smartly dressed with well-coiffed hair and wearing a tie, while in others he's bearded, scruffy, unkempt. Details that are inexplicable to begin with gradually become clear as the film progresses.

It is, of course, an extremely modest affair, but despite that it's remarkably sophisticated and assured. Of the cast, only Lucy Russell seems to have made a subsequent career as an actor. Nolan himself went on to make *Memento* in 2000, and since then has never looked back, with a series of major Hollywood films including *Insomnia* (2002), *Batman Begins* (2005), *The Prestige* (2006), *The Dark Knight* (2008), *The Dark Knight Rises* (2012) and *Interstellar* (2014). Incidentally, the character of the thief played by Leonardo DiCaprio in *Inception* (2010) is also named Cobb.

Following is included in this collection not so much because it's forgotten or overlooked, but because it was only ever known by a small handful of people. The 2012 Blu-ray release has undoubtedly gone a long way to correct that, but it's still a film that's rarely mentioned when Nolan's work is discussed: many seem still to believe *Memento* marked his debut.

Nolan's influence is clearly the film noir of the 1940s and 1950s

37

Force of Destiny

(AUSTRALIA, 2014)

Illumination Films. DIRECTOR/SCRIPT: Paul Cox. ACTORS: David Wenham, Shahana Goswami, Jacqueline McKenzie, Hannah Fredericksen, Seema Biswas, Mohan Agashe, Terry Norris, Kim Gyngell, Deidre Rubenstein, Geneviève Picot. 106 MINS.

Melbourne. Robert (David Wenham), a sculptor, is separated from Hannah (Jacqueline McKenzie), his wife, but remains on friendly terms with her and is very close to Poppy (Hannah Fredericksen), their daughter. Robert is diagnosed with cancer of the liver; doctors give conflicting advice, but it soon becomes clear that he won't survive without a liver transplant. He is placed on a waiting list. During his visits to the hospital he encounters Maya (Shahana Goswami), an Indian woman living in Melbourne. They become romantically involved, and Maya informs Robert that her beloved uncle back home is terminally ill; the pair travel to India together to see him. Back home, during the course of a Christmas dinner with his father (Terry Norris), Hannah and Poppy, Robert gets a phone call from the hospital; a new liver is available.

In almost every respect this extremely emotional film parallels the personal life of Paul Cox in his final years; substitute 'film-maker' for 'sculptor' and the details are abundantly clear. Like almost every Cox film, this simple, humanistic tale is interspersed with directorial 'doodles'—8 mm shots of Venice taken many years earlier, scenes in a forest, a majestic crane flying high in the sky, the shadow of a child, a mother with her son, and so on. What makes *Force of Destiny* one of this very idiosyncratic director's best films, though, are the scenes in which he re-creates incidents and people with whom he personally became involved while in hospital: the efficiency of the doctors, the loving care given by the nurses, and the ordeals faced by other patients and their visitors, including an old man who sings to his wife and places flowers on her bed, or the dying woman who insists on having make-up applied before she's capable of saying goodbye to her daughter.

Cox, a photographer by profession, came to Australia from his native Netherlands in 1963 and made his first feature film in 1975. He completed sixteen more, as well as several documentaries, before his death in 2016. Every film he made contained very personal elements; his actors and technicians were his friends and they all loved him. Some of his films (*Lonely Hearts*, *Man of Flowers*, *My First Wife*, *A Woman's Tale*, *Innocence*) were commercially successful, taking into account the tiny budgets on which they were produced, and several screened at international festivals and in international art house cinemas.

Despite all that, *Force of Destiny*, his final film, struggled to find any distributor or any cinema that would show it. In 2015 it opened the Melbourne International Film Festival—after the film originally selected to open the event was withdrawn—but otherwise screenings have been few and far between. You might argue that cinema audiences probably don't want to see a film about a man suffering from cancer, but the brutal truth is that if the film had been French or Iranian it would have found a more significant audience than Cox was able to attract.

Right up to the time of his death Cox was hoping to make another film; he had written a new screenplay, and claimed he was prepared to direct from a wheelchair if necessary. It didn't happen, and his death was a huge loss not only for the Australian film industry, but for quality cinema worldwide.

38

Garage Days

(AUSTRALIA, 2002)

Mystery Clock Cinema. DIRECTOR: Alex Proyas. SCRIPT: Alex Proyas, Dave Warner, Michael Udesky. ACTORS: Kick Gurry, Maya Stange, Pia Miranda, Russell Dykstra, Chris Sadrinna, Brett Stiller, Andy Anderson, Marton Csokas, Yvette Duncan, Tiriel Mora, Holly Brisley, Matthew Le Nevez, Anne Grigg, Gunther Berghofer. 105 MINS.

Sydney. Freddy (Kick Gurry) dreams—literally—of being the lead singer in a successful rock band. He fronts a group in which his live-in girlfriend, Tanya (Pia Miranda) is bass player, Joe (Brett Stiller) is lead guitar and Lucy (Chris Sadrinna) is the permanently stoned percussionist. Joe is cheating on his girlfriend, Kate (Maya Stange), by having a secret relationship with Angie (Yvette Duncan), a goth. Kate, who is pregnant, walks out on Joe and she and Freddy get together. The band's eager but inefficient manager, Bruno (Russell Dykstra), finds it increasingly difficult to obtain bookings because the live bands that once played in Sydney's suburban pubs are being replaced by DJs and pokies. One night Freddy spots Shad Kern (Marton Csokas), a powerful rock promoter, hanging out with the girlfriend of one of his star clients and blackmails Kern into giving his band a chance. But when Freddy and his band finally get to play at the Homebase festival, they realise they're not as good as they imagined they were.

This fast-paced contemporary comedy represents something rather different from director Alex Proyas, who directed it after *The Crow* and *Dark City* and before *I, Robot*. With the backing of Fox Searchlight Pictures, the film was shot on locations in inner Sydney, mostly Newtown and Enmore, and is directed with plenty of energy and a terrific sense of humour. The plot, which is little more than the story of a bunch of kids who just want to play music together, goes back at least as far as the Judy Garland–Mickey Rooney musicals of the late 1930s.

The opening sequence shows Freddy and the band scoring a triumphant success at a rock festival—but this proves to be what was going through Freddy's mind while he was having sex with Tanya, who is less than impressed with his performance ('I just wanted you to finish') and who produces a dildo right afterwards, saying: 'Watch! You might learn something!' Flashbacks, on deliberately scratchy film, depict Freddy's childhood, with his parents urging him to learn one musical instrument after another, even a sitar. But the day he knew he was destined to be a rock star was in the summer of 1975 when, in the company of his babysitter, he experienced punk for the first time.

Much of the film is very funny as the band members try various ways to raise money. The chief scene-stealer here is Russell Dykstra, whose comic timing is excellent: 'Stop!' he shouts at a passing taxi, and then adds 'In the name of love!' Proyas employs fancy editing, colourful graphics, split screens and hallucinogenic craziness (notably in a scene involving Tanya's wealthy parents). The end credits unfold against scenes in which most of the cast is seen dancing enthusiastically for the camera.

The story's motto is that 'You don't have to be a rock star to feel like a rock star', and it's a bit unusual that the film ends when the band fails to click after finally getting its chance at the big time. *Garage Days* has a great soundtrack of musical numbers including contributions from AC/DC, The Cure and Roxy Music.

For one reason or another, this hugely enjoyable film didn't succeed with either film-goers or music lovers, and a desultory release in Australia resulted in few overseas engagements.

39

Ginger & Rosa

(UK/GERMANY/CANADA/DENMARK, 2012)

Adventure Pictures–BBC Films–Media House–Danish Film Institute. DIRECTOR/SCRIPT: Sally Potter. ACTORS: Elle Fanning, Alice Englert, Alessandro Nivola, Christina Hendricks, Timothy Spall, Oliver Platt, Annette Bening, Jodhi May, Poppy Bloor, Magdalene Mountford. 90 MINS.

England. Ginger and Rosa are born in 1945 in a maternity hospital at the very moment that, on the other side of the world, Hiroshima is being destroyed by an atomic bomb. Their mothers, who are in adjacent beds, become friends. Seventeen years later, in 1962, the girls are inseparable. Ginger (Elle Fanning) lives with her mother, Natalie (Christina Hendricks), a former artist, and her father, Roland (Alessandro Nivola), a left-wing academic and serial womaniser. Rosa (Alice Englert) lives with her mother, Anoushka (Jodhi May), since her father walked out on them. Rosa is a wild child who likes kissing boys, while Ginger is an innocent who still sleeps with her teddy bears. The friends begin to play truant from school; Ginger is traumatised by the Cuban Missile Crisis and starts attending Campaign for Nuclear Disarmament meetings. Her father, Roland, leaves home to live a bachelor existence. One day he invites the girls onto his boat and, to Ginger's horror, seduces Rosa (Ginger can hear what's happening through the thin wall). Despite this, Ginger moves in with her father. Ginger's mother Natalie attempts suicide and Rosa apologises to Ginger for her behaviour.

Sally Potter's early films were strongly feminist in tone and intent, but in recent years she's broadened her approach, and her last two films, *Ginger & Rosa* and *The Party*, have had wide appeal. The former is a throwback to British films of the early 1960s about friendship between young women (*Girl with Green Eyes*, *Smashing Time*). Apparently at least partly autobiographical—Potter was thirteen in 1962—the film, despite its rather curious international casting, rings very true. Elle Fanning (herself only thirteen when the film was made) and Australian Alice Englert (daughter of Jane Campion) are superb as the girls at the centre of the drama, and it's interesting that neither of these very English characters is played by an English actor. Among the key supporting characters are Timothy Spall and Oliver Platt, who play gay friends of the family, and Annette Bening as a left-wing activist who counsels Ginger.

The film authentically evokes a terrifying time in Britain when the threat of nuclear catastrophe loomed large and the crisis in Cuba led many to believe that the world was on the brink of a nuclear Armageddon. Potter vividly describes the different personal approaches of her two protagonists towards this troubling prospect, as Ginger becomes increasingly involved in anti-nuclear politics and other forms of activism, while Rosa adopts a hedonistic, to-hell-with-it-all attitude towards impending disaster.

Scenes in which these impressionable young women endure personal crises are quite heartbreaking and beautifully acted by both Fanning and Englert. Potter makes no bones about the fact that she defines her characters from the start—by the Christian names—in shades of red.

Despite the charm of the film and its gallery of intriguing characters, it was not a box-office success, and was not acquired for cinema release in Australia, which was particularly regrettable given the presence of a talented young Australian in one of the leading roles. Englert's lively, feisty performance as the fun-loving Rosa is one of the film's chief delights.

. . . evokes a terrifying time in Britain when the threat of nuclear catastrophe loomed large

40

The Glass Shield

(USA/FRANCE, 1994)

Glass Shield Productions–CiBy 2000. DIRECTOR/SCRIPT: Charles Burnett. ACTORS: Michael Boatman, Lori Petty, Michael Ironside, Ice Cube, Richard Anderson, Bernie Casey, Victoria Dillard, Elliott Gould, M. Emmet Walsh, Natalija Nogulich, Don Harvey, Gary Wood. 110 MINS.

Los Angeles. John (J.J.) Johnson (Michael Boatman), a newly graduated police officer, is assigned to the Edgemar Sheriff's Office in the city's suburbs. He is the first African-American on the squad, and he soon experiences barely concealed hostility and racism from the mostly white cops who are supposed to be his colleagues, and who follow the lead of their Chief, Massey (Richard Anderson). J.J.'s only ally is another outcast, Deborah Fields (Lori Petty), who is also on the outer. While on patrol with Detective Bono (Don Harvey), J.J. and his partner stop the car driven by Teddy Woods (Ice Cube) for no other reason than that he's black. A gun is found in Woods' car, and he's charged with the murder of a white woman, Mrs Greenspan, some time earlier. During the trial, in which Woods is defended by an African-American lawyer, James Locket (Bernie Casey), J.J. lies under oath when he backs Bono's claim that Woods' car was stopped for a traffic violation. J.J. and Fields suspect that Massey, Baker (Michael Ironside) and other white members of the squad are involved in blackmailing prominent citizens over the crimes they've committed. When it's proved that Woods' gun did *not* kill Mrs Greenspan—the serial number had been changed in the police report—suspicion falls on Mr Greenspan (Elliott Gould) himself, but he is murdered by persons unknown. J.J. and Fields find themselves threatened by their own colleagues.

Charles Burnett is considered by some to be one of America's finest filmmakers. An African-American, his first films *Killer of Sheep* (1978), *My Brother's Wedding* (1983) and *To Sleep with*

Anger (1990) were all semi-autobiographical and independently produced on meagre budgets; they played at film festivals but had little exposure in cinemas. *The Glass Shield* was supposed to be his breakthrough; made on a larger budget, it tells a true story of a young African-American cop who uncovered a world of ingrained racism and corruption within a Los Angeles police department.

Subsequent events involving LA police and their attitudes towards African-Americans have only underlined the truths to be found in Burnett's gripping film. To begin with, J.J. is eager to be part of the team, which is why he backs his white partner in a lie about the reason a black driver was stopped and searched. But he eventually comes to the grim realisation that he will *never* be part of the white men's club that dominates this particular police precinct, and which is led by the sheriff himself. Fields is equally demeaned and patronised by her colleagues, even though—as a law graduate—she's a lot smarter than they are. Being a woman *and* a Jew is just too much for these good old boys to accept. In the beginning the racism is subtle and hardly noticeable; but as J.J. and Fields become more and more involved in the Teddy Woods case, they find themselves in mortal danger. Burnett builds the suspense in these scenes very effectively; his 'heroes' are cops who fear for their lives at the hands of other cops.

Scenes involving J.J.'s family and his fiancée (Victoria Dillard) depict him as an honest and ambitious youth, and Michael Boatman brings a determined steeliness to the character. The film's major flaw is the ending, which is rather abrupt and employs on-screen titles to explain what subsequently happened to the main characters. This strict adherence to the real events was seen as a bit of an anti-climax and didn't help the film's box office.

The Glass Shield was financed by the same French company, CiBy 2000, that financed Jane Campion's *The Piano*. If you say the company name aloud in French (Cee Bee deux milles), you'll find a jokey reference to one of Hollywood's most famous pioneers.

41

Goya's Ghosts

(SPAIN/USA, 2006)

Xuxa Producciones-The Saul Zaentz Company. DIRECTOR: Miloš Forman. SCRIPT: Jean-Claude Carrière, Miloš Forman. ACTORS: Javier Bardem, Natalie Portman, Stellan Skarsgård, Randy Quaid, José Luis Gómez, Michael Lonsdale, Blanca Portillo, Mabel Rivera, Unax Ugalde, Fernando Tielve, Julian Wadham. 114 MINS.

Spain, 1792. The artist Francisco Goya (Stellan Skarsgård) witnesses the upheavals caused by the Inquisition. One of his subjects, Lorenzo (Javier Bardem), is a leading officer of the Inquisition. Goya has also painted Inés (Natalie Portman), the beautiful daughter of a wealthy businessman. Lorenzo wants the Inquisition to become even stricter than it already is, and arranges for the arrest of Inés, who is tortured until she confesses that she's Jewish. While she's helpless in prison, he rapes her. Her father, Tomas Bilbatua (José Luis Gómez), seeks the help of Goya. They succeed in kidnapping Lorenzo and prove to him, also by means of torture, that the innocent are capable of confessing non-existent crimes when subjected to extreme pain. Nevertheless, Inés is kept in prison where she gives birth to a daughter, who is taken away from her. Years pass, the French Revolution occurs and Napoleon's army invades Spain; the Inquisition is disbanded and Lorenzo reinvents himself as a missionary. Inés is released and eventually Goya locates her daughter, Alicia (also Natalie Portman), working as a prostitute. Then the British invade Spain and there's yet another about-turn; the Inquisition is restored. Goya, though now elderly and deaf, continues to paint the people and events he observes.

Czech director Miloš Forman grew up during World War II; his Jewish parents died in the Holocaust, and there are clear allusions to the crimes of the Nazis in the powerful screenplay he and Jean-Claude Carrière (who had often worked with Luis Buñuel) wrote and their depiction of the brutal activities of the Inquisition. Michael Lonsdale portrays the Grand Inquisitor with a dark wit, making him a subtly menacing figure rather than an obvious monster.

Perhaps equally significant is the fact that Forman and Carrière deal with torture as an act of war and intimidation, given that, at the time the film was being made, the Bush administration was known to employ the 'righteous' use of torture in its activities against 'terrorists'. This gave the film a very contemporary connection in 2006.

Goya's Ghosts is not a biography of the great artist but a sweeping historical drama, not unlike the original (non-musical) *Les Misérables*, in which 'ordinary' people are caught up in extraordinary events—the difference being that most of the people in this story are far from 'heroic' characters.

Scenes in which Goya's celebrated paintings are re-created are most beautifully handled by Forman's production team, including cinematographer Javier Aguirresarobe and production designer Patrizia von Brandenstein. Bardem is chillingly good as Lorenzo, while as the artist through whose eyes we see these tumultuous events unfold, Stellan Skarsgård is also excellent.

Goya's Ghosts, a Spanish production made in English, struggled to find international distribution, perhaps because the subject matter was so dark, but also perhaps because the cast lacked really 'big' names. This proved to be the last film made by Forman, who died in 2018. He was responsible for some of the key films of the Czech new wave, as well as directing Hollywood classics such as *One Flew Over the Cuckoo's Nest* and *Amadeus*. It's regrettable that his last film is so little known.

42

Grace is Gone

(USA, 2007)

Plum Pictures–New Crime Productions. DIRECTOR/SCRIPT: James C. Strouse. ACTORS: John Cusack, Shélan O'Keefe, Gracie Bednarczyk, Alessandro Nivola, Marisa Tomei, Mary Kay Place, Doug James, Doug Dearth, Zachary Gray. 82 MINS.

A small town in Minnesota. Stanley Phillips (John Cusack) is a patriotic, God-fearing American who manages a home supplies store. Suffering from poor eyesight, he nonetheless faked the tests to get into the army, where he met Grace, who had been in the military since leaving high school. The pair married and had two daughters before Stanley was forced to leave the army because the truth about his poor eyesight was discovered. Grace, now a Sergeant, was posted to Iraq, and in her absence Stanley devotedly cares for twelve-year-old Heidi (Shélan O'Keefe) and eight-year-old Dawn (Gracie Bednarczyk). One morning, after the girls have left for school, Captain Riggs (Doug Dearth) and an army chaplain (Doug James) arrive at the Phillips home to convey the news that Grace has been killed. The devastated Stanley is unable to bring himself to tell the girls the news when they get home, though Heidi suspects something is wrong. On an impulse, Stanley decides to take a trip to Enchanted Gardens, a theme park in Florida. Along the way they stop to visit Stanley's parents, who are away; Stanley's younger brother, John (Alessandro Nivola), who is anti-Bush and anti-war, tries to get the girls to think for themselves and to question their father's beliefs. Father and daughters reach their destination, but Stanley still hasn't plucked up the courage to tell them their mother is dead.

Grace is Gone is a minor masterpiece, shamefully treated by its distributors. Made four years after the invasion of Iraq, it was to have been directed by Rob Reiner, who left the project for reasons that remain unclear. The film was then taken over by its screen-writer, James C. Strouse, in his directorial debut. Though clearly made in opposition to the George W. Bush administration's war in Iraq, the film makes its points with subtlety. Stanley is a strong Bush supporter who was, he says, proud to see his wife go to war. His brother John, on the other hand, loathes Bush, referring to him as 'that monkey-boy', though he admits he didn't bother to vote in the last election. Heidi asks her father if he ever thought her mother should have stayed home, and Stanley replies: 'She was doing her duty'—to which the girl responds 'What exactly does that mean?' Stanley won't let the girls watch TV news, but an unctuous speech by a smug Donald Rumsfeld is on the screen when a motel TV is switched on.

Young Shélan O'Keefe gives a quite wonderful performance as Heidi, who seemingly grows from a small girl into a young woman before our eyes as the truth gradually sinks in. She catches her father in a lie, but says nothing, and afterwards seems almost to be caring for him as much as he is caring for her. Unable to sleep one night, she goes down to the motel pool where she encounters a boy (Zachary Gray), a little bit older than she is, and their hesitant conversation is a further indication of her growing maturity.

The film is set against a backdrop of Middle America: the highways, the identical shopping malls, the fast-food diners, the motels, even the theme park at which the trio seem to go through the motions of having a good time. The expression on Cusack's face as they leave the park and he realises he can no longer post-pone telling the girls what happened to their mother is almost unbearably moving.

Grace is Gone is a very sad film, and an angry one too. Perhaps American audiences weren't ready for this kind of very personal take on the Iraq War, but the film was barely released anywhere in the world and is now almost totally forgotten.

43

Hero

(USA, 1992)

Columbia Pictures. DIRECTOR: Stephen Frears. SCRIPT: David Webb Peoples. ACTORS: Dustin Hoffman, Geena Davis, Andy Garcia, Joan Cusack, Kevin J. O'Connor, Maury Chaykin, Stephen Tobolowsky, Christian Clemenson, Tom Arnold, Warren Berlinger, James Madio, Susie Cusack, [Chevy Chase]. 118 MINS.

Chicago. Bernie LaPlante (Dustin Hoffman) is a small-time crook, estranged from his wife, Evelyn (Joan Cusack), and ten-year-old son, Joey (James Madio). Bernie is convicted for handling stolen goods, and steals money from his inexperienced lawyer, Donna O'Day (Susie Cusack). Meanwhile Gale Gayley (Geena Davis), star news reporter for local TV station Channel 4, flies to New York to receive an award for her work. On the flight back to Chicago, the plane crashes close to the highway where Bernie, who is out on parole, is driving his old car. A boy about Joey's age pleads with Bernie, who is first on the crash scene, to help find his father in the wreckage; after losing a shoe in the mud, Bernie succeeds in rescuing 54 people, including Gale—whose handbag he steals— before the crashed plane explodes. Late for his appointment with Joey, he leaves without making any contact with the rescue team. Later, after his car has broken down, he's given a lift by John Bubber (Andy Garcia), a homeless Vietnam veteran who lives in his truck. Bernie tells Bubber the story of the plane crash, and when they arrive at their destination he leaves behind his remaining shoe. Bernie attempts to use the credit cards he has stolen from Gale's handbag, but is arrested and imprisoned, and is at first unaware that 'the Angel of Flight 104' is being offered a $1 million reward by Channel 4. Bubber claims to be the hero, offering the shoe as proof. He becomes an overnight celebrity.

More than anything, *Hero* looks back to the feel-good Frank Capra movies of the 1930s, when an 'ordinary' man—usually played by Gary Cooper or James Stewart—found himself capable of doing extraordinary things in a battle against 'the system'. Bernie is a scruffy, conniving, pitiful petty thief, a sort of cousin to the memorable character of 'Ratso' Rizzo Dustin Hoffman played in *Midnight Cowboy* in 1969. But Bernie loves his son, Joey, and that's his redeeming feature; his act of bravery in saving passengers and crew from the crashed plane comes about solely because he wants to help a kid who reminds him of his son. The film is not only an examination of the nature of heroism, it's also a pungent satire on the media and the way the television station involved promotes a tragedy for all it is worth in order to boost ratings (comedian Chevy Chase has an uncredited but quite substantial role as Channel 4's Director of News).

British director Stephen Frears, whose CV includes *My Beautiful Laundrette*, *The Queen*, *Philomena* and *Victoria & Abdul*, made a handful of films in Hollywood, including this one which was based on an original screenplay by David Webb Peoples, who wrote Clint Eastwood's Oscar-winning *Unforgiven* the same year. Few films from major directors with top stars received such a lambasting as this one received on its first release; it was described as 'a doomed venture' by one critic, and attacked for being 'underwritten' and overly contrived.

There are contrivances, but for the most part they're successfully integrated into the intriguing narrative, and the film has enough qualities to merit serious attention. But it seems that, for once, potential audiences followed the critical line and stayed away, though it's also possible that word of mouth reflected annoyance with the film's tricky balancing act between satire and highly emotional drama. Frears and his actors survived the debacle, but the failure of *Hero* appears to have dented Peoples' career—he hasn't been nearly as productive since, with only one major screenplay produced.

44

Honkytonk Man

(USA, 1982)

Warner Bros–The Malpaso Company. DIRECTOR: Clint Eastwood. SCRIPT: Clancy Carlile, based on his novel. ACTORS: Clint Eastwood, Kyle Eastwood, John McIntire, Alexa Kenin, Verna Bloom, Matt Clark, Barry Corbin, Jerry Hardin, Tim Thomerson, Marty Robbins. 122 MINS.

Oklahoma during the Depression. Red Stovall (Clint Eastwood), an alcoholic, tubercular country and western singer, arrives at the farm where his sister Emmy (Verna Bloom) lives with her husband, Virgil (Matt Clark), and their young son, Whit (Kyle Eastwood). Red is heading for Nashville to perform at the Grand Old Oprey, but he lacks the funds to get there. Whit helps him steal some chickens that he proposes to sell. Red is arrested, but Whit helps break him out of jail and decides to accompany his uncle to Nashville. Whit's grandfather (John McIntire) joins them. Arnspriger (Barry Corbin), one of Red's old cronies, persuades him to take part in a robbery in Tulsa, and when that fails Arnspriger's girlfriend, Marlene (Alexa Kenin), joins Red and his nephew on the road. Grandfather decides he's had enough and returns home. Red is becoming increasingly unwell, but soon after arriving in Nashville he's offered a deal with a record company and he seizes one last opportunity to fulfil his lifelong ambition.

Playing well and truly against type, Clint Eastwood's portrayal of a sickly drifter and would-be musician travelling through Middle America with his nephew during the Depression is a very relaxed affair. Eastwood's son, Kyle, responds to his father's direction with a very convincing performance as the boy who adores his uncle, and the film is as much about his education as it is about the adventures of Red. Whit drives the car in which they travel better than Red does and he is constantly resourceful in helping his uncle get out of scrapes, including prison. In fact, as a 'hero' Red is strangely unheroic, and Eastwood Sr seems utterly determined to undermine his 'Man with No Name' or 'Dirty Harry' image with this downbeat portrayal.

Essentially a road movie, the film introduces plenty of colourful characters for the central duo to encounter along the way, including petty criminals and gormless cops. There are digressions throughout the journey, including a visit to a blues club (a terrific sequence), and the film ends with a funeral scene that, with its melancholy beauty, might easily have been staged by veteran John Ford. Bruce Surtees' mellow photography is outstanding.

Eastwood remains one of Hollywood's most classical and frequently inspired filmmakers, and has inherited the mantle of the early professionals like Ford, Howard Hawks and Raoul Walsh. Unlike them, though, he's also an actor of some distinction—and he's very touching here as the sickly protagonist. When the script calls for it, he's also capable of staging an impressive action scene, such as the sequence in which Emmy and Virgil, whose rundown farm is in the middle of the dust bowl, make preparations in the face of a coming storm.

Over the years Eastwood's films have invariably been profitable because he makes them economically and quickly, and because most of them find a ready audience. *Honkytonk Man* proved to be one of his few unsuccessful efforts. It failed at the American box office and was given only a reluctant and very desultory release in Australia. Clearly the actor–director's fan base preferred the dynamic Eastwood to the essentially rather sad and struggling character he plays here.

Essentially a road movie, the film introduces plenty of colourful characters along the way

45

Housekeeping

(USA, 1987)

Columbia Pictures. DIRECTOR: Bill Forsyth. SCRIPT: Bill Forsyth, from the novel by Marilynne Robinson. ACTORS: Christine Lahti, Sara Walker, Andrea Burchill, Anne Pitoniak, Barbara Reese, Margot Pinvidic, Georgie Collins. 115 MINS.

Seattle, 1948. Helen Stone (Margot Pinvidic), whose husband has abandoned her, leaves the city with her young daughters, Ruth and Lucile, and drives to the small town of Fingerbone, where she leaves the girls with her mother, Sylvia (Georgie Collins). She then drives her car over a cliff. In 1954, after the death of their grandmother, the girls are cared for by Sylvia's unmarried sisters-in-law, Lily (Anne Pitoniak) and Nona (Barbara Reese), who find the climate in Fingerbone not to their taste, and make efforts to locate the girls' aunt, Sylvie (Christine Lahti). When Aunt Sylvie eventually shows up, the old ladies promptly depart. Thoroughly unsettled by all these changes, the now adolescent Ruth (Sara Walker) and Lucile (Andrea Burchill) constantly worry that the flaky Sylvie will leave them too. They survive a severe flood in which the ground floor of their house is covered with water. After a period of truancy, Lucile begins to become interested in clothes and the friendship of her schoolmates, while Ruth retreats into the cluttered house, which is filled with old newspapers and empty tin cans. Lucile moves out and is unofficially 'adopted' by one of her teachers, while the local authorities assert that Sylvie is an unfit guardian and seem to be about to take Ruth away from her.

The Scottish director Bill Forsyth scored popular successes with his early films *Gregory's Girl* and *Local Hero*. British film producer David Puttnam, whose company Enigma was responsible for the latter film, was appointed head of the Hollywood studio, Columbia Pictures, in 1986. It was an experiment that didn't last very long, as Puttnam's attempt to make 'serious' films in the Hollywood environment was doomed to failure—but one of the films that *did* get made during Puttnam's one-year tenure at Columbia was *Housekeeping*, which Forsyth adapted from a novel by Marilynne Robinson. It's an unusual film in that men hardly feature in it at all. The narration, spoken by Ruth, describes her grandfather's early life on the plains of America, his later obsession with mountains, and his death in a train crash—but we never see him. The only males on view are three little boys who help push Helen's car out of the mud immediately before she drives off a cliff, leaving them gobsmacked; the headmaster of the local school, who has one brief scene; and the local sheriff, who, prodded on by local churchwomen, makes it clear that he thinks Sylvie is an unfit guardian.

The film is rather mysterious in that motivations are never spelt out, though they're always hinted at. The girls long to know about their parents, but their flighty aunt remains vague on the subject. She's prone to concocting fantasies—such as one about a cottage hidden in the forest where small children live—and she's completely irresponsible, thinking nothing of stealing the rowboat belonging to a fisherman in order to take Ruth out to an island on the lake. Against the most magnificent scenery (filming took place in British Columbia), this curious, and curiously riveting, story unfolds, beautifully acted by the principals and constantly intriguing.

After Puttnam's abrupt departure from Columbia, the executives who replaced him seemed to have little interest in the films he'd initiated, *Housekeeping* among them. It was always going to be a challenging film for a wide audience, structured as it is on small details of unorthodox family life, but it seemed that in the post-Puttnam era no one at the studio really cared to even try to find an audience for it.

46

How I Live Now

(UK/CANADA, 2013)

Passion Pictures–Cowboy Films. DIRECTOR: Kevin Macdonald. SCRIPT: Jeremy Brock, Penelope Skinner, Tony Grisoni, based on a novel by Meg Rosoff. ACTORS: Saoirse Ronan, George MacKay, Tom Holland, Harley Bird, Danny McEvoy, Anna Chancellor. 101 MINS.

England in the near future. Daisy (Saoirse Ronan), a young American, flies into Heathrow Airport and is met by her cousin, fourteen-year-old Isaac (Tom Holland). Armed soldiers are everywhere in evidence and something is very obviously wrong, but nothing is said specifically about the crisis. Daisy has been sent to spend the summer with her British relatives, and she isn't too happy about it. Despite the fact that he's underage, Isaac drives her to the family farm in Wales, where she meets Aunt Penn (Anna Chancellor), who is a government negotiator attempting to prevent a war. Daisy meets Isaac's older brother, Edmond (George MacKay), their younger sister, Piper (Harley Bird) and Joe (Danny McEvoy), a friend of the family. Daisy is an unhappy visitor, worried about a great many things, including whether she might be infected by germs and, more importantly, about her appearance. It's clear that she's attracted to Edmond. Aunt Penn is called away to an emergency meeting in Geneva, leaving the children to fend for themselves. One day, while they're enjoying a swim in a river, they hear an ominous rumble and experience a mighty wind. They discover that there's been a nuclear attack on London. Before long soldiers arrive and forcibly separate the girls from the boys. Edmond makes Daisy promise she'll try to return to the farm and that they'll meet there. Daisy and Piper are billeted in a suburban house and ordered to work on the production of food; but terrorists attack and the girls flee for their lives, attempting to avoid both the soldiers and the invaders and to get back safely to the farm.

This disturbing film is somewhat reminiscent of Jack Clayton's *Our Mother's House* (1967), which is also about children who are left alone to fend for themselves after a tragedy. Kevin Macdonald, a former documentary director known for such films as *One Day in September* (1999) and *Touching the Void* (2003), has taken a novel by Meg Rosoff as his source material to evoke a possible near-future scenario of nuclear warfare and greatly heightened terrorist activity, and how the authorities will react to such threats. The viewer is deliberately given very little information as to what is actually happening. When we realise that a mighty explosion has occurred somewhere in the UK, presumably London, we don't know which nation might have been responsible for the attack. That's not the point; more important is how the children, with as little knowledge of what's going on in the outside world as we have, cope with the frightening situation.

It's not knowing that makes what occurs in the film so very terrifying. There are no answers, no comforting authority figure to tell the children what really happened. This, we feel, is how it might unfold if there really was a nuclear war, and it's a chilling prospect.

The ensemble performances of the child actors are everything you could wish for, with adults almost completely sidelined, apart from the brief appearance of a preoccupied Aunt Penn near the beginning. Saoirse Ronan, who was nominated for a Best Actress Oscar for her role in *Lady Bird* (2017), is particularly good as the American visitor.

The screenplay by Jeremy Brock, Penelope Skinner and Tony Grisoni raised questions that few people, including the critical establishment, seemed prepared to grapple with. This fine film—which is made the scarier by the everyday, matter-of-fact approach to the most terrible events—warranted a much better reception than it received.

47

Impulse

(USA, 1989)

Warner Bros. **DIRECTOR:** Sondra Locke. **SCRIPT:** John DeMarco, Leigh Chapman. **ACTORS:** Theresa Russell, Jeff Fahey, George Dzundza, Alan Rosenberg, Nicholas Mele, Eli Danker, Charles McCaughan, Lynne Thigpen, Shawn Elliott. **109 MINS.**

Los Angeles. Lottie Mason (Theresa Russell) works as an undercover cop, and is currently posing as a hooker. Her boss, Lt Joe Morgan (George Dzundza), is approached by Stan (Jeff Fahey), an Assistant District Attorney, for assistance in locating Frank Munoff (Charles McCaughan) and Tony Peron (Shawn Elliott), potential witnesses in the case against crime boss Hector Luna. Morgan proposes that Lottie be used as bait to trap Munoff and Peron. Lottie and Stan are attracted to one another and start an affair. Lottie, who has already killed a man in the line of duty and who is being investigated by Internal Affairs, is almost killed herself in a tense confrontation with Munoff. Later, by chance, she encounters Peron in a bar and allows herself to be picked up by him, but he is shot dead by an unknown assailant while she is in his house. Afraid that she'll be accused of killing him, she says nothing—and finds herself the subject of a police investigation.

Impulse is a very well-made thriller about an intrepid female cop; unfortunately, and coincidentally, it was released at about the same time as *Blue Steel*, made by another female director, Kathryn Bigelow, in which Jamie Lee Curtis also played a female cop.

Theresa Russell gives a terrific performance as Lottie, the rather sad protagonist who so convincingly enacts the role of a whore while working undercover, and is treated like one by her sleazy boss (Dzundza, wonderfully creepy), who goes through her mail—noting that she's in debt—and who cops a feel whenever he gets the opportunity.

Locke's direction is brisk and lucid, and the scene in which she builds up to the inevitable scene of lovemaking between Lottie and the charming Assistant DA is a model of its kind. She gets fine performances from the entire cast, and the film is handsomely photographed by Australian Dean Semler. Its one significant flaw lies in the screenplay and the overly coincidental encounter between Lottie and one of the men Stan is seeking—but Locke just about manages to make this contrivance work, and the scenes that follow are satisfyingly suspenseful.

Sondra Locke, an actor whose first feature film appearance was in *The Heart is a Lonely Hunter* (1968), met Clint Eastwood when they appeared together in *The Outlaw Josey Wales* (1976). They became a couple and she acted in several of his films over the next few years. In 1986, his company, Malpaso, produced *Ratboy*, the first film Locke directed. By the time she directed *Impulse*, her second film, for Eastwood's home studio, Warner Bros, the relationship was coming to a bitter end in a palimony suit.

Impulse was completed and copyrighted in 1989, but Warner Bros held up the release until April 1990. The reviews were mainly positive, but, in Locke's words—quoted in Patrick McGilligan's excellent unauthorised biography, *Clint: The life and legend* (1999)— the studio 'pretty much dumped it' and along with it, other projects she had in development. The suggestion has been made that the dumping of Locke's film was done to keep Eastwood, the studio's biggest star, on side. Whatever the reason, *Impulse* was afforded the most minimal release in the US and was denied cinema distribution in countries like Britain and Australia, where it might have found an appreciative audience.

Locke has since made a telemovie and a small theatrical feature, *Trading Favors* (1997), which sank without trace, and she has had little work as an actor. Her direction of *Ratboy* and, especially, *Impulse*, suggests that an interesting career has been stalled.

48

In the Bleak Midwinter

(UK, 1995)

Midwinter Films. DIRECTOR/SCRIPT: Kenneth Branagh. ACTORS: Richard Briers, Hetta Charnley, Joan Collins, Nicholas Farrell, Mark Hadfield, Julia Sawalha, Gerard Horan, Celia Imrie, Michael Maloney, John Sessions, Jennifer Saunders, Ann Davies, James D. White. 98 MINS.

London. Christmas is approaching and 33-year-old struggling actor Joe Harper (Michael Maloney) is depressed; he hasn't had a job in ages, he believes he's been rejected for a major role in an upcoming Hollywood sci-fi franchise, and his girlfriend has dumped him. His sympathetic agent, Margaretta D'Arcy (Joan Collins), reluctantly agrees to help him finance a production of *Hamlet*, which he plans to stage in an abandoned church in the village of Hope, where Joe and his sister, Molly (Hetta Charnley), grew up. Molly, now a schoolteacher, still lives there and is spearheading a campaign to save the church from developers. After a series of generally disappointing auditions, Joe picks his cast. He will, of course, play Hamlet; Nina (Julia Sawalha), who refuses to wear glasses though she's terribly short-sighted, is Ophelia; Tom (Nicholas Farrell), who is fussy about his diet and wants to ban smoking from the production, is Laertes. As the King, veteran has-been Henry Wakefield (Richard Briers) is cast opposite gay Terry Du Bois (John Sessions), who will play Queen Gertrude in drag. Carnforth Greville (Gerard Horan) is cast to play multiple roles. Molly helps out with catering and selling tickets and also stands in for her brother during rehearsals, while Fadge (Celia Imrie) joins the company as the set and costume designer. With very little time to rehearse, there are plenty of minor disasters and setbacks, all of them overcome. But on the opening night, Joe is offered a lucrative Hollywood contract on condition he leaves immediately for Los Angeles.

The lovely thing about Kenneth Branagh's *In the Bleak Midwinter*, which he also scripted, is the insight it gives into the 'ordinary' world of actors, and the decidedly unglamorous lives so many of them lead. Almost every member of Joe's company has personal problems of one sort or another, and the ways in which Branagh brings all their stories to satisfying resolutions in time for the Christmas Day finale just about skirts gross sentimentality in favour of genuinely touching scenes of reunion and reconciliation.

Much of the film is very funny, with a great many inside theatrical jokes (Henry, the group's oldest actor, extols the legendary Sir Henry Irving and notes that the great thespian died in Bradford, whereupon Terry remarks that he died in Bradford more than once). The use of Noel Coward's wonderfully witty song 'Why Must The Show Go On?' is a stroke of genius. But, as the title—the first line of a much-loved hymn sung at Christmas services—suggests, there's also a great deal of melancholy. It's not only that compromises have to be made because of a lack of funds, it's also a sad fact that theatres, like churches, are closing down because of a lack of public support.

As the characters, briskly introduced in the opening scenes, gradually each make their own particular impression, the viewer realises that this kind of theatrical endeavour, of working together in a closely knit ensemble, constitutes the closest most of them will get to family life. Arguably the film gets a little too smug in the later stages, but it's hard not to warm to Branagh's generous sentiments.

The film opened in 1995 to very poor business. There were plenty of excuses for this. There were no 'stars', the film was in black and white (in fact, Australian Roger Lanser's monochrome photography is one of its greatest assets) and the title was a turn-off (in America it became *A Midwinter's Tale*). But it remains one of Branagh's most personal and engaging films.

49

In the Electric Mist

(USA/FRANCE, 2008)

Ithaca Pictures–Little Bear. DIRECTOR: Bertrand Tavernier. SCRIPT: Jerzy Kromolowski, Mary Olson-Kromolowski, from the novel by James Lee Burke. ACTORS: Tommy Lee Jones, Peter Sarsgaard, John Goodman, Kelly Macdonald, Mary Steenburgen, Justina Machado, Ned Beatty, James Gammon, Pruitt Taylor Vince, Levon Helm, John Sayles, Alana Locke, Bernard Hocke. 102 MINS (US release version); 117 MINS (French release version).

New Iberia, Louisiana. Part-time detective Dave Robicheaux (Tommy Lee Jones) lives with his wife, Bootsie (Mary Steenburgen), and young daughter Alafair (Alana Locke) in a house by the bayou, where he rents out fishing boats as a sideline. Dave is investigating the savage murders of a couple of prostitutes when he arrests movie star Elrod Sykes (Peter Sarsgaard) for drink driving. Sykes is starring in a movie about the Civil War which is being produced nearby; local identity Julie 'Baby Feet' Balboni (John Goodman), is financing the film. Sykes tells Dave about a manacled skeleton that was discovered close to the film's location. Dave suspects the skeleton belongs to a black man murdered by whites back in the 1960s. As the investigation into the murdered girls proceeds, one of Dave's investigators (Pruitt Taylor Vince) is shot dead, and Sykes' girlfriend and co-star Kelly Drummond (Kelly Macdonald) is also killed after Dave loans her his jacket—he believes the killer was attempting to stop him discovering the truth.

The first film to be made based on one of James Lee Burke's books about Detective Dave Robicheaux was *Heaven's Prisoners* (1996), which starred Alec Baldwin. It was unsuccessful at the box office, but that didn't deter Bertrand Tavernier, one of the finest contemporary French filmmakers, from tackling the sixth book in the series, *In the Electric Mist with Confederate Dead*, as a co-production between his own company and a small American producer. Tavernier consulted extensively with Burke, and shot the film on authentic locations in Louisiana, with a strong cast headed by Tommy Lee Jones, the perfect actor to play Robicheaux.

The film involves a series of killings that occur in this quiet backwater, but also the mystery of a killing that took place years earlier. The recent crimes and the long-forgotten race murder become combined in Robicheaux's investigation, with the chief suspect being the odious Balboni or one of his henchmen. Also falling under suspicion are businessman Twinky LeMoyne (Ned Beatty) and his business partner, Murphy Doucet (Bernard Hocke), who works as a security guard. During the investigation, Dave experiences hallucinations in which he is able to talk to General Hood (Levon Helm), a Confederate officer of the Civil War.

Perhaps it was this supernatural element—taken directly from the book—that unsettled Tavernier's American partner. There was a dispute after the film was completed, and as a result the American version of the film was cut by 15 minutes, a process that was presumably undertaken in an attempt to speed up Tavernier's leisurely, French-style pacing, but which inevitably made the process of the investigation too rushed. Also removed were scenes that commented on the impact of Hurricane Katrina on Louisiana, though a few moments of this survive. Worse, the Americans decided to forgo a cinema release and go direct to DVD; the film didn't make it to cinemas in Britain or Australia. In France it was more successful.

Having seen both versions, it's clear that Tavernier's original cut for French release is far more satisfying. It's a terrific yarn and a tasty whodunit, but its great strength, apart from the excellent cast, is the authentic use of locations—the lush green meadows, the bayous, the small towns where nothing much happens until the murders begin. As a bonus, there's a lovely cameo performance from independent filmmaker John Sayles, who plays the director of the film in which Sykes and Drummond are appearing.

50

In the Land of Blood and Honey
(*U zemlji krvi i meda*)
(USA, 2011)

GK Films. DIRECTOR/SCRIPT: Angelina Jolie. ACTORS: Zana Marjanovic, Goran Kostic, Rade Serbedzija, Branko Djuric, Vanessa Glodjo, Nikola Djuricko, Fedja Stukan, Alma Terzic. 127 MINS.

Sarajevo, 1992. Ajla (Zana Marjanovic), a young Muslim artist, lives with her sister, Lejla (Vanessa Glodjo), who has a small baby. One night at a dance club Ajla meets Danijel (Goran Kostic), a Serb policeman, and they're attracted to one another. As they dance, a bomb explodes, killing many people. Four months later Serb forces led by General Nebojsa Vokojevic (Rade Serbedzija), a fanatical anti-Muslim, enter the city and begin a program of ethnic cleansing, murdering the men and raping the women. Danijel, who is the son of Vokojevic, and who is serving as an officer in the Serb forces, succeeds in saving Ajla from rape. He claims her for himself and eventually provides her with a studio where she can paint and he can visit her for regular sexual interludes. Throughout this period he is an active member of the Serb forces that are committing wholesale atrocities. The General finds out about Ajla and visits her; he sends one of his most brutal men, Petar (Fedja Stukan), to rape her. Danijel discovers this and kills Petar. As UN forces close in, Danijel believes Ajla has betrayed him to her Muslim friends and takes violent action before surrendering as a war criminal.

By any standard this is a remarkable directorial debut from actor Angelina Jolie. She certainly takes plenty of chances with her first film, starting with her choice of subject—a relentless depiction of the plight of an attractive young Muslim woman living in Sarajevo during the bloody Balkan War. She filmed in Bosnia–Herzegovina and Hungary, staging battle scenes with absolute precision and sparing little in depicting the barbarity of this particularly ugly conflict. Australian cinematographer Dean Semler was no doubt of considerable assistance to her in creating the film's powerful imagery.

The film is unusually graphic, both in terms of its violence and, perhaps more surprisingly, its sexual imagery. Ajla finds herself in a terrifying situation. Other women are brutally raped but, because a man she met briefly before the war in a club takes a fancy to her, she is spared—on the condition that she becomes that man's exclusive lover, while knowing he is part of a ruthless and murderous occupation army.

Zana Marjanovic is heartbreakingly effective in this role, conveying the terror and despair of the character with total conviction. Excellent, too, is Goran Kostic as Danijel, who claims to be unhappy at being forced to kill and rape people who were his friends and fellow pupils when he went to school, but who goes along with the wishes and commands of his deeply racist father, a diehard bigot still seeking revenge for the defeat of a Crusader army at the hands of Ottoman Turks in the Battle of Kosovo (1448). The General also is unable to forgive or forget the killing of his mother and siblings in 1944 by Turkish members of the Ustachi (Croatian nationalists), and uses these tragic events of the past as an excuse for his current campaign of terror.

All this Jolie describes in meticulous and at times rivetingly suspenseful detail as she seeks to remind audiences of the tragic events that occurred less than twenty years before she made the film—the three and a half year siege of Sarajevo and the pointless deaths of many thousands of people.

It's really no surprise that the film proved too tough for audiences to swallow. The fact that it was spoken in Bosnian and Serbo–Croatian languages made it artistically authentic, but doubtless was another factor in keeping audiences away. Nor were the reviewers as supportive as they might have been, with some critics seemingly eager to belittle the artistic ambitions of a glamorous superstar. In Australia no distributor was prepared to release the film.

51

In This World

(UK, 2002)

Revolution Films. DIRECTOR: Michael Winterbottom. SCRIPT: Tony Grisoni. ACTORS: Jamal Udin Torabi, Enayatullah, Wakeel Khan, Jamau, Mirwals Torabi, Rasheed, Hossain Baghaeian, Yaaghoob Nosraj Poor, Ghodrat Poor. 90 MINS.

Shamshatoo Refugee Camp, Peshawar, Pakistan, February 2002. The camp is filled with Afghan refugees displaced by the American bombing that followed the Twin Tower attacks in New York five months earlier. Wakeel (Wakeel Khan) determines that his nephew, Enayat (Enayatullah), should seek a better life in London. A people smuggler is arranged, and it's decided that Enayat's younger friend Jamal (Jamal Udin Torabi), who speaks a little English, will go along too. The pair travel in the back of trucks south to Quetta, and then across the border into Pakistan and on through the desert to the Iranian border; but at the border a suspicious guard turns them back because he rightly suspects that they're Afghanis. Back in Pakistan the two make a second attempt, and this time succeed. Eventually, in a hazardous night crossing through Kurdish-held territory in snowy mountain country, they arrive in Turkey and thence to Istanbul. Here they, and other refugees, are hidden in a freight container loaded onto a cargo ship that sails for Trieste; conditions are awful and several refugees, including Enayat, die on the journey. Jamal perseveres and finally manages to get to England, where his future remains uncertain.

This extraordinary docu-drama was filmed between February and June 2002, using a small digital camera, the content of which was later transferred to widescreen 35 mm film. The eclectic Michael Winterbottom—whose filmography includes the Steve Coogan/Rob Brydon *Trip* trilogy, along with assorted thrillers and comedies—worked from a very provisional screenplay by Tony

Grisoni in which only a rough outline of the journey taken by the two young protagonists was in place before filming commenced. The youths themselves, neither of whom had acted before, were found in Peshawar, and their hazardous journey from there into Europe was charted with absolute fidelity. It must have been hazardous, too, for Winterbottom and his camera crew (led by cinematographer Marcel Zyskind), filming as they did with only available light in several countries over a few weeks, starting in Pakistan and continuing on through Iran, Turkey, Italy and France to the UK. The early scenes are especially potent, as the boys travel by truck or occasionally by bus along ancient desert routes, where they see not only camels but also ruined armoured vehicles abandoned by the wayside. The night crossing (filmed with a night vision camera) from Kurdish territory into Turkey is particularly suspenseful, as armed border guards fire on refugees we're unable to see.

Everywhere they go, the young men befriend the locals, especially the children. Though they can't speak the languages of the countries they cross—Jamal's English is pretty basic—they easily mix with the kids to play soccer or other games. When in Trieste, Jamal tries to make a few Euros by selling some useless trinkets he's acquired, and is for the most part rudely brushed aside. At this point the viewer is invited to feel ashamed for the Westerners, with their comfortable lives, who deny even a tiny sum of cash to help this starving refugee fleeing from a conflict that the West itself created.

All the performances from the non-professional actors are naturalistic and unaffected, with the two leads particularly convincing in portraying characters that were presumably very close to themselves.

Despite winning the Golden Bear at the Berlin Film Festival in 2003, Winterbottom's film struggled to find an audience. Who cares, after all, about the plight of refugees?

52

The Journey

(UK, 2016)

Tempo Productions. DIRECTOR: Nick Hamm. SCRIPT: Colin Bateman. ACTORS: Timothy Spall, Colm Meaney, Freddie Highmore, John Hurt, Toby Stephens, Catherine McCormack, Barry Ward, Ian McElhinney, Ian Beattie, Mark Lambert. 94 MINS.

St Andrews, Scotland, 2006. In a private hotel, high-level peace talks are underway as part of the latest attempt to solve the problem of Northern Ireland. Participating are British Prime Minister Tony Blair (Toby Stephens), Irish Prime Minister Bertie Ahern (Mark Lambert), head of the Democratic Unionists Ian Paisley (Timothy Spall), and Martin McGuinness (Colm Meaney), leader of Sinn Fein. The talks have stalled because Paisley steadfastly refuses to meet McGuinness face to face. Paisley demands a break in the talks so he can fly to Belfast and join his wife in their 50th wedding anniversary celebrations. Blair's adviser, Harry Patterson (John Hurt), sees an opportunity to bring the old adversaries together. It is arranged for Paisley and McGuinness to be driven to Edinburgh airport to catch a charter flight to Belfast, but the weather is closing in and time is short. The men are unaware at first that a camera and microphone are concealed in the limo, or that their driver, Jack (Freddie Highmore), is a government agent. Patterson orders Jack to delay the journey in the hope that the men will start talking to one another, which eventually they do. Bitter arguments about the violent past and Paisley's unflinching righteousness gradually give way to a guarded understanding so that, by the end of the journey, an agreement is in sight.

It would be difficult to think of more perfect casting than that of Timothy Spall as Ian Paisley and Colm Meaney as Martin McGuinness, the two bitter enemies who, amazingly, were brought together in 2006 to usher in a long-awaited breakthrough in the politics of Northern Ireland. Nick Hamm's film begins with news-reel footage that serves as portraits of the real men and reminders of the issues involved—the bombings and killings and the angry sectarian conflicts. The authorities have correctly suspected that at last both leaders are just about ready to put the past behind them, though in this fictionalised account of what happened during that journey it's McGuinness—wily, witty, persuasive—who is the more malleable of the two, while Paisley's rigid opposition to anything that to him smacks of Satanism (and that includes the Pope himself, as well as drinking and dancing) makes him very difficult to get through to—though when he finally laughs it's as though a light has suddenly been switched on.

The conversation covers a wide variety of topics, including the cinema (Paisley says the last time he went to the cinema was 1973 and that was to protest against *The Exorcist*). Meanwhile, back in St Andrews, the politicians and their aides—including Gerry Adams (Ian Beattie) and Ian Paisley Jr (Barry Ward)—watch and wait to see what the outcome will be. One of the film's best scenes comes when Jack, after a minor accident in which their car collides with a deer, pulls into a petrol station to refuel, only to discover his credit card has been damaged. McGuinness, as a registered terrorist, has no access to credit, and Paisley doesn't believe in such things as credit cards, but he thoroughly intimidates the hapless young man at the cash register so that the transaction quickly goes through.

Given that the film is basically a conversation piece, the film's visual qualities are strong, and *The Journey* is thoroughly enter-taining for anyone even vaguely interested in the politics of Ireland. Those qualities seem to have been insufficient to have earned the film a cinema release in Australia, apart from a screening at a British film festival.

53

King of the Hill

(USA, 1993)

Wildwood Enterprises–Bona Fide Productions. DIRECTOR/SCRIPT: Steven Soderbergh, based on the memoir by A.E. Hotchner. ACTORS: Jesse Bradford, Jeroen Krabbé, Lisa Eichhorn, Karen Allen, Spalding Gray, Elizabeth McGovern, Cameron Boyd, Adrien Brody, John McConnell. 103 MINS.

St Louis, 1933. Twelve-year-old Aaron Kurlander (Jesse Bradford) lives in a shabby hotel room with his father (Jeroen Krabbé), an unsuccessful door-to-door salesman, his mother (Lisa Eichhorn), who has tuberculosis, and his younger brother Sullivan (Cameron Boyd). A good student, Aaron has a warm relationship with his teacher, Miss Mathey (Karen Allen), and at a school prize-giving he is given a special achievement award. But Kurlander can't make ends meet and Sullivan is sent away to live with relatives. When his father goes on the road and his mother is hospitalised, Aaron is forced to live alone in the shabby hotel where his only 'friend' is Mr Mungo (Spalding Gray), who spends his time with young girls like Lydia (Elizabeth McGovern). Lester (Adrien Brody), a street kid, also befriends the lonely Aaron, but the friendship comes to an end when Lester is arrested by the police.

Steven Soderbergh caused a stir when his first feature, *sex, lies, and videotape,* won the Palme d'Or in Cannes in 1989. His follow-up, *Kafka,* was a major flop, so there was a lot riding on his third feature, *King of the Hill,* an adaptation of a memoir by A.E. Hotchner, who was a friend of Ernest Hemingway. The 'coming-of-age during the Depression' theme is not exactly original, but Soderbergh and his wonderful cast get the very most out of the subject. Taking a leaf from the great Charles Laughton's *The Night of the Hunter* (1955), Soderbergh has the children play their roles naturalistically, while the adults are encouraged to act their roles with just a touch of exaggeration, so that they come across as somewhat larger than life to set them apart from this boy's world. In the case of the buffoonish policeman, overplayed by John McConnell, this doesn't quite come off, but in every other respect it works wonderfully well, with characters like the urbane yet mysterious Mr Mungo beautifully realised.

Aaron is a resourceful boy who wants to help his father keep the family together. He knows that a great deal of rent is owed on the room in the shabby Empire Hotel, and tries to raise money by breeding canaries (a distinct failure) and other far-fetched schemes. He also tentatively reaches out to the opposite sex, though the girl who lives across the way suffers from epilepsy, which is confronting, and the well-to-do girls who attend his school are just too intimidating. Ashamed of the circumstances in which he and his family live, he also makes up stories, saying that his father is an aeroplane pilot or that he works on some kind of secret assignments for the government.

But when he's forced to live alone, fending off the debt collectors and the hotel management, who demand access to Kurlander's room, Aaron is unable to play-act. He's reduced to eating paper to survive, yet he manages to remain cheerful and resourceful.

Soderbergh films this poignant—and ultimately positive—story with great style, and coaxes wonderful performances from both Bradford and Boyd as the brothers. A few years later he would become an 'A' List director (*Out of Sight*, *Erin Brockovich*, *Traffic*, *Ocean's Eleven*), but in 1993 his reputation lay entirely with his first film which, with its edgy sexuality, couldn't have been more different from this period piece involving children and featuring a cast lacking major names. Accordingly the film was afforded the most perfunctory release and quickly disappeared, though it was recently restored and reissued in a pristine Blu-ray version on the Criterion label.

. . . a poignant—and ultimately positive—story

54

Little Dorrit

(UK, 1987)

Sands Films. DIRECTOR/SCRIPT: Christine Edzard, from the novel by Charles Dickens. ACTORS: Derek Jacobi, Alec Guinness, Sarah Pickering, Cyril Cusack, Joan Greenwood, Amelda Brown, Daniel Chatto, Gwenda Hughes, Patricia Hayes, Max Wall, Miriam Margolyes, Bill Fraser, Roshan Seth, John Savident, Michael Elphick, Eleanor Bron, Alan Bennett, Robert Morley, David Thewlis, Murray Melvin, Heathcote Williams, Brenda Bruce, Rosalie Crutchley, Simon Dormandy. Part 1, *Nobody's Fault*, 174 MINS. Part 2, *Little Dorrit's Story*, 183 MINS.

London, the 1850s. *Nobody's Fault*: After the death of his father in China, Arthur Clennam (Derek Jacobi) returns to London for the first time in twenty years. His mother (Joan Greenwood) lives with her servants Affery (Patricia Hayes), who nursed Arthur when he was young, and Flintwinch (Max Wall), Affery's husband. Little Dorrit (Sarah Pickering), a seamstress, also works in the house, but lives in Marshalsea, a debtors' prison, with her father William (Alec Guinness). Arthur sells the family business and invests in a machinery company. He helps the Dorrits in small ways, and discovers that Little Dorrit is heir to an estate and fortune; but his new company collapses and he himself winds up in Marshalsea in the room once occupied by the Dorrits.

Little Dorrit's Story: Little Dorrit is born in Marshalsea. She first glimpses Arthur at his mother's home and falls in love with him, though he's unaware of this. She goes abroad with her father and sister, Fanny (Amelda Brown). Fanny marries Sparkler (Simon Dormandy), the son of Mr and Mrs Merdle (Michael Elphick, Eleanor Bron), the shady couple in whose company Arthur so unwisely invested his money. After the death of her father, Little Dorrit returns to London to locate Arthur.

Little Dorrit was originally published in serial form, one episode per month, in 1855–57. Not one of Charles Dickens' best-known novels, it is one of his most polemical, especially in his indictment of debtors' prisons, like Marshalsea, where bankrupts are forced to stay but are forbidden to work—so that they have no way of repaying their debts. Dickens also pilloried the hopelessly bureaucratic and inefficient Circumlocution Office, a microcosm of official inefficiency.

With its vast array of characters and its burgeoning sub-plots, the book might well have been brought to the small screen as a TV series. Instead director Christine Edzard's bold decision to make it as a six-hour, two-part feature film ensured that almost all of Dickens' characters come alive on the screen. Foremost among them are Dorrit himself, touchingly portrayed by Alec Guinness in one of his last screen performances, and Derek Jacobi whose Arthur Clennam is perhaps his most substantial screen role. Alongside these talents are a great many fine actors who make considerable contributions, notably Miriam Margolyes whose Flora, Arthur's childhood sweetheart, becomes an endearingly comical and totally Dickensian character. Sarah Pickering is a perfect heroine for this savagely critical story of injustice and struggle.

The first part of the film tells the story from Arthur's perspective, and the second from Little Dorrit's. This is a wholly successful device in that it fleshes out all the details of these two richly complex lives. Some scenes are depicted twice, from the two different points of view, adding to the intensity of the drama.

Little Dorrit was entirely filmed in a London studio and Edzard's attention to detail is commendable. When it premiered at the Berlin Film Festival in 1988, with several members of the cast in attendance, the first part screened in the morning and the second in the afternoon. Undoubtedly this is the best way to appreciate the nuances of the drama, with one part closely following the other. Understandably, though, this proved an almost insurmountable challenge for both cinemas and audiences, and as a result this magnificent film has fallen into oblivion.

55

Love at Large

(USA, 1990)

Orion Pictures. DIRECTOR/SCRIPT: Alan Rudolph. ACTORS: Tom Berenger, Elizabeth Perkins, Anne Archer, Kate Capshaw, Annette O'Toole, Ted Levine, Ann Magnuson, Kevin J. O'Connor, Ruby Dee, Barry Miller, Neil Young. 97 MINS.

Portland, Oregon. Private eye Harry Dobbs (Tom Berenger) has a quarrelsome relationship with his girlfriend, Doris (Ann Magnuson), who is jealous of his female acquaintances. Harry is summoned to a bar called Blue Danube by Miss Dolan (Anne Archer), who hires him to follow a man called Rick who, she says, frequents the bar. After she has left, Harry sees a man answering the description Miss Dolan has given him and starts to follow him, not realising that he isn't Rick. In fact he's Frederick King (Ted Levine), a businessman who lives with his wife (Annette O'Toole) and kids in the suburbs. But, as Harry continues to follow King, he discovers the man is living two lives and, as James McGraw, has another wife (Kate Capshaw) and family living on a ranch in another state. While Harry is trailing King/McGraw, he himself is being followed by Stella Wynkowski (Elizabeth Perkins), a private eye hired by Doris to keep an eye on him.

Alan Rudolph grew up in the film industry (his father, Oscar, was a film and TV director) and worked as assistant to Robert Altman on several films, including *The Long Goodbye* and *Nashville*, before starting to direct himself. Of the twenty or so features he's directed, it's safe to say that none of them has been a breakthrough success, perhaps because he never sticks to the rules of genre. *Love at Large* is a private-eye movie without any murders, or any of the usual trappings of this kind of film. The set-up is classic: an alluring but rather mysterious woman hires the gumshoe to follow a man without being too specific about why she wants him tailed—think of Humphrey Bogart in *The Maltese Falcon* and countless other films noir and you get the picture. But from the start we realise that Harry has set out to follow the wrong man: the real Rick (played by singer Neil Young) disappears for much of the movie, only to surface rather dramatically near the end. This, then, could be the basis for a comic spoof of private-eye movies—but *Love at Large* isn't that either. It's often amusing, in a whimsical sort of way, but never laugh-out-loud funny.

Instead it depicts a series of misunderstandings in which the characters too often rely on other people for their knowledge, accepting what they're told rather than what they can see with their own eyes. The film glides and weaves around this unusual premise with great dexterity, contrasting the mean streets of Portland, where it seems to be permanently raining, with the farmland where King/McGraw lives his alternative life—and where we discover his 'wife' is two-timing him with a farmhand, Art (Kevin J. O'Connor). Harry's relationship with the jealous Doris is toxic; Stella, we discover, is also trying to extricate herself from her involvement with Marty (Barry Miller), which is probably why she is studying a book titled *The Love Manual* during the long periods in which she waits in her car observing Harry's detecting from afar. And the sultry Miss Dolan is set up as the quintessential femme fatale who, in any other film of this type, might have faced the hero at the climax with a gun in her hand.

The fact that *Love at Large* refuses to be pigeonholed into any particular category (even if you accept it as a romance, it's a rather peculiar one) doubtless explains the obscurity into which it, and several other films by this beguiling director, has fallen.

56

Love's Labour's Lost

(UK / FRANCE / USA, 1999)

The Shakespeare Film Company–Intermedia Films–Pathé. DIRECTOR/SCRIPT: Kenneth Branagh, from the play by William Shakespeare. ACTORS: Kenneth Branagh, Alicia Silverstone, Natascha McElhone, Nathan Lane, Adrian Lester, Matthew Lillard, Alessandro Nivola, Timothy Spall, Richard Briers, Carmen Ejogo, Emily Mortimer, Geraldine McEwan, Daniel Hill, Richard Clifford, Anthony O'Donnell, Stefania Rocca, Jimmy Yuill, Alfred Bell. 90 MINS.

The Kingdom of Navarre, 1939. The King (Alessandro Nivola) proposes to his three companions, Berowne (Kenneth Branagh), Dumaine (Adrian Lester) and Longaville (Matthew Lillard), that they join him in twelve months of rigorous study, during which period they will not indulge in female company. Dumaine and Longaville agree; Berowne has reservations, but eventually complies. The Princess of France (Alicia Silverstone) and her three ladies in waiting, Rosaline (Natascha McElhone), Maria (Carmen Ejogo) and Katherine (Emily Mortimer), arrive for treaty negotiations with the King, and their alluring presences in the kingdom leads to romantic attachments all round. Meanwhile eccentric Spanish nobleman Don Armado (Timothy Spall) is smitten by the beautiful Jacquanetta (Stefania Rocca), while mature schoolmistress Holofernia (Geraldine McEwan) and Sir Nathaniel (Richard Briers) also discover a taste for romance. News comes of the death of the King of France, as a result of which the four women leave, but all promise to meet again in a year to test the genuineness of their respective lovers.

One of Shakespeare's least performed plays, *Love's Labour's Lost* would pose quite a challenge if it were played straight today. 'Laboured' is a good word to describe its familiar misunderstandings and incorrectly delivered love letters. Kenneth Branagh, in a brilliant move, discards about three-quarters of the original text, keeping only the principal characters, the most significant speeches and the basic plot developments, and relocates it all in a mythical Europe in the period leading up to and during World War II. He transforms what's left of the play into a 1930s-style musical, using ten well-known songs by composers like Irving Berlin, Cole Porter and the Gershwins, and having his cast sing and dance to their hearts' content.

The result is imaginative, briskly paced and thoroughly entertaining. It's true that not all of these actors are professional singers or dancers, but despite that they all, Branagh included, acquit themselves wonderfully well, and to experience Geraldine McEwan sing and dance to 'The Way You Look Tonight' really is a joy. Nathan Lane makes a wonderful contribution as the clownish Costard, channelling slapstick comedians from Bud Abbott to Jimmy Durante with glee, while Timothy Spall's outrageously camp, comically moustachioed Spanish nobleman is something to behold—his big number is 'I Get A Kick Out Of You'.

Branagh parodies Astaire and Rogers musicals with great affection (the plot here is almost as nonsensical as the narrative in, say, *Top Hat*), while Adrian Lester pays homage to Gene Kelly in one sequence. The entire ensemble performs 'There's No Business Like Show Business', while the plaintive 'They Can't Take That Away From Me' is introduced when the lovers are forced to part.

A masterstroke is the use of mock newsreels of the period to bridge the gaps in the plot—newsreels whose jocular commentary precisely echoes the style of narration that was employed at the time. Otherwise the sets and costumes—with each of the four women assigned a principal colour—are delightfully realised.

Sadly, the concept proved too radical for many critics, and the largely negative reviews this thoroughly entertaining film received doomed it at the box office. In Australia it wasn't even released in cinemas.

57

Mad City

(USA, 1997)

Warner Bros. **DIRECTOR:** Costa-Gavras. **SCRIPT:** Tom Matthews. **ACTORS:** Dustin Hoffman, John Travolta, Alan Alda, Mia Kirshner, Ted Levine, Robert Prosky, Blythe Danner, [Bill Nunn], William Atherton, Tammy Lauren, William O'Leary, John Landis. 114 MINS.

Madeleine, California. TV reporter for local station KXBD, Max Brackett (Dustin Hoffman) is assigned, together with his young camera assistant Laurie Callahan (Mia Kirshner), to the local Museum of Natural History for a routine interview with the museum's director, Mrs Banks (Blythe Danner). After the interview is over, but before Brackett has left the building, Sam Baily (John Travolta), a former security guard recently fired by Mrs Banks, enters the museum armed with an automatic rifle and a bag filled with dynamite. He wants his job back, and during the ensuing altercation he accidentally shoots Cliff (an uncredited Bill Nunn), who is now working at Baily's old job as a security guard. A party of school children visiting the museum with their teacher become hostages as a siege unfolds, with Brackett on the inside, but allowed by the trusting Baily to come and go, orchestrating Baily's demands, while at the same time seizing every opportunity to enhance his reputation not only with the local TV station, but with the national network to which it's affiliated. However when the network's senior anchorman, Kevin Hollander (Alan Alda), arrives to take charge, Brackett quickly realises Hollander's aim is to crucify the now contrite Baily and create a truly sensational news story.

The French-Greek director Costa-Gavras, best known for the Oscar-winning political thriller *Z* (1968), made a handful of films in the US, including *Missing* and *Betrayed*. *Mad City* is a frontal assault on the ruthless approach taken by the less scrupulous TV journalists

Devil in the Flesh (1985)—Katia Caballero, Keith Smith (see #29)

Apartment Zero (1988)—Colin Firth (see #4)

Valmont (1989)—Annette Bening, Colin Firth (see #94)

The Favour, the Watch and the Very Big Fish (1991)—Bob Hoskins, Jeff Goldblum (see #34)

Love's Labour's Lost (1999)–Emily Mortimer, Carmen Ejogo, Natascha McElhone, Alicia Silverstone (see #56)

Garage Days (2002)–Russell Dykstra, Kick Gurry, Pia Miranda (see #38)

S1m0ne (2002)—Rachel Roberts (see #85)

Romance & Cigarettes (2005)—dance sequence (see #80)

Grace is Gone (2007)—Shélan O'Keefe, John Cusack, Gracie Bednarczyk (see #42)

Rendition (2007)—Reese Witherspoon (see #74)

In the Electric Mist (2008)—Pruitt Taylor Vince, Tommy Lee Jones (see #49)

AF ARCHIVE / ALAMY

Agora (2009)—Rachel Weisz (see #3)

ENTERTAINMENT PICTURES / ALAMY

Enemy (2013)—Jake Gyllenhaal (see #30)

PICTORIAL PRESS LTD / ALAMY

Sunshine on Leith (2013)—George MacKay, Antonia Thomas (see #87)

PICTORIAL PRESS LTD / ALAMY

She's Funny That Way (2014)—Imogen Poots, Owen Wilson (see #84)

AF ARCHIVE / ALAMY

Truth (2015)—Cate Blanchett, Robert Redford (see #91)

AF ARCHIVE / ALAMY

on occasions when they not only report on, but also manipulate, a 'hot' story. The film seems inspired by the 1951 Billy Wilder movie *Ace in the Hole*, which took a similarly caustic approach to the journalistic profession. In *Mad City*, a TV network covering a police siege involving hostage schoolchildren and a distraught blue collar worker who has just lost his job, films interviews with the man's alleged friends and neighbours, and then edits them in such a way as to give the worst possible impression of the gunman.

Meanwhile the journalist on the spot, Brackett, sensing an opportunity to be promoted within the TV network from which he'd previously fallen from grace after an unfortunate on-camera meltdown, coaches the gunman—who, as superbly played by Travolta in his best screen role, is barely articulate and is instantly apologetic for his foolish and dangerous actions—in order to prolong the siege, and thus the newsworthiness of the event. When Baily agrees to let a couple of the children go free, Brackett advises him that one of them should be African-American to make up for the fact that the guard he wounded was black.

Costa-Gavras adds conviction to this at times bitterly humorous drama by including several easily recognisable real-life TV anchors, among them Larry King and Jay Leno, and he also probes the uneasy nexus between the TV news crews and the police who are attempting to bring the siege to a positive conclusion.

The scariest thing we see is the way hordes of journalists, with their bulky cameras and boom mikes, rush to harass anyone who might have anything at all to do with the event unfolding—like scavengers attacking some helpless animal.

Hoffman has never given a bad performance, and his portrayal of Brackett—ambitious, wily, manipulative but strangely sympathetic—is among his best.

The film was pilloried by most American critics and failed at the box office; it went straight to video in Australia. Costa-Gavras has not worked in America since.

58

The Meyerowitz Stories
(New and Selected)

(USA, 2017)

Netflix Original–IAC Films. DIRECTOR/SCRIPT: Noah Baumbach. ACTORS: Adam Sandler, Ben Stiller, Dustin Hoffman, Emma Thompson, Elizabeth Marvel, Grace Van Patten, Candice Bergen, Adam Driver, Judd Hirsch, Rebecca Miller, Matthew Shear. 110 MINS.

New York. Septuagenarian Harold Meyerowitz (Dustin Hoffman), a sculptor, lives with his third wife Maureen (Emma Thompson), in a cluttered three-storey house. Bitter because he has never been afforded the recognition he believes to be his due, the grumpy Harold has an ambivalent attitude towards his three children. Danny (Adam Sandler), who once showed promise as a musician, is drifting aimlessly through life, but is proud of his daughter Eliza (Grace Van Patten), who has enrolled at film school. Jean (Elizabeth Marvel) lives alone, while Matthew (Ben Stiller) has found success in the finance business in LA. Both Danny and Matthew are recovering from broken marriages, while Jean has always been single. Matthew and his father are planning to sell the New York house, and its entire art collection, at a knock-down price, while Danny is bitterly opposed to this. Harold is persuaded to participate in a retrospective of his work at Bard College, where he taught for many years, and where Eliza studies film. But the old man suffers a stroke and is hospitalised. This brings the quarrelling siblings closer together, and both of them speak for their father at the show's opening.

This is the best film to date from Noah Baumbach, a director who, in movies like *The Squid and the Whale*, *Greenberg* and *While We're Young*, has specialised in exploring the collateral effects of selfish behaviour. Divided into chapters, the film—as its title proclaims—is structured around a series of family anecdotes: the inebriated Maureen serving up an inedible fish dish for Danny and Eliza; Matthew attempting to have a restaurant lunch with his crotchety father, while the old man regularly antagonises both waiters and other diners; the hospital experience where there seems to be no continuity of either doctors or nurses; the snobbery and politics of the art scene. Much of this is extremely funny in a Woody Allen kind of way, with running gags and non-sequiturs in abundance (at one point, Harold complains that in his opinion the reason the Republicans control the government is a result of the public's indifference to art). But it's also painful. Speaking of their father, Danny tells Matthew: 'He loves everything *you* do.' 'He doesn't tell *me*,' replies Matthew. 'He tells *me*!' cries the under-appreciated Danny.

The performances are simply wonderful—Hoffman has rarely been better than he is here as the curmudgeonly old self-promoter whose self-absorption has seriously affected the lives of his children. But the next generation offers hope in Grace Van Patten's lovely performance as the skittish Eliza, who cheerfully sends home for her father and grandfather to view copies of the provocative film-school movies she has created (*Pagina Man* about a man with a penis as well as a vagina is her latest creation).

The Meyerowitz Stories is included here as an example of Netflix Original productions. Netflix's stated policy is to screen their own productions only on Netflix—and they will apparently never be made available on DVD or Blu-ray. They do allow a few festival screenings, and *Meyerowitz* had a brief cinema release in the UK, so there are exceptions—but in Australia, it seems that unless you're a Netflix subscriber you won't see this or other outstanding films, including *Beasts of No Nation* and *Okja*. As a result these films inevitably will fall into the 'forgotten' category, which seems a terrible shame.

. . . the best film to date from Baumbach

59

Mike's Murder

(USA, 1984)

The Ladd Company. DIRECTOR/SCRIPT: James Bridges. ACTORS: Debra Winger, Mark Keyloun, Darrell Larson, Brooke Alderson, Paul Winfield, Robert Crosson, Daniel Shor, William Ostrander. 109 MINS.

Los Angeles. Betty Parrish (Debra Winger) works in a bank and lives alone in a small house in the suburb of Venice. She has met Mike Chuhutsky (Mark Keyloun) at the local tennis courts and they enjoyed a one-night stand; but though charming and good-natured, Mike proves to be very unreliable and it's months before she sees him again. When she does, he's in trouble and needs to hide out. He asks Betty to drive him to a house in the hills and promises to call her soon. Three months later he phones and asks her for a date that night. She waits for him but he never shows up. Next morning she receives a phone call from Sam (Robert Crosson), who says he's a friend of Mike and that Mike was murdered the previous night. Shocked and horrified, Betty ventures to the house in the hills where she'd taken Mike the last time they met; there she meets Phillip (Paul Winfield), who tells her he was Mike's lover. She goes to Mike's apartment and encounters the police examining copious bloodstains. Later that night Mike's friend Pete (Darrell Larson), who, together with Mike, had stolen a small amount of cocaine from The Mob and who is in fear for his life, turns up at Betty's house.

In 1979 *The China Syndrome*, the fourth film directed by former screenwriter James Bridges, became a phenomenal success; it was followed by another hit, *Urban Cowboy* (1980) and then, in 1982, Bridges wrote and directed *Mike's Murder*, starring Debra Winger, who had scored a hit with *An Officer and a Gentleman* the same year. In *Mike's Murder*, Winger plays a single woman who gradually comes to realise her life is in danger because of her brief relationship with the eponymous Mike, a small-time drug dealer who has made the mistake of trying to cheat The Mob. The early scenes, set in the suburban streets and apartments of a sun-drenched Los Angeles, evoke for Betty the magic of falling in love, followed by the disillusionment when she realises how fickle and unreliable Mike really is. She consoles herself with Richard (Daniel Shor), but can never quite get Mike out of her mind, as she admits to her sympathetic girlfriend, Patty (Brooke Alderson). When by chance they meet again and she drives Mike to the house in the hills, she still doesn't comprehend that the man she has a 'thing' for is placing her in danger. After she receives the news of Mike's murder, the most everyday events take on a sinister turn. A car parked on the street near her house looks threatening, a phone that suddenly rings shocks her, a stranger arriving on her doorstep seems confronting—simple events like these are filmed by Bridges in such a way as to create nerve-jangling suspense, and the climactic scenes are truly terrifying without being in any way explicit. Bloody violence is hinted at, but visual excess is carefully avoided.

This is probably Debra Winger's finest screen performance. She's in practically every scene and her sensitive, vulnerable presence is enchanting, especially as the events around her become darker and more sinister.

When the film was completed in 1982 the studio shelved it. Perhaps they felt it wasn't explicit enough, or that the supporting cast was composed of unknown actors, or that it was too down-beat. Two years later it limped into cinemas for a limited American release (I was fortunate enough to see it at a cinema in Beverly Hills during its one-week run), but to the best of my knowledge it never made it to cinemas in English-speaking countries outside the US and Canada. It's a shame that such an unusual and original thriller was dumped in this way. Bridges went on to make just two more films before his death in 1993 at the age of 57.

60

Mississippi Grind

(USA, 2014)

Electric City Entertainment. DIRECTORS/SCRIPT: Anna Boden, Ryan Fleck. ACTORS: Ben Mendelsohn, Ryan Reynolds, Sienna Miller, Analeigh Tipton, Alfre Woodard, James Toback, Robin Weigert. 109 MINS.

Dubuque, Iowa. Gerry (Ben Mendelsohn) is a sad loner who works in a desultory kind of way selling real estate. A gambling addict, whose addiction brought about the end of his marriage years earlier, Gerry thinks he's met a kindred spirit in Curtis (Ryan Reynolds), who seems far more together than he is. The pair form a team and decide to head for New Orleans to participate in a high-stakes poker game organised by a big-time gambler, Tony Roundtree (James Toback). Gerry quits his job and the two men set off in his car, heading down the river and gambling at every opportunity. In St Louis, Curtis reconnects with Simone (Sienna Miller), a prostitute who works on the riverboats. Gerry spends an evening with Vanessa (Analeigh Tipton), Simone's roommate, and tells her about his ex-wife and his daughter. Although Gerry already owes money to Sam (Alfre Woodard), a loan shark, this doesn't stop him gambling, and in Memphis he loses everything he has, though he keeps this a secret from Curtis. Gerry insists on a side-trip to Little Rock, where he visits his ex-wife, Dorothy (Robin Weigert), who has remarried. He briefly sees his daughter again for the first time in a long while. The reunion is very tense, and when Gerry leaves he steals some money and also a photograph of the girl. In New Orleans, Gerry and Curtis have a falling out when they lose at the racetrack, but Gerry is undeterred and makes a concerted effort to win at the casino.

The performance of Australian actor Ben Mendelsohn in his first starring role in an American movie would be reason enough to see this compelling road movie which features a couple of gambling addicts, one relatively relaxed and carefree, and the other deeply desperate.

The two meet in a beautifully staged pre-title sequence, which is set in a smoky room filled with diehard gamblers. Gerry, a regular, is, like the other locals, intrigued by the charming stranger, Curtis, who unexpectedly orders a glass of expensive bourbon for him and chatters casually about himself. In contrast, Gerry is quietly desperate; he owes a lot of money 'to everyone', as he admits with a rueful grin—Mendelsohn plays the role with a hangdog brilliance in what is arguably his best screen performance. The scene in which he visits his ex-wife, who makes it painfully clear how utterly worthless she thinks he is and how she despises him for abandoning their daughter, is beautifully handled and sits in stark contrast to the strangely touching scene in which Gerry bonds with the seemingly vulnerable Vanessa, who shows him simple magic tricks, while he responds by playing an Erik Satie piece on the piano.

The film has links to past movies about gamblers, notably Robert Altman's *California Split* and Karel Reisz' *The Gambler* (both 1974): the latter was scripted by James Toback, who portrays the formidable Roundtree here.

Although the writers–directors are clearly condemning the gambling industry, they have such sympathy for their characters, and especially for Mendelsohn's perpetual loser, that they can't resist a surprisingly upbeat ending. Nevertheless, the final image, of a battered and bloodied Gerry attaching to the windscreen of his car the photograph of his daughter that he stole from his ex-wife, is almost unbearably poignant.

The 'happy ending', however, wasn't enough to rescue the film from the obscurity into which it fell after its launch at the Sundance Film Festival. It was granted the most limited cinema release in Australia, with the result that few people were given the chance to see an extraordinary performance from one of the country's finest actors.

61

Molokai: The story of Father Damien

(BELGIUM/THE NETHERLANDS, 1999)

ERA Films-Jos Stelling Productions. DIRECTOR: Paul Cox. SCRIPT: John Briley, from the biography by Hilde Eynikel. ACTORS: David Wenham, Aden Young, Tom Wilkinson, Kate Ceberano, Chris Haywood, Leo McKern, Derek Jacobi, Sam Neill, Kris Kristofferson, Peter O'Toole, Alice Krige, Thom Hoffman, Keanu Kapuni-Szasz, Michael Pas, Dirk Roofthooft. 119 MINS.

The Hawaiian Islands, 1872. Belgian missionary Father Damien (David Wenham) volunteers to work for three months in the leper colony on the island of Molokai. The colony is separated from the rest of the island by Pali, the mountainous cliffs that rise steeply up from the tiny leper community. Bishop Maigret (Leo McKern) warns Damien not to get too close to the lepers, and especially not to touch them—advice the missionary ignores. Damien becomes passionately devoted to the cause of the lepers and remains on the island for most of the rest of his life, apart from a brief trip to Honolulu to make confession and to meet Princess Liliuokalani (Kate Ceberano). He contracts the disease himself, and dies in 1889 at the age of 49.

ERA, a Belgian production company, invited Dutch-born Australian filmmaker Paul Cox (see also #37) to film the story of Father Damien, who was canonised in 1995. A screenplay had already been written by John Briley, who had won an Oscar in 1982 for his screenplay for *Gandhi*, a biography of another real-life hero, which was directed by Richard Attenborough. Cox was accustomed to writing his own films and to have almost complete control over their production. Though he was keen to tell Damien's story, he was aware that he'd be working under the orders of film producers based in Europe.

The decision to film in the still-existing leper colony on the island of Molokai was crucial to the success of the film, as was the casting of Australian actor David Wenham, who is compelling in this arduous role. The difficulties associated with the film's production were many, but Cox quickly befriended the leaders of the colony, who gave him their full support—support that proved to be vital when the producers, unhappy with the footage shipped back to Brussels, attempted to replace Cox with another director.

For what would be the most expensive film ever produced by a Belgian company up to that time, some insurance was deemed necessary by ERA, and a roster of well-known actors was cast, some without Cox's approval, in minor roles. Peter O'Toole is very effective as a dying Englishman who has no faith; Tom Wilkinson gives a strong performance as a priest who comes to assist Damien; Kris Kristofferson portrays the island's administrator; Sam Neill is the Prime Minister; Alice Krige is a nun who answers a call for help; Kate Ceberano is the Hawaiian Princess, who visits the colony to offer support.

Significant roles are played by Cox regulars: Chris Haywood is a bombastic character who mellows with age and illness; Aden Young is a doctor who decides, after a while, that he can't bear the stress of living and working in the colony. Nino Martinetti, Cox's frequent collaborator behind the camera, was in charge of the location photography, and the widescreen format was used for the first time on a Cox film.

After Cox had edited the film into a 'director's cut', the producers re-edited it, reducing it by some 10 minutes, and removing material that included some of Cox's beloved footage of the lepers themselves. The film opened in Brussels in March 1999, to indifferent reviews and poor box-office. Cox was able to restore some, but not all, of the cut footage and the film had its first Australian screening at the Melbourne International Film Festival in July 2000, after which it had a limited but not very profitable commercial run. Despite its flaws, it's a film that deserves re-appraisal.

62

Moonlight Mile

(USA, 2002)

Touchstone. DIRECTOR/SCRIPT: Brad Silberling. ACTORS: Jake Gyllenhaal, Susan Sarandon, Dustin Hoffman, Holly Hunter, Ellen Pompeo. 117 MINS.

A small New England town, 1973. Joe Nast (Jake Gyllenhaal) arrives for what was expected to be his wedding to Diana Floss; instead he and Diana's parents, Ben (Dustin Hoffman) and Jojo (Susan Sarandon) attend her funeral—Diana was fatally shot while sitting in the diner across the street from her father's real estate office. The killer was aiming at his wife, who was sitting beside Diana, and who was also shot—but, unlike Diana, she survived. Ben and Jojo insist that Joe stay on with them after the funeral, and, because he has no particular place to go or employment prospects, he reluctantly agrees to join Ben in his business, a position Ben had offered him before the tragedy. The uneasy atmosphere in the bereaved household, with Jojo, a writer and recovering alcoholic, occasionally exploding in anger and sorrow, proves stifling for Joe—until he meets Bertie (Ellen Pompeo), a young woman whose fiancée has been fighting in Vietnam but hasn't been heard of for three years.

Brad Silberling was a television director who, prior to this beautiful film, made a couple of supernatural movies (*Casper* and *City of Angels*). His screenplay for *Moonlight Mile* was inspired by the murder of his actress girlfriend in 1989, and how he coped with the loss. This personal experience no doubt explains the shifting moods of the film, as comedic elements keep intruding even in the face of tragedy and bereavement. When Joe, Ben and Jojo leave for Diana's funeral, the driver of their hire car turns on the ignition and the radio blasts out some totally inappropriate music. At the wake, Diana's beloved dog suddenly throws up in close proximity to the guests. Jojo's friends shower her with self-help books with titles like *Grieving for Grown Ups*.

In his first adult role—after his breakthrough movie, *Donnie Darko*—Gyllenhaal perfectly captures the bemusement, displacement and indecision of Joe's character. At times his performance is reminiscent of Dustin Hoffman in *The Graduate* as he tries to decide between staying with Ben and Jojo, acting as a kind of surrogate child to them in place of their dead daughter, or cut his losses and start a new life with Bertie. But Bertie is every bit as mixed up as Joe; she can't or won't accept the fact that her fiancé, Cal, isn't coming home, and as a result she lives an artificially lonely existence. As for Ben, he's pathetically eager for Joe to join him in his struggling real estate business, and looks on him as the son he never had. There's a great scene in which he enters the diner where his daughter was killed and starts questioning the startled and embarrassed staff about what actually happened that day. While Jojo explodes with grief and anger on occasion, Ben for the most part keeps his grief bottled up, which makes the scene in the diner particularly revealing.

The film's other key character is the DA (Holly Hunter), who feels that Joe's testimony at the killer's trial will be of vital importance in securing a conviction.

If the film has a flaw it's that we don't know very much about Joe; his own family never gets a look-in. But this proves a minor concern in light of the film's main themes.

This is one of those films with a great soundtrack of songs from the period that perfectly fit the mood. Even those few people who went to see it in 2002 probably missed Silberling's touching dedication that appears on screen after the end credit crawl: 'For all our loves … departed, or yet to arrive …'

Despite the popularity of its leading actors, the film was poorly received at the time. Perhaps its theme—admittedly a tricky one to market—was a turn-off for audiences.

63

The More Things Change . . .

(AUSTRALIA, 1985)

Syme International. DIRECTOR: Robyn Nevin. SCRIPT: Moya Wood. ACTORS: Judy Morris, Barry Otto, Victoria Longley, Lewis Fitz-Gerald, Peter Carroll, Louise Le Nay, Owen Johnson. 95 MINS.

Rural Victoria. Connie (Judy Morris) and Lex (Barry Otto) are attempting to combine city and country living. They've acquired a small farm about two hours' drive from Melbourne. Connie is the breadwinner—she works for a publisher in the city and commutes every day—while Lex has given up his job and is attempting to work the farm with the aim of making them and their small son, Nicholas (Owen Johnson), self-sufficient. It's getting too much for him, so Connie decides to find someone who can help with the chores in exchange for free room and board. The person chosen for this is Geraldine (Victoria Longley), who is pregnant but not, unfortunately, by her fiancé, Barry (Lewis Fitz-Gerald). The arrangement works well for a while, but Connie becomes increasingly irritated by Lex's laid-back attitude and his growing closeness to Geraldine, who has decided to put the baby out for adoption after it's born. Barry pays a visit and they all get on well with him. The baby is born, Geraldine and Barry marry, and Geraldine changes her mind about letting the baby go. But the marriage of Connie and Lex is no longer so secure.

The More Things Change . . . unfolds over a period of about six months, during which time the lives of the principal characters change dramatically. The film, a marital comedy–drama, successfully explores the pressures on all concerned in this sort of arrangement, and does so with insight and flashes of humour.

The idea for the film came from producer Jill Robb, and the screenplay was written by Moya Wood, with uncredited assistance from Michael Brindley. It turned out to be the only feature film directed by Robyn Nevin, well known for her work as director in the theatre, and equally well known as one of Australia's finest actors. In my book *The Avocado Plantation* (1990), I detailed the difficulties Nevin experienced during the film's production, some of which were physical (Barry Otto broke his ankle a couple of days into shooting) and some of which stemmed from the fact that Nevin was new to the role of film director. She was greatly assisted by the film's cinematographer, Dan Burstall, who had, himself, worked as a director.

Despite these challenges, the film works wonderfully well. The characters are painfully real, and the situations in which they find themselves proved to be increasingly familiar in the 1980s as city couples opted for a 'sea change' and experimented with different lifestyles. The farmhouse in which Connie and Lex live is a small one, and the bathroom/toilet is located in a very public area, so there's not a great deal of privacy. One of the more amusing scenes has a technician from Telstra mistake the obviously pregnant Geraldine for Lex's wife; they don't disabuse him, so that when Connie returns he's thoroughly confused.

Geraldine, who appears to be a shy young woman despite her complicated love life, finds the domestic situation difficult at first, especially as she is easily able to overhear the increasingly bitter squabbles between Connie and Lex. When she changes her plans and she and Barry decide to keep her baby girl, she tells Connie: 'We're going to do lots of things—like you two,' a line that turns out to be sadly ironic given that the marriage of Connie and Lex is in the process of collapsing.

The More Things Change . . . is a modest, honest film, attractively photographed and beautifully acted. However, it made little impact at the cinema box office, and now seems to have disappeared.

. . . a marital comedy-drama

64

Mullet

(AUSTRALIA, 2000)

Porchlight Films. DIRECTOR/SCRIPT: David Caesar. ACTORS: Ben Mendelsohn, Susie Porter, Andrew S. Gilbert, Belinda McClory, Tony Barry, Kris McQuade, Peta Brady, Wayne Blair, Paul Kelman, Steve Le Marquand, Aaron Blabey. 89 MINS.

Coollawarra, New South Wales. Eddie (Ben Mendelsohn), nicknamed Mullet, returns to his home town on the NSW South Coast, after a three-year absence, during which time nobody, not even his parents (Tony Barry, Kris McQuade), knew where he was living. During his absence Tully (Susie Porter), the girl he left behind, has married Pete (Andrew S. Gilbert), his brother, who is the local cop. Mullet shacks up in an abandoned caravan, buys an old car, and starts fishing for mullet in the river, selling the fish to his sister Robbie (Peta Brady), who runs the local fish shop and is dating Jack (Wayne Blair). Mullet's return brings a great many unresolved tensions to the surface. Tully and Pete quarrel, and Kay (Belinda McClory), who has run the local pub since her mother ran off with a man, is angry that Mullet won't have sex with her. Matters come to a head at a family barbecue where Tully reveals that she's pregnant.

David Caesar, one of Australia's best directors, is a master at exploring the lives of 'ordinary' Aussies, and *Mullet* is one of his best films. Once again, Ben Mendelsohn gives an exceptional performance in the title role. His character, we learn, was always considered the 'brainiest' of the three children of constantly bickering parents, and when he left town three years before the start of the film, everyone assumed he'd gone either to London or to America to make a name for himself. Instead, it turns out, he's been in Sydney working as a copywriter for an advertising agency, most of the money he earned has 'gone up his nose', and that he only left the agency because he got the sack. He returns home, hitching a ride on the back of a truck, looking unkempt and lost. (His father reckons that his long hair makes him appear like 'a rat looking through a straw broom', just one of the wonderfully colourful expressions in Caesar's screenplay.)

Nobody in town can understand why he left and why he's back. 'Was it me?' asks Tully. 'It was everything,' he replies, though Coollawarra (population 1491) is obviously a place where prospects are limited to say the least—the best thing that's happened since his son left, according to his father, is the installation of a flush toilet.

The characters are all beautifully realised. Susie's Porter's Tully, who adored Mullet before he abandoned her without a word, is clearly not entirely content with domestic life with the decent but dull Pete. Robbie talks openly about her sexual problems, while Kay reveals that she's had joyless sex with half the men in town. As for Mullet's mother, she thinks her son should just go away and leave them all in peace.

Like *Mississippi Grind* (#60), the final shot of the film is of Mendelsohn sitting in the driver's seat of a stationary car facing an uncertain future. In this case the warm-hearted but lonely Kay holds out a possible solution, but will he seize the day or will he simply drift away like he did the last time?

The ensemble cast is superb, and some of the actors achieve their finest work under Caesar's direction—Tony Barry and Kris McQuade as the parents are exceptionally good. Yet this honest, affectionate and ultimately very moving film failed to attract much of an audience, proving again that it's very hard indeed to predict what will 'work' in cinemas and what won't.

65

Ned Kelly

(AUSTRALIA/UK, 2003)

Endymion Films–Working Title (Universal). **DIRECTOR:** Gregor Jordan. **SCRIPT:** John Michael McDonagh, from the novel by Robert Drewe. **ACTORS:** Heath Ledger, Orlando Bloom, Naomi Watts, Geoffrey Rush, Rachel Griffiths, Joel Edgerton, Laurence Kinlan, Philip Barantini, Kiri Paramore, Kerry Condon, Kris McQuade, Emily Browning, Geoff Morrell, Charles 'Bud' Tingwell, Saskia Burmeister, Peter Phelps, Russell Dykstra, Nicholas Bell. **109 MINS.**

Country Victoria, the 1870s. As a boy, Ned Kelly is constantly falling foul of the law, but as he gets older (played by Heath Ledger) he resolves to stay on the straight and narrow and obtains a job on the estate of an English landowner, Richard Cook (Nicholas Bell), whose wife, Julia (Naomi Watts), is attracted to him. In his spare time he takes part in bare-knuckle fights. The local police are constantly harassing the Kellys mainly, it seems, because they're Irish. Widowed Ellen (Kris McQuade) and Ned's sisters, Kate (Kerry Condon) and Grace (Emily Browning), all find themselves hassled by police officers. One night, when Ned is secretly spending time with Julia, a drunken policeman tries to molest Kate and is thrown out by her son, Dan (Laurence Kinlan). Ned is blamed, and in his absence his mother Ellen is sent to prison. In revenge, Ned forms a gang with Dan and his mates Steve Hart (Philip Barantini) and Joe Byrne (Orlando Bloom). When police arrive at the location where the bushrangers are hiding, a gun battle ensues, resulting in the deaths of the law officers. Ned and his gang begin to rob banks, sharing their loot with the poor people of the district. Superintendent Francis Hare (Geoffrey Rush) hunts down the bushrangers, and Ned is eventually trapped at the inn in Glenrowan.

After a big success with the crime comedy *Two Hands* (1999, with Heath Ledger and Rose Byrne), Gregor Jordan made a film in

Europe (see #17), before returning to Australia to make yet another film about the legendary Ned Kelly, this one based on Robert Drewe's book (not the rather more popular Peter Carey treatment of the legendary outlaw). The screenplay adaptation was by John Michael McDonagh, who later became known as the director of such significant Irish films as *The Guard* (2011) and *Calvary* (2013).

Since the trail-blazing *The Story of the Kelly Gang*—which, in 1906, was arguably the world's first feature-length film—the Kelly story has been an oft-told tale, most famously by Tony Richardson in 1970 with Mick Jagger in the lead (yet another version of the story, based on the Carey book, has not yet gone into production at the time of writing). Jordan's decision to avoid the trap of turning the story into a popular adventure yarn pays off in one respect; the film's grim, lowering, wintry tone, and its bitter depiction of an Irish (Catholic) family hounded by the Victorian Establishment, harassed by the Law and driven to crime and banditry as a direct result, is probably closer to the truth. In any event, sequences like the climactic confrontation at Glenrowan, staged in pouring rain, evoke the great Japanese director Akira Kurosawa in their painfully physical approach to violence.

Ledger is a very impressive Ned, and a strong supporting cast is employed, with Geoffrey Rush a standout as the implacable Hare. British cinematographer Oliver Stapleton brings the events vividly to life, and much of the film was shot on the locations where the Kelly Gang actually operated.

As was the case with *Burke & Wills* (see #20), a simple knock-about parody of the story, Abe Forsythe's *Ned*, was released at about the same time, and ten years earlier there had been another parody, *Reckless Kelly*, written and directed by Yahoo Serious. However, the film's disappointing box-office returns were probably due more to the downbeat approach taken by Jordan than anything else. Maybe Jordan's film is too ambitious to achieve popular appeal—or maybe Australians are just too familiar with the story.

66

Nobody's Fool

(USA, 1994)

Paramount Pictures–Capella International. DIRECTOR/SCRIPT: Robert Benton, from the novel by Richard Russo. ACTORS: Paul Newman, Melanie Griffith, Bruce Willis, Jessica Tandy, Dylan Walsh, Pruitt Taylor Vince, Gene Saks, Josef Sommer, Philip Seymour Hoffman, Philip Bosco, Elizabeth Wilson, Margo Martindale, Jay Patterson, Alex Goodwin. 109 MINS.

The small town of North Bath, New York State, in winter. Donald 'Sully' Sullivan (Paul Newman), aged 60, lodges with his elderly former schoolteacher, Miss Beryl (Jessica Tandy), and works on and off for Carl Roebuck (Bruce Willis), owner of the Tip Top Construction Company. Sully is suing Carl over an injury he received on the job, but his inept lawyer, Wirf (Gene Saks), seems incapable of winning this or indeed any case. Sully and his best friend, Rub Squeers (Pruitt Taylor Vince), regularly gamble with Carl, who habitually cheats on his long-suffering wife, Toby (Melanie Griffith). Unexpectedly, Sully, who walked out on his wife and children years earlier, is reunited with his son Peter (Dylan Walsh), who has lost his teaching job and whose own marriage is in trouble. Sully also meets his grandson, Will (Alex Goodwin).

Robert Benton's reputation as both a screenwriter (*Bonnie and Clyde*) and director (*Kramer vs. Kramer*) is an impressive one, and this unassuming film, made late in his career, represents some of his best work. Set in a small community in upstate New York in mid-winter, the film quietly explores the lives of various characters who manage to live in harmony with one another, despite their differences and occasional conflicts. Completely unsentimental, the film homes in on the complicated relationships between parents and children—Sully and Peter, Peter and Will, Miss Beryl and her obnoxious son Clive, Josef Sommer, who is attempting to open a theme park in town—as well as between people who succeed in remaining friends despite the conflicts in which they're involved—such as Sully's running battle with Carl over money due to him, a disagreement that never prevents them playing cards together. Also beautifully realised is Sully's warm relationship with Toby, Carl's neglected wife; they flirt and talk about going away together—something it's abundantly clear they'll never actually get around to doing—though clearly they are very comfortable with one another.

Jessica Tandy—in her last screen role—brings warmth and dignity to the part of wise old Miss Beryl; the film is dedicated to her. Also notable in an early role is Philip Seymour Hoffman as Raymer, the young policeman with whom Sully has regular altercations. As Sully's incompetent, one-legged attorney, Gene Saks—better known as a director of comedy films like *The Odd Couple* and *Mame*—also gives a winning performance.

Benton's adroit way with dialogue is used to advantage. Peter advises his errant father: 'You know what Mom's worst fear is? That your life has been fun,' and when Sully gets Peter to help him drug Carl's Doberman so that he can break into his property and steal his snow-blower, the younger man complains, 'I'm a member of Greenpeace and I just helped you poison a dog.'

Despite a successful launch in competition at the Berlin Film Festival, and warm praise from some important critics (Andrew Sarris named it as his choice for best film of the year), *Nobody's Fool* seems to have been perceived as too slight to grab the attention of mainstream audiences and, over the years, seems to have been pretty much forgotten despite its many qualities.

Benton's adroit way with dialogue is used to advantage

67

The Old Man Who Read Love Stories

(FRANCE/AUSTRALIA/SPAIN/THE NETHERLANDS, 2000)

Fildebroc–Magnetic Hall–Sociedad Kino Visión–Odusseia Films. **DIRECTOR/SCRIPT**: Rolf de Heer, from the book by Luis Sepúlveda. **ACTORS**: Richard Dreyfuss, Timothy Spall, Hugo Weaving, Cathy Tyson, Victor Bottenbley, Fede Celada, Luis Hostalot, Guillermo Toledo. 111 **MINS**.

The Amazon. Antonio Bolivar (Richard Dreyfuss) has lived alone for most of his life on the fringe of the little village of El Idilio, located on the bank of a tributary of the great river. He came to this remote place with his wife, who subsequently died of malaria, and he himself almost died from snakebite, but was nursed back to health by members of the local Indian tribe. The tribe's leader, Nushino (Victor Bottenbley), befriended him and he was accepted as a member of the tribe until white men attacked them and Bolivar was expelled from their midst. This was when he moved to the village, which is governed by Luis Agalla (Timothy Spall), the Mayor, a pompous blowhard with an attractive servant, Josefina (Cathy Tyson). At election time Bolivar is obliged to prove that he can read, which he cannot, in order to vote. Rubicondo (Hugo Weaving), the dentist, and Josefina, his mistress, point him in the direction of romantic novels of the Mills & Boon variety and he becomes obsessed with these books, painstakingly trying to understand exactly what they mean. The community is menaced by a female jaguar, whose cubs were killed by a hunter (who was given a hunting permit by the Mayor); the hunter becomes one of the animal's victims, but there are others. Bolivar believes that the animal may be pursuing him.

Dutch-born Australian director Rolf de Heer has several things in common with his compatriot, Paul Cox. Both make emotionally involving films about outsiders and lonely people, and both preferred, as far as possible, to remain fully independent. After

Bad Boy Bubby (1993), *The Quiet Room* (1996) and *Dance Me to My Song* (1998), all of which dealt with marginalised characters, de Heer was approached by a French producer to film Luis Sepúlveda's book about a lonely old man living in the jungles of the Amazon. It's interesting to compare the resulting film with Cox's *Molokai* (see #61), which was filmed in Hawaii a year earlier. Both films find their directors out of their comfort zones, no longer in complete control of their material. Both succeed in rising to the challenges involved.

The Old Man Who Read Love Stories was filmed in French Guiana and, despite the potentially thrilling subject matter—a hunt for a jaguar that is killing local people—the mood is gentle and elegiac. Basically, this is a story of courage and integrity as the old man confronts the various challenges that face him. While Timothy Spall turns the venal Mayor into almost a caricature, Hugo Weaving and Cathy Tyson perfectly inhabit their roles as the cheerful dentist and the woman who brings a form of education into the life of the illiterate protagonist through the pulp fiction they loan him. But it's Richard Dreyfuss, far from the sort of role he played in Hollywood in films like *Jaws*, *Close Encounters of the Third Kind* and *The Goodbye Girl*, who impresses most of all. His subtle, mellow performance is imbued with innate charm, serenity and quiet authority. Beautiful work by French cinematographer Denis Lenoir adds to the enjoyment.

The film premiered at the Melbourne International Film Festival in July 2001, and subsequently played at a handful of other film festivals before what proved to be a sadly limited theatrical release. It seems to have fallen into the trap of being seen as not commercial—a film with a Hollywood 'name' in the lead and a story about a hunt for a savage beast is supposed to be far more action-packed than this—and at the same time it was deemed to be not sufficiently serious for the art house crowd. It deserves rediscovery.

68

Open Range

(USA, 2003)

Touchstone Pictures–Tig Productions. **DIRECTOR:** Kevin Costner. **SCRIPT:** Craig Storper, from a novel by Lauran Paine. **ACTORS:** Robert Duvall, Kevin Costner, Annette Bening, Michael Gambon, Michael Jeter, Diego Luna, James Russo, Abraham Benrubi, Dean McDermott, Kim Coates, Peter MacNeill. **137 MINS.**

Montana, 1882. 'Boss' Spearman (Robert Duvall) has moved his cattle to a free range area with the help of three cowboys: Charley Waite (Kevin Costner), the burly Mose (Abraham Benrubi) and Button (Diego Luna), a Mexican teenager. Mose is despatched to purchase supplies at the nearby town, but fails to return. Boss and Charley ride into town to search for him and find that Sheriff Poole (James Russo) has thrown Mose in jail on a charge of fighting. Denton Baxter (Michael Gambon), owner of much of the town and the land around it, tells the men that free rangers are not welcome, but nevertheless Mose is released and his injuries are treated by Doc Barlow (Dean McDermott) with the assistance of Sue (Annette Bening). Boss and Charley assume Sue is the doctor's wife, but she turns out to be his sister. Some time later armed men attack the camp of Boss and his men; Mose is killed and Button is injured. Boss and Charley take Button to the doctor's house and then confront Baxter, Poole and their men in a showdown.

When I was an eager young film-goer, westerns and musicals constituted the most popular Hollywood genres. Hardly a week went by without the release of a new western of one sort or another, and some of the best-regarded films of the period were westerns (*High Noon* and *Shane* among them). After the late 1960s the popularity of the western went into a steep decline, to be superseded by science fiction and superhero movies. Like the western, Kevin Costner is an actor, and occasional director, whose fortunes have abruptly faded away, who went from being a box-office superstar and Oscar winner for *Dances with Wolves*—a western—in 1990 to being viewed as a has-been seemingly overnight, though actually it was the large-scale flop *Waterworld* (1995), followed by Costner's second film as director, the disastrous *The Postman* (1997), that effectively killed his career.

Despite this, Costner's affection for the western is equalled only by that of Clint Eastwood among contemporary filmmakers, and *Open Range* uses all the classic elements of the genre: the beautifully photographed landscapes with riders and cattle placed in a vast prairie, shot by cinematographer James Muro; the rugged pioneer and his small group of men; the small town with its weak sheriff, kindly doctor and nervous inhabitants; the powerful landowner who believes himself to be above the law. These characters, and others like them, have been a staple of the western since the earliest days of cinema, but Costner breathes fresh life into what might have been tired old clichés.

For one thing, Robert Duvall's Boss—whose real name, we discover, is Bluebonnet!—is a wonderfully nuanced character who keeps his past a secret even from his closest friends. The stock character of the town's most attractive (single) woman is given depth in Annette Bening's richly detailed portrayal. And Michael Gambon's powerful rancher, a transported Irishman, is a deliciously unusual villain. There are other original details: the town, which is prone to being flooded after heavy rain, is not yet quite completed and the climactic gun battle takes place among the half-finished buildings. Arguably the main drawback to the film's complete success is Costner's rather languid pacing.

But audiences in 2003 simply weren't interested, either in westerns or in Costner. The film flopped, and at the time of writing, Costner hasn't directed again.

69

Out of the Blue

(CANADA, 1980)

Robson Street. DIRECTOR: Dennis Hopper. SCRIPT: Leonard Yakir, Brenda Nielson. ACTORS: Linda Manz, Dennis Hopper, Sharon Farrell, Raymond Burr, Don Gordon, Eric Allen, Fiona Brody, David Crowley, Joan Hoffman, Carl Nelson, Francis Ann Pettit. 93 MINS.

America's Midwest. Ten-year-old Cindy Barnes, nicknamed 'CeBe', wearing a Halloween costume, is a passenger in the truck being driven by her father, Don (Dennis Hopper), when he crashes into a packed school bus, killing several children. Five years later, CeBe (Linda Manz) is nervously awaiting her father's release from prison. Devoted to the memory of Elvis and a dedicated follower of punk, she lives with her flighty mother, Kathy (Sharon Farrell), a waitress sexually involved with both her boss, Paul (Eric Allen), and Don's best friend, Charlie (Don Gordon). Though she still takes a teddy bear to bed, and sucks her thumb, the prickly CeBe smokes (both tobacco and marijuana), drinks and is a fearless challenger of authority. One evening, coming home late, she realises for the first time that her mother is a heroin addict. She hitches a ride to another city and becomes involved in a series of underground experiences, including becoming a groupie for a punk band. After she is caught driving a stolen car, with three naked girls as passengers, she's returned to her mother and undergoes counselling from Dr Brean (Raymond Burr). Don is released and gets a job at a garbage dump, but the father of one of the children he killed harasses him. Events lead to a tragic climax in which incidences from the past, previously hidden, emerge.

Dennis Hopper's first film as director, *Easy Rider* (1969), was an unprecedented success—a low-budget film by a first-time director that was a massive hit the world over. Given carte blanche by a major studio, Universal, to repeat the experiment, Hopper failed lamentably with *The Last Movie* (1971), a stoner's indulgence that almost nobody went to see. Nine years later he was cast as Don Barnes in the Canadian film, *Out of the Blue*, and when Leonard Yakir, the film's co-screenwriter and original director, dropped out at the start of the shoot, he took over behind the camera.

The result is a tough, sometimes difficult to watch, but extremely impressive examination of the legacy handed down by the hippy generation to their children. Only late in the film do we realise that why CeBe acts the way she does is in no small part due to the fact that she was a victim of incest at the hands of her appallingly irresponsible father. In the meantime she always seems able to extricate herself from the dangerous situations in which she places herself, successfully escaping the sleazy characters she meets, or avoiding the advances of her father, who is usually too drunk or stoned to know just what he's doing (Hopper gives a brilliant performance in a role as one of the screen's most despicable parents). Sharon Farrell, too, is remarkable as CeBe's mother, an obviously unhappy woman who is only too easily seduced by any man who is nice to her.

Best of all is Linda Manz who, three years after her first screen role in Terrence Malick's *Days of Heaven*, gives a quite extraordinary performance as the fifteen-year-old who acts with all the confidence of an adult. 'Disco sucks,' she confidently proclaims. 'Kill all hippies!' But, poignantly, she notes that her heroes died on her: Elvis and Sid Vicious. And that her father also—involuntarily— abandoned her for years.

The musical soundtrack mostly consists of songs by Neil Young, including 'Thrasher' and 'My My, Hey Hey (Out of the Blue)', as well as Presley's 'Heartbreak Hotel'.

Perhaps because it was produced by a small Canadian company without international distribution in place, the film quickly disappeared, despite the generally fine reviews it was accorded—one critic called it 'the most successful feature film to deal with punk'.

70

Pawno

(AUSTRALIA, 2015)

Toothless Pictures. DIRECTOR: Paul Ireland. SCRIPT: Damian Hill. ACTORS: John Brumpton, Damian Hill, Malcolm Kennard, Mark Coles Smith, Maeve Dermody, Kerry Armstrong, Tony Rickards, Ngoc Phan, Daniel Frederiksen, John Orcsik, Naomi Rukavina, Mark Silveira, Brad McMurray, Jesse Velik, CoCo Rickards. 87 MINS.

The Melbourne suburb of Footscray. Les Underwood (John Brumpton) owns a pawnshop on a busy side street. Danny Williams (Damian Hill) works as Les's assistant and walks his boss's dog when things are quiet in the shop. During a 24-hour period, several dramas occur in and around the pawnshop—the exterior of which has been daubed with the words 'Shylock Motherfucker', a sentiment viewed with grim resignation by Les when he arrives for work. His old friend Harry Wilkinson (Tony Rickards), a very lonely widower, hangs around at the shop most of the day. Among the others who come and go are Paige Turner (Daniel Frederiksen), a transgender woman who has two sons at home; Jennifer Montgomery (Kerry Armstrong), who is searching for her teenage son, who has gone missing; 'Poodles' (John Orcsik), who pawns his camera, forgetting there's a card inside containing porno material; Jason (Brad McMurray), a tough guy who needs to pawn his watch; and Harsha (Mark Silveira), an Indian dentist forced to deliver pizzas because he can't get Australian accreditation, but who nonetheless is willing and able to help relieve Les of a painful tooth. Meanwhile Danny is drawn to Kate (Maeve Dermody), who works in the local bookshop alongside her friend Holly (Naomi Rukavina), and Les frequents a Vietnamese restaurant run by Lai (Ngoc Phan), his girlfriend. Out on the street good-natured layabouts Carlo (Malcolm Kennard) and Pauly (Mark Coles Smith) have an opinion on just about everything.

Beautifully scripted by Damian Hill, with some input from director Paul Ireland, and elegantly photographed in the Scope ratio by Shelley Farthing-Dawe, *Pawno* is one of the finest examples of entirely independent Australian cinema, having been made—on a tiny budget—with no government support. From the very beginning, when Paige quietly weeps in the shop after being abused by some kids out on the street and is comforted by Les, the generosity of spirit that pervades the entire movie is heartening. 'People come in here bullshitting and leave pissed off' is Les's summation of pawnshop life, while the sad, lonely Harry remarks that 'you get a bag of allsorts in here'. Each character, however brief his or her contribution, is scripted with pinpoint accuracy, and the ensemble acting is impeccable, with Armstrong especially notable as the mother desperately seeking news of her missing son.

The film's only miscalculation is a scene in which Les, with little apparent motive, turns on Jason and beats him; the incident seems out of character. But otherwise the journeys taken by this melting pot of multiracial, pan-sexual characters rings completely true throughout.

Some of the other characters glimpsed on the street, including the sweet toothless girl who sings and the black bongo drum players, appear to be real-life denizens of Footscray, and Ireland and Hill integrate them seamlessly into the fictional drama.

The advantage of making a film with complete independence is that no one is going to second-guess you. The disadvantage is that, especially now, it is incredibly difficult to secure distribution or exhibition in what has become an extremely crowded and competitive market. After some difficulty, the filmmakers managed to secure a small distributor, and as a result the film was given a limited release in a handful of cinemas. It is a shame it wasn't seen much more widely.

71

The Pledge

(USA, 2000)

Morgan Creek Productions. DIRECTOR: Sean Penn. SCRIPT: Jerzy Kromolowski, Mary Olson-Kromolowski, based on the screenplay *Es geschah am hellichten Tag*, by Friedrich Dürrenmatt. ACTORS: Jack Nicholson, Robin Wright Penn, Patricia Clarkson, Benicio Del Toro, Dale Dickey, Aaron Eckhart, Helen Mirren, Tom Noonan, Michael O'Keefe, Vanessa Redgrave, Pauline Roberts, Mickey Rourke, Sam Shepard, Lois Smith, Harry Dean Stanton. 124 MINS.

A small town in Nevada. On the day of his retirement from the police force, detective Jerry Black (Jack Nicholson) responds to a call reporting the discovery of the body of Ginny Larsen, an eight-year-old girl, who has been raped and murdered. Black brings the news of their daughter's murder to her parents, and makes a solemn pledge to her mother, Margaret (Patricia Clarkson), 'on his soul's salvation', that he will find the killer. His colleague, Stan Krolak (Aaron Eckhart), is convinced that mentally challenged Native American Toby jay Wadenah (Benicio Del Toro) is the killer and forces a confession out of him; Wadenah kills himself with a police gun. Black isn't convinced Wadenah was the killer, and though now retired from the force he continues his investigation. He talks to the dead girl's grandmother (Vanessa Redgrave) and to some of her friends, and after meeting with Jim Olstad (Mickey Rourke), whose daughter has gone missing, becomes convinced that a serial killer is operating in the district. Neither Krolak nor his boss, Pollack (Sam Shepard), believes him, and so he decides to set a trap for the killer, using the daughter of Lori (Robin Wright Penn), a waitress with whom he has formed a relationship, as bait.

In 1958, Swiss author Friedrich Dürrenmatt wrote an original screenplay, *It Happened in Broad Daylight*, which was brought to the screen by Hungarian director Ladislao Vajda. Sean Penn's remake, which re-locates the story from Switzerland to Nevada, is infinitely superior to Vajda's film. Jack Nicholson gives one of his finest performances as the burnt-out cop who makes a most solemn pledge and is determined, even obsessed, with fulfilling it, no matter what the cost. This leads him to abandon his home and his friends and to set up an elaborate trap for the killer he's certain is out there, somewhere—but in doing so, he betrays the woman with whom he has formed a new relationship; she's beautifully portrayed by Robin Wright Penn.

The ambiguity of his obsession is the core of the film, which was scripted by Jerzy and Mary Kromolowski. Black is a tragic figure because the only way he can fulfil his pledge to the bereaved Mrs Larsen is to behave with ruthless disregard for the lives and safety of others.

Chris Menges' exceptional photography is just one of the film's many assets. There are several intriguing cameo performances—Helen Mirren as a doctor, Harry Dean Stanton as the owner of the garage Black purchases as part of the trap he plans to set for the killer, Tom Noonan as a religious fanatic, and others. The film's conclusion is tragically ironic, and there's little doubt that this is one of the screen's most interesting attempts to explore the themes of crime and punishment.

Despite generally enthusiastic reviews, and the presence of Jack Nicholson in the lead, the film was only a modest box-office success and has since, along with Sean Penn's other films, been pretty much sidelined. The reasons for this remain unclear, but perhaps the subject matter proved too intense for audiences, especially given the 'normal' everyday settings in which these horrific events unfold.

72

Power

(USA, 1986)

Lorimar Productions–Polar Entertainment. DIRECTOR: Sidney Lumet. SCRIPT: David Himmelstein. ACTORS: Richard Gere, Julie Christie, Gene Hackman, Denzel Washington, Kate Capshaw, E.G. Marshall, Beatrice Straight, Fritz Weaver, Michael Learned, J.T. Walsh, Matt Salinger, Omar Torres. 111 MINS.

Washington. Media consultant and lobbyist Pete St John (Richard Gere) is in the middle of a gubernatorial and senate election campaign. His clients include the Governor of Washington State, who is seeking re-election despite the bad publicity she attracted when she divorced her husband; and also a bumbling candidate for Governor of New Mexico. St John is saddened to hear that his friend and client, Ohio senator Sam Hastings (E.G. Marshall), is retiring due to ill health. One of Hastings' platforms has been to encourage the development of solar energy, and St John is now approached by the shady Arnold Billings (Denzel Washington) on behalf of his candidate for the vacant Ohio seat, Jerome Cade (J.T. Walsh); Billings does not reveal that he's in the pay of a Middle East oil-producing country. St John takes Cade as a client, but has second thoughts when Ellen (Julie Christie), his ex-wife and a journalist, discovers that Billings was blackmailing Sam's wife, Claire (Beatrice Straight), and that Sam had reluctantly agreed to retire in order to protect his wife. Meanwhile St John's mentor, Wilfred Buckley (Gene Hackman), is promoting another Ohio candidate, Phillip Aarons (Matt Salinger), an idealistic college professor and environmentalist.

Like Richard Brooks' *Wrong is Right* (see #101), Sidney Lumet's drama about the decline of the American political process in the era of tabloid TV and advertising hype is amazingly prescient. One of its themes is the danger of the influence of a foreign power on an American election, something that hit the headlines exactly

30 years after the film was made. Another is the fact that the manipulators behind the scenes care only about getting their man or woman elected. No thought is given to their policies or the morality of their causes. Money is all that matters, and behind-the-scenes PR people, like St John, are very well paid—he earns $25,000 per month, plus expenses. The key figure of naive, idealistic Aarons, who believes in the future of renewable energy among other things, has been reflected more recently in the positions held by politicians like Bernie Sanders and Jeremy Corbyn: like them, Aarons doesn't win the election, but he comes second and, in this case, beats the most 'manufactured' and reactionary candidate.

All this is totally fascinating and more than somewhat depressing. Lumet, through the machinations of St John, shows how TV footage is easily manipulated to convey exactly the opposite message to the truth. Cynicism abounds, candidates are pre-packaged, engineered, rehearsed, made over until whatever made them human beings has almost entirely disappeared and they've become mere puppets—often, the film suggests, under the influence of sinister external commercial interests. Candidates, someone says, 'are pre-digested, like TV dinners'. These things are, it seems, truer than ever today.

Political films are rarely successful. (You have to go back to Frank Capra and *Mr. Smith Goes to Washington*, which is referenced here, to find a truly popular film about politics.) Arguably, Lumet and writer David Himmelstein didn't make things any easier by packing in so much detail, and featuring so many different clients that St John is attempting to get elected—the film's opening sequence is set in Mexico, where there's a bomb blast at a political rally, and St John advises his candidate how to make use of the tragedy in his future public appearances.

Richard Gere gives a smooth performance as the manipulative St John, and Denzel Washington, in only his third screen appearance, impresses as the smooth, sinister, double-dealing Billings.

73

Queen & Country

(UK/IRELAND/FRANCE/ROMANIA, 2014)

Sparrowglen Ltd–The British Film Institute–Irish Film Board–Le Pacte–Merlin Films. DIRECTOR/SCRIPT: John Boorman. ACTORS: Callum Turner, Caleb Landry Jones, David Thewlis, Richard E. Grant, Pat Shortt, Brían F. O'Byrne, Tamsin Egerton, Vanessa Kirby, Sinéad Cusack, David Hayman, Aimee-Ffion Edwards, Gerran Howell. 115 MINS.

England, 1952. Bill Rohan (Callum Turner), aged eighteen, is called up for military service. He leaves his family home on an island in the Thames near Shepperton Film Studios and reports to the army base at Aldershot. He meets and befriends Percy Hapgood (Caleb Landry Jones), and they go through basic training together. They are both promoted to sergeant and, instead of leaving for Korea as they feared, they are assigned to teach recruits how to use typewriters. They fall foul of Sergeant-Major Bradley (David Thewlis), a stickler for the regulations. Bill meets the mysterious 'Ophelia' (Tamsin Egerton), who won't give him her real name; Percy takes up with Sophie (Aimee-Ffion Edwards), a nurse. The friends are given leave for the Coronation in 1953, and Percy joins Bill at his family home where he meets his sister, Dawn (Vanessa Kirby), who has left her husband and children in Canada. During the Coronation telecast, Bill sees 'Ophelia' in Westminster Abbey, where she is one of the Queen's ladies in waiting.

One of Britain's best filmmakers, John Boorman's last film to date is a sequel to one of his most popular, the autobiographical *Hope and Glory* (1987). *Queen & Country* actually begins with a scene from the earlier film in which, in 1943, young Bill rejoices because his school has been hit by a German bomb and all the kids have been given a day off ('Thank you, Adolf!'). Nine years later Bill is enduring compulsory military service and experiencing the pangs of first love.

The film is light-hearted and often funny, though it avoids the broad caricatures of army life depicted in farcical British films like *Private's Progress* or *Carry on Sergeant*. Instead the various incidents that Bill and Percy experience seem drawn directly from Boorman's own recollections of his military service: the crazy scheme to steal the regimental clock in order to annoy the RSM (Brían F. O'Byrne) being the most significant of them.

Callum Turner is fine as Bill, but the revelation here is American actor Caleb Landry Jones (later to make an impression in films like *Three Billboards Outside Ebbing, Missouri*), who adopts an utterly convincing British accent and plays the opportunistic Percy with great skill. Tamsin Egerton is suitably mysterious as the tantalising 'Ophelia', while Aimee-Ffion Edwards is deliciously down to earth as the pragmatic Sophie. Also outstanding is David Thewlis' hidebound Sergeant-Major, a simple and, in the end, rather tragic man for whom the army is his entire life.

It's in the details of life in Britain in the early 1950s that the film succeeds so beautifully, notably the scene in which Bill's father (David Hayman) unpacks his first television set on which the family plans to watch the Coronation, and the difficulties he experiences in getting the aerial in just the right place on the roof—an assignment that occupies several family members—so that a dodgy black and white image can eventually be received. The proximity of the family home to Shepperton Film Studios leads neatly into the conclusion, in which Bill/Boorman takes his first steps as a film director.

The film is so authentically 'English' it's hard to believe that all of the scenes in the military camp were filmed, for financial reasons, in Romania!

After its premiere at Cannes in 2014 it took a year before the film opened in Britain, and to date it has never screened in cinemas in Australia.

74

Rendition

(USA, 2007)

Anonymous Content. DIRECTOR: Gavin Hood. SCRIPT: Kelley Sane. ACTORS: Jake Gyllenhaal, Reese Witherspoon, Alan Arkin, Meryl Streep, Peter Sarsgaard, Omar Metwally, Igal Naor, J.K. Simmons, Moa Khouas, Zineb Oukach. 122 MINS.

The capital city of an unnamed North African country. A suicide bomb explodes in the central square and among the victims are CIA operatives. Anwar El-Ibrahimi (Omar Metwally), an Egyptian-born chemical engineer living in America and married to Isabella (Reese Witherspoon), has been attending a conference in Cape Town. He boards a plane to fly to Chicago. After the plane lands at O'Hare airport, but before he is able to pass through immigration, Anwar is arrested by CIA operatives and is 'renditioned' to a North African country, where he undergoes interrogation and torture, carried out by Fawal (Igal Naor). His ordeal is overseen by a CIA 'observer', Douglas Freeman (Jake Gyllenhaal). When Anwar doesn't arrive home, Isabella, who is pregnant, seeks help from the authorities and is informed that he never boarded the plane. Desperate, she contacts her former boyfriend, Alan Smith (Peter Sarsgaard), an aide to Senator Hawkins (Alan Arkin), and, through their influence, she eventually discovers that Anwar is being held by the CIA.

In 2007, four years after the Coalition of the Willing's 2003 invasion of Iraq—carried out ostensibly to remove Saddam Hussein's weapons of mass destruction—a handful of American films were made about the conflict and its international implications, among them Brian De Palma's *Redacted* and Paul Haggis' *In the Valley of Elah*. *Rendition* is the best of this group, an unflinching indictment of the CIA's abuse of power and the methods by which innocent people were caught up in the pervading mood of hysteria.

This was the first American film made by South African director Gavin Hood, who scored an international success with his award-winning *Tsotsi* (2005), and it's a tense, gripping and thought-provoking movie. Kelley Sane's screenplay unfolds on more than one level. There's Anwar himself, an innocent man suffering interrogation and torture who, in the end, offers as the names of 'terrorists' members of the Egyptian national football team because he can't think how else to end the pain and humiliation—a sharp reminder that torture is not always effective as a means of obtaining information, apart from any moral considerations as to its use. Then there's Isabella, desperately seeking news from her husband who seems to have vanished from the face of the earth, and the brick walls she comes up against. Behind the scenes there's CIA Chief Corinne Whitman, chillingly played by Meryl Streep, on whose orders these 'renditions' are being carried out. There's Freeman, a decent man forced to watch the brutal methods his country has farmed out to Egyptian torturers. And there's Fawal, the torturer, who is himself targeted by a terrorist group and whose daughter, Fatima (Zineb Oukach), has a boyfriend who might be using her to get at her father.

All these threads are beautifully woven together, and the film even manipulates the order in which the narrative unfolds as a means to deliver some genuine shocks and surprises. Like some of the other films dealing with the current events in Arab countries, *Rendition* was filmed in Morocco, to convincing effect.

Despite the potency of the film's message, even audiences who might have been attracted to its point of view seem to have stayed away—in fact not one of the films made in the aftermath of the invasion has made any impact on the box office, with the exception of the Oscar-winning *The Hurt Locker* (2008). Hood subsequently made another very powerful film about Allied activities in the Middle East, *Eye in the Sky* (2015).

Return Home

(AUSTRALIA, 1989)

Musical Films. DIRECTOR/SCRIPT: Ray Argall. ACTORS: Dennis Coard, Frankie J. Holden, Ben Mendelsohn, Micki Camilleri, Rachel Rains. 86 MINS.

Mitchell Park, South Australia. Noel (Dennis Coard) has been working in a high-pressure executive position in an insurance office in Melbourne for several years. His marriage has ended and he decides to take leave from work and return to the beachfront suburb of Adelaide where he grew up, and where his brother, Steve (Frankie J. Holden), runs a petrol station and car repair workshop with the administrative help of his wife, Jude (Micki Camilleri). The business is struggling, but Noel enjoys living in his brother's house, getting to know his two small children, and observing the work of Steve's young apprentice, Gary (Ben Mendelsohn). Gary, a cheerful, rather irresponsible young man, has alienated his girl-friend Wendy (Rachel Rains), but wants to get back together with her. Steve and Jude are having difficulty paying their bills, and the petrol company that supplies them is refusing to deliver fuel. Noel suggests they become part of a franchise, but Steve angrily rejects the idea, though Jude is more responsive. Gary and Wendy get back together again, and Steve tells Gary he'd like him to stay on after his apprenticeship is completed. Noel's vacation concludes and he returns to Melbourne—but then decides to quit work in the city and return home permanently to Mitchell Park.

Ray Argall was better known as a cinematographer of low-budget Australian films when he wrote and directed this small, intimate and extremely fine drama. Photographed by Mandy Walker on 16 mm, the film has autobiographical elements. Argall had spent much of his youth in suburban Adelaide and, like Gary, had a passion for hot cars. The film was shot on a tiny budget ($350,000), and on completion was invited to the Berlin Film Festival.

Much of what makes this little story so compelling is in the way Argall explores the suburb itself, frequently inserting an overhead shot that shows its position in relation to the city of Adelaide not far away. A new shopping centre has effectively drained the life out of the smaller businesses, none of which seem to be doing very well, the exception being—ironically these days—the video rental store; Steve even contemplates turning his repair room into a video store, though in hindsight it's clear that it wouldn't be very long before that kind of business, too, would virtually disappear.

Argall explores the relationships between the four main characters with affection. The scenes in and around the garage are minutely observed, together with the frustration experienced when impatient clients get abusive. Interestingly, the expected scene of a family reunion with the brothers' parents never materialises, leaving the viewer to wonder about this omission. It would seem to have been a good opportunity for a scene that would give the viewer more information about the background of the brothers, yet Argall has clearly made a decision not to introduce the parents at all.

The performances are exemplary. Coard, a relative newcomer to acting after spending fifteen years working for Telecom, is relaxed and charming as the man who solves a mid-life crisis by returning to his roots, while Holden, Mendelsohn and Camilleri are all superbly naturalistic.

The film seems to have been too 'minimalist' for audiences, too lacking in 'big scenes'. Despite very positive reviews, including rare five stars each from Margaret Pomeranz and myself on *The Movie Show* on SBS television, it soon disappeared from cinemas and has since been virtually forgotten. Argall only made one more film—*Eight Ball* (1991)—which was not in the same class as this very attractive debut.

76

Reunion

(FRANCE/WEST GERMANY/UK, 1989)

Les Films Ariane-TAC-CLG Films. DIRECTOR: Jerry Schatzberg. SCRIPT: Harold Pinter, from the novel by Fred Uhlman. ACTORS: Jason Robards, Christien Anholt, Samuel West, Françoise Fabian, Maureen Kerwin, Barbara Jefford, Bert Parnaby, Shebah Ronay, Dorothea Alexander, Frank Baker, Tim Barker, Imke Barnstedt, Gideon Boulting, Alan Bowyer, Jacques Brunet, Rupert Degas, Robert Dietl, Alexandre Trauner. 100 MINS.

New York. Henry Strauss (Jason Robards), a 70-year-old New York lawyer, decides to return to Stuttgart, his home town, for the first time since he left for America in 1933. Then named Hans (Christien Anholt), he was the son of Jakob (Bert Parnaby), a Jewish doctor who was awarded the Iron Cross for gallantry during the Great War. At high school Hans befriended Konradin von Lohenburg (Samuel West), who was from an aristocratic family. Nazism was on the rise, and when Konradin took Hans to meet his cousin Gertrud (Shebah Ronay), he was embarrassed at her support for Hitler. Eventually matters reached the point where even Dr Strauss, who was convinced that 'the land of Goethe, Schiller and Beethoven would not fall for "that rubbish"', came to appreciate the reality of the impending danger, sending Hans to America, before he and his wife (Barbara Jefford), committed suicide. In the present, Henry discovers there is still anti-Semitism in Germany when he visits the elderly Gertrud (Dorothea Alexander) and she refuses to talk to him. He visits the grave of his parents, which is located in the most humble section of a public cemetery. And, on a visit to his former school, he finally discovers the fate of his friend, Konradin.

The year 1989, when *Reunion* was released, was the 50th anniversary of the start of World War II, so—despite the fact that many dozens of films had previously been made about the Nazi era—it seemed fitting that Jerry Schatzberg, the talented director of *The Panic in Needle Park* and *Scarecrow*, should tackle the subject. Screenwriter Harold Pinter adapted a novel by Fred Uhlman about a man who tried to forget everything about his homeland until he made a reluctant return for the first time in 55 years. Henry himself admits that he hasn't read or spoken a word of his native language during his long years of exile, and many of his ingrained prejudices and reservations are proved correct by the lukewarm experience he receives from taxi drivers, bureaucrats and the elderly cousin of his old friend.

Schatzberg, a former fashion photographer, approaches this material in interesting ways. Bruno de Keyzer's cinematography is de-saturated throughout the lengthy central flashback sequence, while in the scenes that take place in the present, colour is often used in a stylised fashion—for example in the sequence where Henry visits the archive in which his parents' belongings are still stored (his guide in this sequence is played by the film's very distinguished veteran production designer, Alexandre Trauner).

Robards gives a commanding performance as the elderly German who now thinks of himself as American, and whose cynicism is ingrained. (Speaking to a colleague on the phone, who mentions that he fought in Germany, Henry responds: 'On which side?') The scenes set in 1932–33, as Nazism gradually impacts more and more upon the daily lives of a group of young friends, are vividly handled, especially in the sequence where the pretty and charming Gertrud unthinkingly reveals her anti-Jewish feelings and then asks Hans if he's certain he *is* a Jew. As the friends, Christien Anholt and Samuel West are excellent.

After a launch at the 1989 Cannes Film Festival, *Reunion* struggled to find distribution. Some critics complained that this sort of story had often been told before, which of course is true, but in no way diminishes the achievement of Schatzberg and Pinter.

77

Ride with the Devil

(USA, 1999)

Universal Pictures-Good Machine. DIRECTOR: Ang Lee. SCRIPT: James Schamus, from the novel by Daniel Woodrell. ACTORS: Tobey Maguire, Skeet Ulrich, Jewel, Jeffrey Wright, Simon Baker, Jonathan Rhys Meyers, James Caviezel, Tom Guiry, Tom Wilkinson, Jonathan Brandis, John Ales, Matthew Faber, Margo Martindale, Mark Ruffalo, John Judd. 138 MINS.

The Missouri–Kansas border, 1861. With the outbreak of the Civil War, a community is divided. Jake Roedel (Tobey Maguire), nicknamed Dutchman, sides with the South, while his father Otto (John Judd) favours the North. When the father of Jake's best friend, Jack Bull Chiles (Skeet Ulrich), is killed, the young men join the Bushwhackers, a gang of Southern guerrilla fighters led by Black John Ambrose (James Caviezel). Another member of the gang is George Clyde (Simon Baker), whose loyal slave, Daniel Holt (Jeffrey Wright), fights alongside his master even though his sympathies are with the Union. Jake falls in love with Sue Lee (Jewel), a widow, and they marry. But an oasis of peace is shattered when, in 1863, the Bushwhackers, now led by William Clarke Quantrill (John Ales), stage a bloody attack on the town of Lawrence, Kansas.

Made by the enormously versatile Taiwanese director Ang Lee between his films *The Ice Storm* and *Crouching Tiger, Hidden Dragon*, this magnificently staged adaptation of Daniel Woodrell's 1987 novel *Woe to Live On* is, like all of this director's best work, mainly concerned with intimate details. Whereas another director might emphasise the sweep and spectacle of Civil War combat, Lee probes into the personal lives of his characters. To be sure, the film, superbly shot by Frederick Elmes, has plenty of spectacular action, and it reaches a climax with a sequence—the attack on the town and people of Lawrence—worthy of Sam Peckinpah. The massacre in Lawrence, which is well documented, was one of the lowest points in American history, and Lee doesn't flinch from showing it in all its barbarity.

But it's the small details in the adaptation by James Schamus that most resonate. The ways in which this bitter quarrel over slavery and the Northern Union's domination over the Southern Confederacy impacts on friends and neighbours are what give the film its considerable power.

Scenes in which Jake befriends the former slave, Daniel Holt, provide the heart of the film; Holt, out of loyalty to his master George Clyde—a good role for Australian actor Simon Baker—comes to realise that he's on the wrong side, and is eager to discover what freedom actually means. And Sue Lee, well acted by the singer known only as Jewel, is, according to this reading of the film, an embryonic feminist.

Lee and Schamus present a revisionist view of the Civil War, acknowledging crimes committed on both sides, and accepting the fact that Quantrill's guerrillas included among their number more than a few hardened killers. Yet *Ride with the Devil*, among the very best films made about this tragic war, is as much about freedom and liberation as it is about war crimes and pointless chivalry.

By the end of the 1990s it was increasingly difficult for films like this—a thoughtful and serious epic—to find an audience when the cinemas in shopping malls were increasingly being filled with sci-fi extravaganzas and dumb comedies. Times were changing and, sadly, *Ride with the Devil*, for all its considerable qualities, proved to be a victim of those changes.

Ride with the Devil is among the very best films made about the Civil War

78

River of Grass

(USA, 1995)

Plan B–Cozy Productions. DIRECTOR/SCRIPT: Kelly Reichardt. ACTORS: Lisa Bowman, Larry Fessenden, Dick Russell, Stan Kaplan, Michael Buscemi, Lisa Robb, Tom Laverach, Bert Yaeger, Frances Reichardt, Carol Flakes, George Moore. 76 MINS.

Dade County, Florida. Cozy (Lisa Bowman) was abandoned by her mother when she was ten and was raised by her father, Jimmy Ryder (Dick Russell), a one-time jazz drummer now employed as a cop. As a teenager, Cozy had married a man she didn't love and they had two children. Jimmy loses his gun, which falls from his holster, and is found by Lee Ray Harold (Larry Fessenden), who decides to keep it. Lee Ray is not happy with his current domestic situation, in which he is living with his grandmother. One night Cozy leaves her kids at home and heads for a bar where she meets Lee Ray. He takes her to the home of a supposed friend where, he tells her, there's a swimming pool; they're surprised by the homeowner. Cozy fires at him and believes she's killed him (she hasn't). The pair flee, but they never manage to get out of Dade County.

Jean-Luc Godard once famously said, in effect, that all you need for a movie is a boy, a girl and a gun—and those are the simple ingredients of Kelly Reichardt's beguiling first feature. The plot, though filled with more incident than most of the director's subsequent, minimalist features (*Old Joy, Wendy and Lucy, Meek's Cutoff, Night Moves, Certain Women*), is familiar enough. A bored young woman with a troubled childhood abandons her family in an attempt to escape to a new life with a handsome stranger ('I wondered if there was any other person on this planet as lonely as me—turned out there he was living a county away' says Cozy in the film's voice-over narration). The irony is that the pair never get very far, but become stuck in the dreary little motels that dot the highways of this unattractive corner of America; the title, we learn, is the Native American name for the Florida Everglades.

It's basically quite a sad little story. Unsurprisingly, Lee Ray turns out not to be Cozy's knight in shining armour, but instead a hopeless loser. Yet there's a strongly romantic core to the film and an appealing sense of humour. In order to pay for their escape, the young couple steal the collection of LP records owned by Lee Ray's grandmother and try to flog them; her father Jimmy is actually hanging out at a record store when Lee Ray comes in with the records to sell, but neither one makes the connection. The most frightening thing that happens to the couple occurs when Cozy encounters a palmetto bug—a sort of cockroach—in the bathroom of one of the motels, and Lee Ray attempts to shoot it. Just as the lovers think they're in the clear and heading off on one of those highways that lead to a new life somewhere over the horizon they find themselves at a tollgate and don't have the cash to pay, so they're forced to turn around, back the way they came. And they're about to rob a convenience store when a gunman barges in and does it before they even realise what's happening.

Lisa Bowman is not your typical ingénue, and Larry Fessenden's Lee Ray is more of a dreamer than a man of action (Fessenden also edited the film and was responsible for the sound design). As Cozy's policeman dad, Dick Russell provides another offbeat characterisation in a film that's filled with unexpected elements. *River of Grass* has a loose, relaxed structure that's strangely appealing, while the song track, including a lovely version of the old Billie Holiday song, 'Travelin' Light', adds to the mood.

This is not so much a forgotten film as an unknown one. Reichardt came to the attention of festival-goers ten years later with *Old Joy*, and her work—though always in a very minor key—has become more prominent in the years since then. Few had seen *River of Grass* until it was restored and given a very limited international release a couple of years ago. It has proved to be a delightful discovery.

Road to Nhill

(AUSTRALIA, 1997)

Gecko Films. DIRECTOR: Sue Brooks. SCRIPT: Alison Tilson. ACTORS: Bill Hunter, Lynette Curran, Monica Maughan, Patricia Kennedy, Tony Barry, Paul Chubb, Matthew Dyktynski, Terry Norris, Alwyn Kurts, Lois Ramsey, Denise Roberts, Kerry Walker, Bill Young. 95 MINS.

Pyramid Hill, Victoria. Bob (Bill Hunter), the local agricultural supply merchant, recounts the story of an accident involving four members of the local ladies' bowling team. Margot (Lynette Curran) is driving Nell (Monica Maughan), Jean (Patricia Kennedy) and Carmel (Lois Ramsey) on the road from Nhill when the car flips and overturns. With some difficulty, Margot, Nell and Carmel succeed in escaping from the car, but Jean is trapped, held upside down by her seatbelt. First on the scene is Maurie (Paul Chubb), a pig farmer, who alerts the emergency services—but the ambulance team confuses the Nhill Road with the road to Nhill, and heads off in the wrong direction. Jean is finally released from the wreck, with no help from the hopeless Maurie who, after long delays, takes her home to her elderly husband, Jack (Alwyn Kurts). Though he's solicitous, and eventually takes her to hospital, Jack is eager not to miss out on his own bowls game. Ted (Terry Norris), head of the local Country Fire Authority, insists on taking his wife, Carmel, home in the fire engine. Nell's husband, Jim (Tony Barry), fruitlessly pursues the ambulance in the wrong direction. Vegetable farmer Brian (Bill Young) takes Nell and Margot—who he fancies in a shy, awkward sort of way—with him, delivering Nell to hospital (where Jim finally locates her), and eventually taking Margot to the home she shares with her lesbian partner, Alison (Kerry Walker). He insists on showering the women with unwanted vegetables. Bret (Matthew Dyktynski), the local cop, knows nothing about the incident because, despite the fact that he's married with two young children, he's dallying with another woman at the time of the incident.

This was the first feature from Sue Brooks, who was born in Pyramid Hill. She subsequently made *Japanese Story* and *Looking for Grace*. *Road to Nhill* is a delightfully dry comedy about resourceful women and ineffectual, selfish men. Chief among these are Chubb's gormless Maurie and Bill Young's Brian, who is eager to please and thoroughly decent, but too insensitive to realise that Margot is gay. The film deftly captures the awkwardness of the men as they face an unexpected and possibly serious crisis, and the ways in which the more practical women deal with it. Alwyn Kurts is memorable as Jack, Jean's elderly husband, who appears to be in the early stages of dementia (though asked repeatedly not to serve tea with milk, he continues to do so). As Bob remarks, 'It was funny, but if someone had been hurt it wouldn't have been funny at all'—a misplaced comment because, as we discover, someone *is* badly hurt as a result of the crash.

A bitter, feminist anti-male tract? Not at all, because the film is filled with affection and compassion for all its characters, all of them beautifully written and acted. The humour is minimalist, but effective, and arguably the film's only flaw is the unnecessary addition of the voice of 'God'—ironically spoken by avowed atheist Phillip Adams—who comments from above on what's happening below ('The forces of uncertainty are tamed and life goes on!'). Nicolette Freeman's handsome photography captures the drought-stricken landscapes of rural Victoria, and employs some striking overhead shots that help to locate where the various characters are situated. There are two music themes, one bright and chirpy, the other jazzy and melancholy.

The film's lack of commercial success, and thus its comparative obscurity, probably derives from the fact that the comedy is so underplayed and the pacing, reflective of small towns, so leisurely.

80

Romance & Cigarettes

(USA, 2005)

GreeneStreet Films. DIRECTOR/SCRIPT: John Turturro. ACTORS: James Gandolfini, Susan Sarandon, Kate Winslet, Christopher Walken, Steve Buscemi, Bobby Cannavale, Elaine Stritch, Mandy Moore, Mary-Louise Parker, Aida Turturro, Eddie Izzard, Barbara Sukowa, David Thornton, Amy Sedaris, P.J. Brown. 106 MINS.

Queens, New York. Chain smoker Nick Murder (James Gandolfini), a steelworker, is married to Kitty (Susan Sarandon), a seamstress. They have three grown daughters, Baby (Mandy Moore), Constance (Mary-Louise Parker) and Rosebud (Aida Turturro). Nick is having an affair with Tula (Kate Winslet), a girl from Lancashire who works at Agent Provocateur, a shop that sells sexy lingerie. Kitty finds out about the relationship and enlists the help of her cousin, Bo (Christopher Walken) to take revenge on Tula, while Nick reluctantly agrees to be circumcised to please his demanding girlfriend. Baby announces she wants to marry local Elvis lookalike Fryburg (Bobby Cannavale). Nick decides to break with Tula, and Kitty reluctantly takes him back, but he is diagnosed with lung cancer.

The third film that actor John Turturro directed was apparently written while he was playing in the Coen Brothers' *Barton Fink*, and the Coens are listed among the producers of *Romance & Cigarettes*, an almost unclassifiable, audacious combination of bawdy vulgarity, romantic musical, romance and tragedy. The film is nothing if not unexpected, and the surprises extend to the members of the illustrious cast, and the incorporation of singing and dancing on actual locations.

The first instance of this comes when Nick, thrown out of the house by Kitty, launches into a mournful rendition of Engelbert Humperdinck's 'A Man Without Love', singing karaoke style while the original recording plays in the background, and then dancing (!) out onto the street, where he is joined by various passers-by. Other famous songs to be given this kind of treatment are Tom Jones' 'Delilah' (performed by Christopher Walken with considerable panache), Cyndi Lauper's 'Prisoner of Love' (Kate Winslet and a chorus of pregnant women), and Bruce Springsteen's 'Red-Headed Woman'.

The dialogue is raw, to say the least, and seems to have been influenced by Charles Bukowski, whose writing is directly quoted at one point. The superb cast throw themselves into this unlikely melting pot with brio. Winslet's flame-haired, under-garbed, Liverpudlian-accented Tula has to be seen (and heard) to be believed, while Walken and Steve Buscemi, as Nick's sex-obsessed workmate, are hilarious. Almost stealing the film in the one scene in which she appears is Elaine Stritch, who plays Nick's mother, and who refers to her son derisively as 'Nicholas Nicotine'. When asked how she is, she cheerfully admits that 'Every breath is a victory'.

Gandolfini, at the time in the middle of his successful role in the TV series *The Sopranos*, plays the crass, crude but innately sentimental Nick with elan, and the film takes a surprisingly dark turn in the later stages when his constant smoking catches up with him. 'Two things a man should be able to do,' he proclaims at one point. 'Be romantic and smoke his brains out.' The fact that Gandolfini died aged only 51 in 2013 makes the scenes of his illness even more poignant.

Of the five films John Turturro has directed to date, *Romance & Cigarettes* is by far the craziest, and for much of its length the most eye-poppingly entertaining, though the storyline itself is surprisingly thin. Yet the director and his willing cast reach out to the limits to provide something utterly fresh and daringly different.

Too different, as it turned out, to be accepted by many critics and by cinema audiences.

81

Running on Empty

(USA, 1988)

Lorimar Film Entertainment–Double Play. DIRECTOR: Sidney Lumet. SCRIPT: Naomi Foner. ACTORS: Christine Lahti, River Phoenix, Judd Hirsch, Jonas Abry, Martha Plimpton, Ed Crowley, L.M. Kit Carson, Steven Hill, Augusta Dabney, David Margulies. 116 MINS.

Suburban Florida. Annie (Christine Lahti) and Arthur Pope (Judd Hirsch), political activists who campaigned against the Vietnam War, have been on the run from the FBI since 1971 when they blew up a napalm-producing centre, badly injuring a janitor they didn't expect to be there. Their sons, seventeen-year-old Danny (River Phoenix) and ten-year-old Harry (Jonas Abry), have become reconciled to moving away from their homes and friends at a moment's notice and finding new homes and assuming new identities, with the assistance of a network of sympathisers. Their latest move takes them from Florida to New Jersey, where the boys enrol in school, and Danny's interest in music becomes evident. He is encouraged by his teacher, Mr Phillips (Ed Crowley), and falls in love with Lorna (Martha Plimpton), Phillips' daughter. He secretly goes to New York to audition at Julliard music school, but can't supply the personal records they require. He poses as a pizza delivery boy to glimpse his maternal grandmother (Augusta Dabney) in her home, but she doesn't recognise him. One of the Popes' fellow radicals, Gus Winant (L.M. Kit Carson), is killed by the FBI, and tensions rise as the conflicted Danny has to decide whether he will continue to stay with his family or branch out on his own.

This unofficial companion piece to *Daniel* (see #27), made five years earlier, continues Sidney Lumet's fascination with the effect on children of the actions of their politically radical parents. The focus here is almost entirely on Danny, beautifully played by River Phoenix, a talented and likeable kid who begins to question his future with his fugitive parents. The scenes between Phoenix and Martha Plimpton, are unusually convincing and tender. Indeed, all the performances are wonderful, with Christine Lahti enormously impressive in scenes such as the one in which she meets her wealthy, conservative father (Steven Hill) and attempts to explain the reasons for her past actions and to seek his help.

Lumet never glosses over the fact that the actions the Popes took in 1971 had serious repercussions for the unfortunate janitor, who was blinded and crippled in the explosion. But he also emphasises their sincerity in opposing—as did so many during those turbulent times—the violent American involvement in Vietnam, with all of its tragic consequences. As a result the Popes are exiles in their own country, and their entirely innocent children are paying a heavy price for their parents' radicalism.

The ways in which the family members are able, at first, to integrate into the small-town community without suspicion are completely convincing. Arthur finds blue-collar work, Annie gets a job as receptionist in a medical centre, and the boys go to school. When they leave Florida in the opening scenes, they're forced to abandon their beloved dog, yet the kids are surprisingly resigned and resilient about this sort of thing, unquestioningly accepting the instructions of their parents. And the parents adore their boys; they're good with them, as far as it's possible for them to be—yet they know that if Danny is to pursue his dream to become a musician, he will leave the family and they may never see him again. (Early in the film Arthur learns that his mother has been dead for four weeks, and when Annie meets her father it's the first time they've seen one another for many years.)

Despite the growing popularity of River Phoenix, who died at the age of 23, five years after *Running on Empty* was made, the film was never a great success, probably because it was seen as too political—and as we've seen, political films rarely succeed at the box office.

82

The Search

(FRANCE/GEORGIA, 2014)

La Petite Reine-Sarke Studio. DIRECTOR/SCRIPT: Michel Hazanavicius, based on Richard Schweizer's screenplay, *The Search* (1948). ACTORS: Bérénice Bejo, Annette Bening, Maksim Emelyanov, Abdul Khalim Mamutsiev, Zukhra Duishvili, Lela Bagakashvili, Yuriy Tsurilo. 149 MINS.

The Second Chechen War, 1999. In the village of Nazran, an unseen Russian soldier uses a video camera to record the destruction of the community and the massacre of its people, including a couple whose little son, Hadji (Abdul Khalim Mamutsiev), carrying his baby brother, wanders away from the carnage, traumatised. The boy leaves his brother on the doorstep of a farmhouse, and the baby is eventually found by his older sister, Raïssa (Zukhra Duishvili), who continues to search for Hadji. The boy, meanwhile, has wandered into an orphanage run by Helen (Annette Bening), an American aid worker, and is eventually adopted by Carole (Bérénice Bejo), a French NGO worker attached to the Human Rights department of the European Union. Carole finds it difficult to get through to the shattered child, who seems unable to speak. A parallel story features Kolia (Maksim Emelyanov), a Russian youth who is arrested for drug possession and drafted into the army, where he is treated brutally by officers and men alike. Meanwhile, Raïssa, who has given up hope of finding her brother, prepares to leave the area.

A complete change of pace from a director who had hitherto specialised in comedies, including some very popular French-language spy spoofs and the internationally popular silent film, *The Artist* (2011), *The Search* was inspired by a 1948 Hollywood film of the same name directed by Fred Zinnemann. This told the story of an American soldier, played by Montgomery Clift, who helps an orphaned German boy find his mother. In Hazanavicius' film, Clift's role is effectively the character given to Carole, while the equivalent of Helen was played in the original by Aline MacMahon. Interestingly, the Kolia character—not present anywhere in the 1948 film—seems to parallel the kind of role Montgomery Clift played in both *From Here to Eternity* (1953) and *The Young Lions* (1958)—that of a sensitive young man brutalised by his military training and by the bullying that comes with it.

In bringing the sorry story of the Chechen conflict to a wide cinema audience, Hazanavicius is certainly to be commended, even though he does take an overly didactic approach and expands the running time to a rather uncomfortable two and a half hours. Yet there is much to commend this film. It is spoken mainly in English, with some Chechen dialogue also, and it was filmed entirely in Georgia.

In a key scene, Carole addresses a meeting of Foreign Affairs ministers and advisers, with an impassioned speech drawing their attention to the horrors of the Chechen conflict. To say that her audience is indifferent to what she has to report is to understate the case, since some are chatting among themselves while others are asleep.

There are no shades of grey. The Russian soldiers are monsters who are depicted as both racists and religious bigots: they refer to the hapless Chechens as 'terrorists' and 'blacks' and offer no mercy to the terrified civilians.

Hazanavicius pulls no punches here—the war is unbelievably horrific and its effect on innocents like Hadji is incalculable. The kindness of volunteer helpers like Helen and Carole is commendable, but will never be enough.

The Search was given a mixed reception when it premiered in competition at Cannes in 2014, and seems not to have travelled much, if at all, outside Europe. It's worthy of serious reflection as, despite its flaws, its themes are important and timely.

83

The Sessions

(USA, 2012)

Fox Searchlight Pictures–Such Much Films. DIRECTOR/SCRIPT: Ben Lewin, inspired by a magazine article by Mark O'Brien. ACTORS: Helen Hunt, John Hawkes, William H. Macy, Moon Bloodgood, Annika Marks, Rhea Perlman, Adam Arkin, Robin Weigert, W. Earl Brown, Blake Lindsley, Rusty Schwimmer. 95 MINS.

Berkeley, California, 1988. Mark O'Brien (John Hawkes), in his late 30s, has been paralysed from the neck down due to the polio he contracted as a child. He survives with the help of carers, and an iron lung that he can only leave for short periods of time. A poet and journalist, Mark is aware that his sexual organs are in working order but he remains a virgin. His most recent carer is disagreeable and thoughtless, and he replaces her with Amanda (Annika Marks), who is both kind and beautiful; but when Mark tells her he loves her, she quits. Her replacements are Vera (Moon Bloodgood) and the burly Rod (W. Earl Brown). Mark is commissioned to write an article about the use of a sex surrogate, and—after obtaining approval from Father Brendan (William H. Macy), his priest—he succeeds in hiring the services of Cheryl (Helen Hunt), a married woman who takes her part-time job very seriously, allowing sexual intimacy only as part of a series of six sessions. During the first four sessions, Cheryl gently prepares the fearful Mark for sex, and at the fourth session he achieves penetration. Cheryl decides to end the sessions at this point and Mark is devastated, but is now able to approach Susan (Robin Weigert), a doctor at the hospital he attends.

Despite the subject matter, and the fact that Helen Hunt—in a brave and beautiful performance—frequently appears naked on screen, there's nothing prurient about Australian director Ben Lewin's bold and magnificent—and very personal—film. Lewin himself was crippled by polio as a child, but that hasn't stopped him living a normal life as a family man and also directing films, though *The Sessions* marked a comeback after almost twenty years in which he was unable to make a film for the cinema.

Given his intimate interest in and connection to the story of Mark O'Brien, who died at the age of 49, it's no surprise that *The Sessions* is such a tender and moving film experience. It's also most unusual given the predilection of American films, even many independent ones, to wallow in violence but shy away from the most intimately sexual material—certainly little is left to the imagination in this film, yet Lewin and his superb actors triumph over all possible criticisms of exploitation.

Some time is given over to an exploration of Mark's Catholicism and his resulting feelings of guilt, making the role of the sympathetic priest, played with great good humour by William H. Macy, so integral to the drama. Mark blames himself for the fact that his parents had to spend most of their lives caring for him, and this feeling of guilt continues to affect him now that he's middle-aged.

Lewin's screenplay is based on the character's own magazine article, 'On Seeing a Sex Surrogate', and Hawkes is superb in the role, succeeding in convincing in not only the physical details, but also the emotional and intellectual ones. And Hunt as the housewife with a most unusual part-time occupation gives a truly astonishing performance.

Perhaps it's no great surprise that a film as candid, raw and uncompromising as this one had difficulty attracting an audience.

It's no surprise that *The Sessions* is a tender and moving film experience

84

She's Funny That Way

(USA, 2014)

Lagniappe Films–Red Granite–Three Point Capital. DIRECTOR: Peter Bogdanovich. SCRIPT: Louise Stratten, Peter Bogdanovich. ACTORS: Owen Wilson, Imogen Poots, Jennifer Aniston, Rhys Ifans, Kathryn Hahn, Will Forte, Austin Pendleton, George Morfogen, Lucy Punch, Jake Hoffman, Cybill Shepherd, Colleen Camp, Tatum O'Neal, Quentin Tarantino. 93 MINS.

New York. Isabella ('Izzy') Paterson (Imogen Poots), a celebrated actress being interviewed by a journalist, reveals candidly how her career began. Using the name 'Glo Stick', she had worked as a high-class prostitute and her clients were often celebrities. One day she is assigned to a Manhattan hotel room to have sex with 'Derek Thomas', who is actually Arnold Albertson (Owen Wilson), a famous Broadway director about to start casting and rehearsals for a new play, *A Grecian Affair*. Izzy tells Arnold about her acting ambitions. The next day she turns up at the theatre to audition for a role in the play. Arnold is horrified, particularly because his wife, Delta (Kathryn Hahn), is the play's star. But Izzy very much impresses the play's author, Josh Fleet (Will Forte), as well as Delta. Meanwhile one of Glo Stick's clients, a Judge (Austin Pendleton), has hired a private eye, who happens to be Josh's father, to follow her. Josh is dating Jane Claremont (Jennifer Aniston), a therapist. Meanwhile the male star of the play, Seth Gilbert (Rhys Ifans), is concealing the fact that he and Delta had enjoyed an affair when they were recently together in London. Coincidentally, all these characters decide to eat at the same restaurant one evening, leading to revelations and embarrassments.

She's Funny That Way is a wonderfully old-fashioned comedy, inspired by French farce and classic movies. Peter Bogdanovich is famously a film buff whose early hits, including *The Last Picture Show* (1971), *What's Up, Doc?* (1972) and *Paper Moon* (1973), all drew heavily on the work of some of the great directors of Hollywood's past. Bogdanovich fell out of fashion after a couple of flops, but has continued to make modestly budgeted comedies and romances—and this is one of his best. It was based on a screenplay he'd written many years earlier with his former wife, Louise Stratten, and when he finally found the backing to make it, in 2014, he hadn't worked on a feature since *The Cat's Meow* in 2001. Apart from the influence of French bedroom farces, the film is clearly inspired by the vintage films of directors like Ernst Lubitsch, whose work is directly referenced with a clip from *Cluny Brown* (1946). The plot is full of innocent sexual encounters, misunderstandings and coincidences, and it rattles along without wasting any time. It's also a showcase for a terrific cast in which Imogen Poots and Owen Wilson obviously relish the chance to play such classic romantic/comedic characters.

The restaurant scene, in which all the major characters find themselves embarrassingly dining at the same place, is a classic of its kind, beautifully directed and acted. There are delights among the supporting cast as well, with Bogdanovich's former muse, Cybill Shepherd, turning up as Izzy's mother, and Tatum O'Neal, who made her name in *Paper Moon*, also putting in an appearance. Plus there's an amusing cameo appearance at the very end from none other than Quentin Tarantino.

The film was made independently and on a very modest budget, with both Wes Anderson and Noah Baumbach lending their support as independent producers. After a successful world premiere at the Venice Film Festival, it was poorly distributed in most countries, perhaps because it was seen as just too retro. As a result the audiences that might have embraced this deliciously sexy comedy were probably not even aware that it was screening.

85

S1m0ne

(USA, 2002)

New Line Cinema. DIRECTOR/SCRIPT: Andrew Niccol. ACTORS: Al Pacino, Catherine Keener, Pruitt Taylor Vince, Winona Ryder, Jay Mohr, Jason Schwartzman, Stanley Anderson, Evan Rachel Wood, Rachel Roberts, [Elias Koteas]. 117 MINS.

Hollywood. Film director Viktor Taransky (Al Pacino) is furious when the outrageous demands of Nicola Anders (Winona Ryder), the temperamental star of his new movie, *Sunrise Sunset*, lead to her exiting the production before its completion. An encounter with Hank Aleno (uncredited Elias Koteas), a dying CGI (computer-generated imagery) genius, ends with Hank bequeathing to Viktor his last invention: S1mulation One software. Nine months later Viktor has completed the movie using 'Simone', a digitally created computer animation. 'Simone' becomes an international sensation and Viktor immediately 'stars' her in a second film, *Eternity Forever*, making 'her' even more popular. Because she's never seen, and never gives interviews, tabloid journalists, including Max Sayer (Pruitt Taylor Vince) and Milton (Jason Schwartzman), go crazy trying to find her whereabouts. Viktor fakes TV interviews in which 'Simone' is never actually present, and sets up a hotel room so that it appears as if his 'star' has enjoyed a wild night, allowing the hacks of the press to find her underwear. Meanwhile the head of Amalgamated Film Studios, Elaine Christian (Catherine Keener), Viktor's ex-wife, whom he still loves, is also puzzled by the elusiveness of the star. 'Simone' shares the Best Actress Oscar with herself for her two starring roles and becomes *Time* magazine's Person of the Year. But for Viktor she has become a monster.

Hollywood at the start of the digital revolution is the setting for this clever, inventive comedy. Al Pacino gives a tremendously funny performance as the egotistical director ('nostalgic for an era you weren't even born in', as his ex-wife tells him) who finds himself able to use advanced new technology to create a mythical movie star, acting the role himself while 'she' digitally follows all his moves and sounds. It's a great concept, beautifully worked out and written ('It's not every day you're fired by the mother of your child,' moans Viktor when Elaine shuts down his movie), and ultimately the crazy idea is taken to its logical conclusion. When Viktor decides 'Simone' has become too powerful, he attempts to destroy her career with a black and white art film, *I Am Pig*, which she is credited with directing, and which involves her eating from a trough—but the public still loves her unreservedly, and that includes Viktor's sweet daughter, Lainey (Evan Rachel Wood), who is more computer savvy than he is. He tries to rob his creation of her popularity by having her espouse far-right causes (she claims to love to eat fried dolphin and not to believe there's a hole in the ozone layer), but nothing diminishes her popularity. Like Frankenstein, Viktor (who shares a first name with that famous monster's creator) comes to rue the day he brought his creature into the world.

New Zealand-born Andrew Niccol came to fame with his screenplay for Peter Weir's *The Truman Show* (1998) and, almost at the same time, wrote and directed his own first feature, *Gattaca* (1997). As a comedy on the cult of celebrity and the encroaching digital future of cinema—where the long-dead Peter Cushing can be 'resurrected' to appear in scenes opposite Ben Mendelsohn in *Rogue One: A Star Wars story* (2016)—*S1m0ne* has elements of brilliance, not least the fact that, at its base, it has a plot that goes right back to *Metropolis* for inspiration. The film did not find success with the public, for reasons that remain rather obscure. Niccol has subsequently made some interesting films, but nothing that has quite reached this level.

86

The Straight Story

(USA / FRANCE, 1999)

The Picture Factory–Le Studio Canal+. DIRECTOR: David Lynch. SCRIPT: John Roach, Mary Sweeney. ACTORS: Richard Farnsworth, Sissy Spacek, Harry Dean Stanton, Everett McGill, John P. Farley, Kevin Farley, Jane Galloway Heitz, Joseph A. Carpenter. 111 MINS.

Laurens, Iowa. A 73-year-old widower, Alvin Straight (Richard Farnsworth) lives with his daughter, Rose (Sissy Spacek), whose children have been taken from her by the welfare department on the grounds that she can't look after them. After suffering a fall that has resulted in a damaged hip, Alvin—whose eyesight is failing— is warned by a doctor at the local hospital that he needs to take better care of himself. Despite this, when he hears that his elder brother, Lyle (Harry Dean Stanton), who lives 300 miles away in Mount Zion, Wisconsin, has suffered a stroke, Alvin is stubbornly determined to travel to see him. Unable to drive a car, he hooks a trailer onto his motorised lawnmower and sets off. The lawnmower soon breaks down, but he replaces it with a 'new' (1966) replacement and continues the journey, meeting a variety of people along the way, until he finally reaches the home of his brother and succeeds in patching up a quarrel that had divided them years earlier.

The Straight Story is quite unlike anything David Lynch has made before or since. All it has in common with his most cel-ebrated films is his interest in small-town America, but here there are none of the sinister connotations to be found in *Twin Peaks* (1989) or *Blue Velvet* (1986). On the contrary, *The Straight Story* is a wonderfully mellow experience and a delight from start to finish, thanks in no small part to the lovely performance of Richard Farnsworth, who died a year after the film's release.

The richness is in the detail. During the course of his achingly slow journey, old Alvin encounters a cross-section of 'ordinary'

170

Americans. He gives a lift to a pregnant teenage runaway, and counsels her about the importance of family. He meets a woman troubled by the fact that, during the course of her daily drive to work, she frequently encounters deer on the road and often accidentally hits them ('Every week I plough into a deer, and I love deer!'). He meets volunteer fire fighters and a coachload of tourists. A family allows him to camp in their garden while his motor-mower is being repaired at the local garage by identical twin brothers who constantly fight with one another. Most importantly he meets, in a bar, a man who, like himself, is a World War II veteran, and they share some painful memories of that conflict.

When he finally reaches his destination, he and his brother have nothing much to talk about—but it doesn't really matter. It's enough that Alvin took the time and effort to travel all that way, and, though he doesn't put it in words, Lyle is clearly touched to see him. The two old men sit on the porch of Lyle's wooden house in a companionable silence.

Alvin's odyssey is beautifully photographed by veteran British cinematographer Freddie Francis in luscious widescreen colours. The landscape—the cornfields, the endless vistas—is majestic, even though the people who inhabit it are, for a Lynch film, startlingly ordinary.

The film was made before some cinemas targeted older audiences with films about elderly people visiting exotic Indian hotels and the like. It was no surprise, perhaps, that Lynch fans found it all too bland (which it isn't), but at the time there seemed to be no other audience left for this admittedly small but touchingly eccentric road movie.

. . . . a wonderfully mellow experience
and a delight from start to finish

87

Sunshine on Leith

(UK, 2013)

DNA Films. DIRECTOR: Dexter Fletcher. SCRIPT: Stephen Greenhorn, based on his play. ACTORS: Peter Mullan, Jane Horrocks, George MacKay, Antonia Thomas, Freya Mavor, Kevin Guthrie, Jason Flemyng, Paul Brannigan. 100 MINS.

Edinburgh. After serving in Afghanistan, where one of their mates, Ronnie (Paul Brannigan), has been very badly injured, Davy (George MacKay) and Ally (Kevin Guthrie) return home to pick up their lives. Ally had been dating Davy's sister, Liz (Freya Mavor), before they went away and now hopes to marry her; but Liz is reluctant to commit and decides she wants to travel before settling down. Davy meets Liz's friend Yvonne (Antonia Thomas), who comes from the south of England. The parents of Davy and Liz, 'Rab' (Peter Mullan) and Jean (Jane Horrocks) are about to celebrate their silver wedding anniversary, when Rab is made aware of the fact that he is the father of a daughter he never knew about, the result of a brief fling he had after his marriage to Jean. At a celebratory party, Jean accidentally finds out about the daughter, and realises Rab had been unfaithful to her years earlier. They quarrel, and Rab suffers a heart attack. Liz decides to leave to live and work in Florida, and Rab, recovering in hospital, encourages her. Ally decides to re-enlist.

The Proclaimers—Charlie and Craig Reid—are immensely popular Scottish singer–songwriters and *Sunshine on Leith*, which Stephen Greenhorn scripted from his own stage show, combines some of their best-known songs, including 'I'm Gonna Be (500 miles)', which provides the rousing climax. The film is a strangely touching dramatic story about cross-generational relationships. While feeling vaguely guilty that their mate, Ronnie, has been permanently crippled by a roadside bomb in Afghanistan, Davy and Ally attempt to settle back into civilian life. Ally, confident all along that Liz will marry him, is shattered when she makes it clear she won't, while Davy's attraction to the delightful Yvonne is tempered by the fact that she may soon return South of the Border, somewhere the patriotically Scottish Davy simply doesn't want to be. Meanwhile the parents, a seemingly happy and devoted couple, go through an extreme crisis thanks to the revelation of Rab's old infidelity and the presence of a long-lost daughter.

These characters are presented realistically so that we care about their problems. Shoehorning the plot into a musical was a challenge that former actor turned director Dexter Fletcher surmounts surprisingly well. At first it's a little disconcerting when Davy and Ally break into song as they walk through the streets of Leith, Edinburgh's harbourside suburb, but Fletcher makes it work—and there's a nice in-joke as The Proclaimers themselves make a brief appearance in this sequence. Subsequent musical numbers—in a pub, an art gallery, a hospital—are all skilfully integrated into the narrative and by the time we reach the film's terrific climax— spectacularly filmed below Edinburgh Castle near the Princes Street railway station entrance—the film's sense of optimism has become infectious.

Not everyone was convinced, however, and many of the reviews were lukewarm or even hostile. Partly this attitude seems due to the ambivalence many people feel today towards original movie musicals, especially musicals that unfold in realistic settings. Perhaps this was the reason the film failed to make much of an impact on its original release.

But if ever a film deserved to be re-assessed it's this one, not least for its spectacular photography—by George Richmond—of one of Europe's most beautiful cities. *Sunshine on Leith* works because its characters are so human, so flawed, so real, and because the songs they sing are so beguiling and so rousingly enjoyable.

88

Taking Sides

(GERMANY/FRANCE/UK/AUSTRIA, 2001)

MPB-Little Big Bear-Satel Film. DIRECTOR: István Szabó. SCRIPT: Ronald Harwood, based on his play. ACTORS: Harvey Keitel, Stellan Skarsgård, Moritz Bleibtreu, Birgit Minichmayr, Ulrich Tukur, Hanns Zischler, Armin Rohde, August Zirner, Robin Renucci, R. Lee Ermey. 110 MINS.

Germany, 1946. Wilhelm Furtwängler (Stellan Skarsgård), conductor of the Berlin Philharmonic Orchestra during the Nazi period, is being investigated by Major Steve Arnold (Harvey Keitel) who, before joining the army, was an insurance investigator. Furtwängler denies he was ever a member of the Nazi Party, and his statement is supported by members of the orchestra. Arnold, who cares little for art or culture, openly despises Furtwängler and refuses to believe that he was above politics. An informer claims that Furtwängler made anti-Semitic remarks and that he once sent Hitler a telegram on his birthday. Arnold's two assistants are shocked at the way the American treats the musician: they are Emmi (Birgit Minichmayr), whose father was executed after the plot to assassinate Hitler, and Lieutenant David Wills (Moritz Bleibtreu), a German Jew who escaped to America before the war. Furtwängler is eventually exonerated, but never again allowed to conduct music in the US.

Hungarian director István Szabó, born in 1938, made his reputation with a series of emotionally rich, very personal films that were produced under the Communist regime in his native Hungary in the 1960s. He is better known, however, for his award-winning epic, *Mephisto* (1981), about the fate of a famous pre-war German actor and his compliance with the Nazi regime. *Taking Sides* was made at a time when Szabó, along with many other fine directors of his generation, was finding it extremely difficult to finance his films. Like his best work, it has a personal element to it: Furtwängler believed art and politics should be separated, as did Szabó himself when he made films under the rigid Communist control in place in Hungary in the 1960s and 1970s. Like the actor played by Klaus Maria Brandauer in *Mephisto*, Furtwängler continued to work as an artist—the conductor of one of Germany's most prestigious orchestras—with the support of Nazi officials, but unlike the actor in *Mephisto*, there seemed to have been no delight in or acceptance of Nazism on Furtwängler's part.

Furtwängler, superbly played by Swedish actor Stellan Skarsgård, was only one of many German artists who were investigated by Americans after the war. Ronald Harwood's screenplay, based on his play, poses difficult questions, but on the whole comes down in favour of the artist. Much of the drama stems from the fact that Major Arnold, played with bombastic skill by Keitel, is, in artistic terms, a philistine and completely out of tune with the attitudes of the musician. Scenes in which he rails against Furtwängler are powerfully presented. In Arnold's view, the very fact that Furtwängler stayed on in Germany and worked there throughout the Nazi period means that he was 'taking sides', and therefore condoning his political masters. Could the same be said for Szabó?

Taking Sides is a small-scale film, mostly set in a single room, with production design by Ken Adam, the man who designed *Dr. Strangelove* (1963). However, it's far from being a theatrical experience, thanks to Szabó's adroit use of close-ups in key scenes.

Unfortunately, the film was not a great success. Some time after it was released, Szabó himself was accused of acting as an informer against other film professionals working in Communist Hungary. He rejected the accusations, and other directors working at the time came forward to explain that, whenever they were permitted to travel overseas for a film festival or other event, they were interrogated on their return by the secret police. This was the atmosphere in which directors like Szabó were obliged to work in the Communist era.

89

The Three Burials of Melquiades Estrada

(USA/FRANCE, 2005)

EuropaCorp–Javelina Film Company. DIRECTOR: Tommy Lee Jones. SCRIPT: Guillermo Arriaga. ACTORS: Tommy Lee Jones, Barry Pepper, January Jones, Dwight Yoakam, Julio Cesár Cedillo, Melissa Leo, Levon Helm, Mel Rodriguez, Cecilia Suárez. 121 MINS.

Van Horn, Texas. Pete Perkins (Tommy Lee Jones), an unmarried rancher whose property is close to the Mexican border, hires illegal immigrant Melquiades Estrada (Julio Cesár Cedillo) to work for him and they become close friends, even going out on a double date when they take a pair of married women to a motel. Pete's date, Rachel (Melissa Leo), works as a waitress in her husband's diner and is also romantically involved with the sheriff, Belmont (Dwight Yoakam), while Melquiades' companion is Lou Ann (January Jones), recently arrived from Cincinatti with her husband, Mike Norton (Barry Pepper), who works for the border patrol. Mike, who has no scruples about bashing 'wetbacks', including women, accidentally shoots and kills Melquiades, and buries the body, which is subsequently dug up by coyotes. Pete learns the identity of his friend's killer and kidnaps Mike, forcing him to travel by horseback with Melquiades' exhumed body, to bury him in his home town. But the journey involves a number of unexpected situations and surprises.

The first of only two features to date directed by actor Tommy Lee Jones was written by Guillermo Arriaga, best known for his screenplays for Alejandro González Iñárritu—*Amores Perros* (2000), *21 Grams* (2003) and *Babel* (2006). And, like those films, it forces the viewer to experience the same situation from more than one perspective. At first we don't realise that the body discovered by coyotes is that of the outgoing, friendly Melquiades, who has become such a close friend of his employer, the taciturn Pete. Later, when we see his killing, we are shown the viewpoint of both the victim and the killer.

Nothing is quite what it seems. The young border patrol officer from Ohio, very well played by Barry Pepper, seems at first a decent young husband, but his sadistic streak soon asserts itself and his unhappy wife leaves as soon as the going gets tough. Complex, too, is the character of Rachel, who is happily married, yet equally happy to have sex with two of the township's most prominent men.

On the journey south, captor and prisoner encounter a blind old man (Levon Helm) who listens to Mexican radio stations but speaks no Spanish. He begs Pete to shoot him because his son, who used to visit him and bring him food, hasn't been around for a long time. When Norton is bitten on the foot by a rattlesnake and taken to a local woman for treatment, he discovers that she was one of the 'wetbacks' he'd punched in the face a few days earlier. And when Pete and Norton finally arrive at the place Melquiades described as his home, nobody there has heard of him.

Beautifully photographed by Chris Menges, this is a modern western that casts a rancid eye on relations between Mexicans and Texans on the border between the two countries. It's ironic that the most sympathetic character is Melquiades Estrada himself, with most of the Americans portrayed unsympathetically. At the same time, Pete's warm and genuine friendship with Melquiades is, as he himself realises, the most positive element in his life.

After it screened in competition in Cannes in 2005, the film—which was entirely financed by French director Luc Besson's EuropaCorp—struggled to find much of an audience, some said because of a title many couldn't pronounce, but more probably because of a narrative that has no neat and tidy resolutions. Jones has since directed *The Homesman* (2014), an equally interesting film, and an almost equally overlooked one.

90

Timecode

(USA, 2000)

Red Mullet Productions. DIRECTOR/SCRIPT: Mike Figgis. ACTORS: Stellan Skarsgård, Saffron Burrows, Salma Hayek, Jeanne Tripplehorn, Danny Huston, Julian Sands, Holly Hunter, Kyle MacLachlan, Leslie Mann, Alessandro Nivola, Glenne Headly, Xander Berkeley, Richard Edson, Mia Maestro, Daphna Kastner, Steven Weber. 97 MINS.

Hollywood. Emma (Saffron Burrows) leaves a session with her shrink and goes to the office of Red Mullet Studios, a film company founded by her philandering husband, Alex Green (Stellan Skarsgård), to tell him she's leaving him. Meanwhile Rose (Salma Hayek), Alex's latest girlfriend, is travelling to the studio in a chauffeur-driven car with her rich lover, Lauren (Jeanne Tripplehorn). Cherine (Leslie Mann) unsuccessfully auditions for director Lester Moore (Richard Edson), and later meets Emma in a bookshop and takes her home. Rose and Alex have sex behind a screen in the studio's theatrette. Lester decides to cast Rose in his new film. Maverick director Ana Pauls (Mia Maestro) arrives to pitch her latest idea to Alex and his staff, but Lauren—who had secretly placed a microphone in Rose's handbag and so knows all about her exploits with Alex, turns up with a gun.

An end credit on Mike Figgis' audaciously experimental *Timecode* explains that the film was shot with four digital cameras in continuous takes, starting at 3 p.m. on 19 November 1999. Each camera essentially follows a different character. The four images are presented on a split screen divided into four equal squares. The actors improvised their lines around a story outline provided by Figgis, who was one of the camera operators. Sometimes the characters overlap, so that two cameras are covering the same moment but from different angles. There is no editing.

Essentially, then, this is an experimental movie made on a larger than usual budget and employing a cast of professional actors, some of them very well known. During the course of filming, there are three earthquakes that temporarily bring a halt to the action (in one of these, Lauren calls out to 'Salma', the name of the actor rather than to 'Rose', the name of the character Salma is playing).

When the film starts, the viewer is likely to be confused by the multiple images and the conversations taking place that aren't always obviously audible. But in post-production Figgis juggled the sound skilfully so that whenever an important dialogue exchange takes place, the audio for that quarter of the screen is enhanced and that of the other three quarters reduced, so it's always pretty clear what's happening.

In fact the plot, which includes a smattering of Hollywood insider jokes (the film for which Lester Moore is seeking to cast a leading lady is titled *Bitch from Louisiana*), is a fairly slim one. But Figgis doesn't take his own pretensions too seriously. Avant-garde director Ana Pauls' pitch to the astounded Red Mullet executives describes a film exactly like the one we're watching, and her concept is greeted with dismissive laughter by Alex.

Since *Timecode* was made, other digitally filmed movies have been shot in continuous takes with no editing (an experiment first employed by Alfred Hitchcock on *Rope* in 1948, though then he was shooting on film, and the maximum length of a take at the time was defined by the maximum 10 minutes of a roll of 35 mm film with which a camera could be loaded). Figgis' achievement with *Timecode* is to make a thoroughly entertaining film that was on the cutting edge of what was then the new technology.

Sadly *Timecode* seems to have been ahead of its time and found only limited audiences. Since then, the career of Figgis—who previously made *Leaving Las Vegas* (1995) among others—seems to have slowly petered out.

91

Truth

(USA/AUSTRALIA, 2015)

Mythology Entertainment. DIRECTOR/SCRIPT: James Vanderbilt. ACTORS: Cate Blanchett, Robert Redford, Dennis Quaid, Topher Grace, Elisabeth Moss, Bruce Greenwood, Dermot Mulroney, Stacy Keach, Noni Hazlehurst, Rachael Blake, Andrew McFarlane, Felix Williamson, Helmut Bakaitis, Nicholas Hope, Philip Quast, Steve Bastoni. 125 MINS.

New York, 2004. President George W. Bush is running for re-election. Mary Mapes (Cate Blanchett) is a senior producer for the CBS TV current affairs program *60 Minutes*, and has recently put to air a story about the treatment of Iraqi prisoners in Abu Ghraib. Mapes hears a rumour that, during the Vietnam War, Bush had pulled strings to get himself drafted into the Texas Air National Guard—and thus avoid being posted to a war zone—but that he hardly ever reported for duty. Long-time *60 Minutes* presenter, the legendary Dan Rather (Robert Redford), is briefed, and Mapes assembles a team of investigators including Mike Smith (Topher Grace), a radical freelancer, Roger Charles (Dennis Quaid), a military expert, and Lucy Scott (Elisabeth Moss), a professor of journalism. As the investigation proceeds, everything the team discovers seems to suggest the story is true, but there's no actual proof—until Bill Burkett (Stacy Keach), a retired Texas Air National Guard officer, reluctantly provides the team with copies of evidence that Bush did, indeed, shirk his obligations during the war. The story goes to air on September 8 and the response is immediate, with the right-wing media attacking Mapes, Rather and CBS relentlessly. Doubt is shed on the accuracy of the proof provided by Burkett, and Mapes is fired. Rather resigns.

Most movies about journalists working to uncover a sensational and controversial story—*All the President's Men* (1976), *Spotlight* (2015), *The Post* (2017)—end in the triumph of the fourth estate, but not this one. Although writer–director James Vanderbilt, adapting Mary Mapes' book, *Truth and Duty: The press, the president and the privilege of power* (2005), clearly believes that the CBS team was sincere and, in fact, correct in its pursuit of the President, the results were a personal and professional disaster for all the key players. Lacking a conventional happy ending, it's perhaps not much of a surprise that the film failed to find an audience.

This was Vanderbilt's first and, to date, only foray into direction; he's better known as the screenwriter of David Fincher's superb investigative thriller, *Zodiac* (2007). But Vanderbilt does a fine job with the rather complex material, telling the story entirely from the point of view of the increasingly beleaguered *60 Minutes* team and building to a devastating climax.

The film was almost entirely made in Sydney, which explains the large number of Australian actors in supporting roles. Most notably, these include Noni Hazlehurst, who gives one of her finest performances as the anxious wife of the sickly Burkett, and Rachael Blake as Betsy West, a senior CBS employee. The film was photographed by Mandy Walker, edited by Richard Francis-Bruce and designed by Fiona Crombie, Aussies all.

Given the strong local involvement, it's disappointing that the local distributor—no doubt influenced by the film's poor box-office returns in America—dumped it without ceremony and very little in the way of publicity. Even the cast and crew screening, traditionally arranged by the distributor for the benefit of the local actors and crew members who worked on the production, was refused, which is almost unheard of. No wonder, then, that the film sank without trace.

Yet it showcases one of Cate Blanchett's finest performances as Mapes, and tells with skill and precision a cautionary tale about how the power of the press can be overwhelmed by the even greater power of politics.

92

25th Hour

(USA, 2002)

40 Acres and A Mule Filmworks. DIRECTOR: Spike Lee. SCRIPT: David Benioff, based on his novel. ACTORS: Edward Norton, Philip Seymour Hoffman, Barry Pepper, Rosario Dawson, Anna Paquin, Brian Cox, Tony Siragusa, Levani. 134 MINS.

New York City, a few months after 9/11. Monty Brogan (Edward Norton) is a low-level drug dealer, whose customers have mostly been students. He is facing a seven-year prison term after being arrested by Drug Enforcement Administration officials; his associate, Kostya (Tony Siragusa), assures him that it was his girlfriend, Naturelle Riviera (Rosario Dawson), who betrayed him to the authorities—only she, Kostya claims, knew the exact location in his apartment where the drugs were hidden. Over the 24 hours that represent his last day of freedom, Monty contemplates suicide and looks back over his wasted life, remembering how he met Naturelle. He meets up with two of his best friends, Jacob (Philip Seymour Hoffman), a schoolteacher who is involved with one of his pupils, Mary (Anna Paquin), and Francis (Barry Pepper), an investment banker who lives in an apartment that directly looks down on Ground Zero, where the Twin Towers formerly stood. He is summoned by Nikolai (Levani), his drug supplier, who reveals that it was actually Kostya, not Naturelle, who betrayed him—and he is handed a gun. But Monty refuses to kill Kostya. Instead, fearing that he'll be subjected to gay rape in prison, he persuades Francis to smash his face to a pulp. Monty's father James (Brian Cox), a former fire fighter now bartender, drives his son to the prison and, during the journey, 'imagines' another, very different, life in Texas for his son.

Scripted by David Benioff from his own novel, *25th Hour* was the first Hollywood studio picture to refer directly to the events of

September 11, 2001, and the first production to be granted access to Ground Zero. In a sense, the story of Monty's last day at liberty before serving a long prison term is the story of New Yorkers in the aftermath of the terrorist event that changed the world. Nothing is secure anymore; everyone is living under an implied threat that things have radically changed for the worse. The homophobia of the federal agents is just one of the striking elements of this grim drama. Another is the pathetic relationship between the teacher and his very advanced pupil—a startling performance from NZ former child actor Anna Paquin.

Right from the start, Spike Lee emphasises the void left behind by the demolished Twin Towers; the opening credits unfold over the Manhattan skyline at night with two beams of light projecting heavenwards from the location where the towers once stood. James' bar contains a shrine dedicated to the fire fighters who were killed that day. The air of doomed romanticism extends even to Monty's name—his mother had adored the film *A Place in the Sun*, and named him after its lead actor, Montgomery Clift.

The film opened in America a few weeks before the end of 2002 and, despite the skill which Spike Lee has brought to the material, it was poorly received. Many commentators and reviewers questioned who would really want to see a movie in which the audience is asked to have sympathy for a drug dealer? That, of course, is missing the point, because the film is about a great deal more than that—it's about coping with a catastrophic disaster and finding a way to continue living. Monty faces a void of seven years in his life, and is terrified of the sexual violence the DEA officers gleefully inform him is in store for him. Combining all these themes is a challenge superbly met by Lee—but it proved too much of a challenge for audiences at the time.

93

Until the End of the World
(*Bis ans Ende der Welt*)

(GERMANY/FRANCE/AUSTRALIA, 1991)

Road Movies Filmproduktion–Argos Films–Village Roadshow Pictures. DIRECTOR: Wim Wenders. SCRIPT: Peter Carey, Wim Wenders. ACTORS: William Hurt, Solveig Dommartin, Sam Neill, Rüdiger Vogler, Jeanne Moreau, Max von Sydow, Chick Ortega, Eddy Mitchell, Ernie Dingo, David Gulpilil, Justine Saunders, Chishu Ryu, Elena Smirnova, Allen Garfield, Lois Chiles, Jimmy Little, Rhoda Roberts. 158 MINS (release version); 275 MINS (original version).

Europe, 1999, eight years into the future. An Indian satellite containing a nuclear bomb has gone out of control; America is threatening to shoot it down. Many think this will mean the end of the world. Claire Tourneur (Solveig Dommartin) travels from Venice by road to Paris, en route befriending a couple of bank robbers and acquiring their loot. She gives a lift to Trevor (William Hurt), who is trying to evade Burt (Ernie Dingo), a bounty hunter. In Paris, Claire reunites with her boyfriend, Eugene (Sam Neill). Attracted to Trevor, whose real name is Sam, Claire travels with him to Lisbon, Berlin, Moscow, Beijing, Tokyo, San Francisco and eventually Sydney, followed by Eugene and also by Phillip Winter (Rüdiger Vogler), a private detective. In the outback near Coober Pedy, Sam is reunited with his parents, scientist Henry (Max von Sydow) and his blind wife, Edith (Jeanne Moreau).

I included this unwieldy epic in this book because, on paper, it looks astonishingly exciting. It's surely the only film in history to include scenes shot on four different continents, and one of Australia's most distinguished authors, Peter Carey, is credited with co-scripting alongside the German director of such classics as *Alice in the Cities* (1974), *Kings of the Road* (1976), *Paris, Texas* (1984) and *Wings of Desire* (1987). At the time of the film's release, much attention was given to the fact that it had been reduced, presumably by the distributors, from the director's cut of 4 hours 35 minutes to just over two and a half hours. This, we were informed, explained the reason for the scrappy structure, the obvious gaps, and the narration—spoken by Sam Neill—that papers over the missing bits. Having finally located and viewed the longer version I can affirm that it's just as scrappy and just as filled with gaping holes in the narrative—only it's a good deal longer.

The combination of a sci-fi fantasy, a love story and a road movie ought to be right up Wenders' alley, but something has gone badly wrong with this ungainly affair. The story is decidedly strange: Trevor/Sam is recording images of friends and family that can be played to his mother via a device that will allow her to see them, but the recording process is affecting *his own* sight. The peripheral characters—Sam Neill's jilted lover who just has to keep following the woman who left him; the drum-playing French bank robber (Chick Ortega), who also winds up in outback Australia; the German private eye—seem little more than self-indulgent padding. Wonderful Aboriginal actors including David Gulpilil are largely wasted.

However it all looks great, thanks to Robby Müller's fluid camerawork, and it sounds terrific, too, with a music track filled with songs by David Byrne, Patti Smith, U2, Elvis Costello, k.d. lang, Lou Reed, Nick Cave and many others. But it's just too indigestible, too chaotic and much, much too long, even in the release version.

So why include it here? It was, unsurprisingly, an enormous flop back in 1991, and bankrupted one of the production companies that supported it. It's annoying, self-indulgent and crazy. And yet … there's a certain grandeur to this cinematic folly, and there is so much talent involved that it would be pretty difficult not to find some enjoyment from it on some level.

94

Valmont

(FRANCE/UK, 1989)

Renn Productions–Timothy Burrill Productions. **DIRECTOR:** Miloš Forman. **SCRIPT:** Jean-Claude Carrière, from the novel by Choderlos de Laclos. **ACTORS:** Colin Firth, Annette Bening, Meg Tilly, Fairuza Balk, Siân Phillips, Jeffrey Jones, Henry Thomas, Fabia Drake, T.P. McKenna, Isla Blair, Ian McNeice, Ronald Lacey, Vincent Schiavelli, Nils Tavernier. **137 MINS.**

France, 1781. Fifteen-year-old Cécile de Volanges (Fairuza Balk) is removed from the convent where she has lived for most of her life, in preparation for her arranged marriage to Gercourt (Jeffrey Jones), Commander of the Royal Guard. Gercourt's mistress, the widowed Marquise de Merteuil (Annette Bening), is furious that her lover clearly plans to abandon her in favour of his new young wife, and plots revenge. She enlists the help of a former lover and notorious womaniser, the Vicomte de Valmont (Colin Firth), and asks him to seduce Cécile prior to her wedding. However he is, at first, uncooperative, because he's engaged in attempting to seduce the virtuous Madame de Tourvel (Meg Tilly), wife of a judge. Cécile, meanwhile, has fallen in love with her music teacher, Chevalier Danceny (Henry Thomas). The Marquise and Valmont plot to bring Cécile and Danceny together so that the girl will lose her virginity, but the plot fails. De Tourvel succumbs to Valmont, but for one night only.

Les Liaisons Dangereuses, the novel by Choderlos de Laclos, which consists entirely of letters written to and from the various characters involved, has been filmed three times, once by Roger Vadim in 1960, who updated the story to the present, and twice in 1989, by Stephen Frears and by Miloš Forman. The Frears version, titled *Dangerous Liaisons*, starred John Malkovich, Glenn Close, Michelle Pfeiffer and Uma Thurman and opened in cinemas first, so that by the time the Forman film was completed it had been completely overtaken by its rival. Both films are actually very good indeed; the casting of the main characters in the Frears film, which was adapted by Christopher Hampton, employed actors who were a little older than those in Forman's film, which was scripted by Jean-Claude Carrière.

Sumptuously photographed by the director's regular collaborator Miroslav Ondricek, *Valmont* boasts exceptional performances from Colin Firth as the cheerfully decadent Valmont, Annette Bening as the manipulative Marquise, and Fairuza Balk, outstanding as the naive innocent at the centre of the drama. Arguably Meg Tilly, as the supposedly faithful wife, is less effective than Michelle Pfeiffer was in this role, but it's fascinating to see the little boy from *E.T.*, Henry Thomas, cast as Cecile's youthful swain, Danceny.

The settings and costumes are opulent and the minor characters, especially Fabia Drake as Valmont's elderly aunt, are all excellent. Interestingly, Forman and Carrière made some changes to the narrative that principally affect the conclusion of the drama, as a result providing a rather more upbeat ending than is found in either the book or the other two films.

It's unfortunate that these two films by Forman and Frears went into production at more or less the same time, because one was always going to overwhelm the other. By the time *Valmont*—an independently made French–British co-production—was completed it was clear that distributors would not be very interested in a second version of an already popular story—and neither Firth nor Bening were as well established at the time as they would later become. As a result the film was almost unseen. It opened in France, but scarcely anywhere else, though it had very brief screenings in the UK a couple of years later. It deserved better.

95

Waiting

(AUSTRALIA, 1990)

Filmside Productions Limited–Australian Broadcasting Corporation. **DIRECTOR/SCRIPT:** Jackie McKimmie. **ACTORS:** Noni Hazlehurst, Deborra-Lee Furness, Frank Whitten, Helen Jones, Ray Barrett, Fiona Press, Denis Moore, Noga Bernstein, Matthew Fargher. **90 MINS.**

Rural New South Wales. Clare (Noni Hazlehurst) is nine months pregnant. She lives in an isolated shack in the bush with an outside dunny, and her only neighbour is the elderly Frank (Ray Barrett), who lives in a caravan nearby. Her best friends gather to celebrate the birth. Sandy (Helen Jones) and Michael (Frank Whitten), a political science teacher, have arranged with Clare to be the surrogate parents of the baby, and she was actually impregnated by Michael ('It took ages!'). The couple already have two adopted sons, one Aboriginal, the other Asian. Diane (Deborra-Lee Furness), a fashion journalist who has spent six years in London, arrives together with her latest lover, Bill (Denis Moore). Terry (Fiona Press), a radical feminist filmmaker, also makes an appearance, bringing with her Rosie (Noga Bernstein), her teenage daughter; Terry plans to make a movie about the birth using equipment she's 'borrowed' from a women's cooperative. In between torrential rain showers, these bickering friends joke, quarrel, cook and consume meals, drink lots of booze, swim naked in the nearby lake—and wait for the baby that never seems to arrive. And then Clare starts to have second thoughts about whether she will relinquish the child after it's born.

Jackie McKimmie's second feature, after some acclaimed shorts, is an engaging ensemble piece permeated with a strong dose of feminism. The opening scene shows Hazlehurst, who was genuinely pregnant during filming, emerging naked from the lake where she swims every day, and this sets the scene for a frank and very Aussie movie about friendship, rivalry, sexual politics and infidelity.

Clare is an artist whose paintings cover the walls of the rather dilapidated shack in which she lives. She has just won a competition to study in Paris, and she can't wait to fulfil her obligation as surrogate to Michael and Sandy and hand over the baby as soon as it's born. She also misses her ex-lover, Steve (Matthew Fargher), who has abruptly left her. Clare is bohemian and at the same time very practical. Not so her friends. Terry is obsessed with shooting a film it's doubtful many people will see (her aim, she says, is to 'make the birth of a child into a work of art'), while her daughter Rosie seems to have more common sense than her mother, as well as most of the other adults. Sandy is a compulsive mother—not content with adopting two boys, she yearns for the baby she's unable to have herself. It was her suggestion that Michael have sex with Clare to get her pregnant, and she's just discovered that he also had sex with Diane, even though Michael is hardly anyone's idea of a great lover. As for Diane, she's unable to be without a man for any period of time, and even flirts with the local cop when Rosie and one of the boys get into trouble. Furness has some of the best lines ('I need a valium to get my legs waxed') and delivers them with aplomb.

McKimmie keeps the pace of the movie barrelling along as the sudden influx of all these people turns Clare's little house into chaos. Steve Mason's photography makes the most of the cluttered interiors, and the breathtakingly beautiful landscape outside; the film was shot around Cessnock in New South Wales. The soundtrack is augmented with various different renditions of 'Que Sera, Sera', the song Doris Day made famous in Hitchcock's *The Man Who Knew Too Much* (1955).

Waiting is a quietly enjoyable film, but it performed only modestly at the box office, and has since virtually disappeared from view. To date McKimmie has only made one more feature film, *Gino*, in 1993.

96

Walk the Talk

(AUSTRALIA, 2000)

Jan Chapman Productions. DIRECTOR/SCRIPT: Shirley Barrett. ACTORS: Salvatore Coco, Sacha Horler, Nikki Bennett, Carter Edwards, Robert Coleby, Skye Wansey, John Burgess, Jon English, Nicki Wendt, David Franklin, Bille Brown. 111 MINS.

The Gold Coast, Queensland. Joey Grasso (Salvatore Coco) is a naive, eager hustler who lives off his long-suffering girlfriend, Bonita (Sacha Horler), and the $1 million she has recently received in compensation for an accident that left her a paraplegic. Joey attends a motivational conference, where he meets Nikki Raye (Nikki Bennett), a single mum and would-be singer, who is possessed of a limited talent. Even Nikki's father (Carter Edwards), himself an entertainer who plays gigs on the Gold Coast, mocks his daughter's modest prowess as a singer. Undaunted, Joey forms a talent agency and 'employs' Bonita as his 'girl Friday', with Nikki as his sole client. Despite all Joey's efforts, only one gig eventuates—a Thursday lunchtime performance at a bowling club, which comes to an abrupt conclusion when an elderly bowler expires during Nikki's number. Undeterred, Joey conceives a wild idea to obtain publicity for Nikki: he fakes her kidnapping, which certainly attracts publicity, though the end results aren't what anyone anticipated.

Like the characters in Shirley Barrett's award-winning first feature, *Love Serenade* (1996), Joey is an eccentric who isn't aware of his own eccentricities. On the contrary, he considers himself to be just an ordinary person. He's ambitious and he won't take no for an answer, but he's incapable of seeing himself as others see him—as a hopeless loser with a pushy streak. Salvatore Coco is terrific in this role, and *Walk the Talk* is an incisively scripted satire whose themes include the fleetingness of fame and the credulity of the public. The Gold Coast locations, photographed by Mandy

Walker in pastel shades, are seen here as a world of mediocrity: tacky restaurants serving bad food, second-rate clubs and entertainment provided by third-rate performers. But this is home territory for Joey, who believes there's no such thing as a failure, and who is pathetically confident in his own abilities as a promoter. As for Nikki, a divorced mother of two, she just wants to be famous. Nikki Bennett is, in actuality, a professional singer, and quite a talented one.

The film was entirely financed by the Hollywood company, DreamWorks—after record producer David Geffen saw and admired *Love Serenade*—but after viewing the finished product, the studio decided not to release it. It was subsequently acquired for Australian distribution by 20th Century Fox, but the box-office returns were negligible.

Some found Barrett's caustic satire mean-spirited, while others found Joey's personality unduly abrasive. In fact everything about this tough, terrific film is acutely observed and handled, and Barrett merited a better reception than she received. Alongside the strong contributions of Coco and Bennett, Sacha Horler is very fine in what could have been a thankless role, and there's a great cameo from Jon English as a record producer unimpressed with Joey's methods.

It would be ten years before Barrett, a genuinely original voice among Australian filmmakers, was able to make another film—*South Solitary*—and sadly that, too, failed to make much of an impact.

Everything about this tough, terrific film
is acutely observed and handled

97

The War Zone

(UK, 1999)

Portobello Pictures. DIRECTOR: Tim Roth. SCRIPT: Alexander Stuart, based on his novel. ACTORS: Ray Winstone, Tilda Swinton, Lara Belmont, Freddie Cunliffe, Kate Ashfield, Aisling O'Sullivan, Colin J. Farrell. 98 MINS.

The coast of Devon, southern England. A couple, known only as Mum (Tilda Swinton) and Dad (Ray Winstone), together with their two teenaged children, Jessie (Lara Belmont) and Tom (Freddie Cunliffe), have left London and moved to an isolated house near the sea. Not long after they've settled in, Dad drives Mum, who is about to give birth, and the kids to the nearest hospital in the middle of the night. The car crashes, and though none of them is badly hurt, they all suffer from abrasions. Mum gives birth to a daughter. Returning home one day, Tom peers through the bathroom window and sees Dad and Jessie sharing a bath. Jessie assures her brother that nothing untoward occurred. In a bar, Jessie meets Nick (Colin Farrell in his first major role, billed on the credits with a middle 'J'); Tom joins them for a campfire on the beach, but Jessie and Nick leave him alone when they go off to make love. Later, when searching through Jessie's personal effects, Tom finds Polaroid photos of her, naked, together with their father. Tom follows his sister to a concrete bunker, originally built during the war, on a nearby cliff-top; there he videotapes his sister having sex with her father. Later, Dad takes Jessie and Tom on a business trip to London; Jessie introduces Tom to her friend, Carol (Aisling O'Sullivan), who tries to seduce him. The baby falls ill and Tom suspects that Dad might have interfered with her.

The first, and to date the only, film directed by actor Tim Roth is a bitter, uncompromising family drama adapted from a book by Alexander Stuart. The family placed under the microscope here is certainly a troubled one, though not at first sight. Dad, who is forever on the phone talking business, seems to be a dealer in second-hand goods, and he spends most of his time at home. The reason why he and Mum decided to move to this remote part of Devon, far from London, is never explained—though there are hints aplenty. Tom, through whose angry eyes we witness the unfolding drama, is troubled with acne and teenage angst; Jessie seems far more mature and relaxed. Oddly, nudity seems to be the norm in this family—Dad walks around the house naked at night, while on more than one occasion Tom visits Jessie in her bedroom as she lies, naked, on top of the bed.

When Tom first claims to see Jessie and Dad sharing a bath, we have only his word for it—and the film is open to the interpretation that his fevered adolescent imagination might have led him to conjure up such a shocking image. But later events confirm his first traumatic discovery, and the scene in which Dad has sex with Jessie is harrowing to say the least.

This is all very grim, but elevated by the exceptional performances. Winstone as the bluff, charismatic Dad; Swinton as the strangely innocent mother; and Belmont and Cunliffe as the siblings who are concealing shocking secrets—all of them are excellent. Farrell makes a considerable impression in his brief role. Also impressive is the classically styled widescreen photography by Seamus McGarvey.

No doubt the subject matter kept audiences away from this chilling depiction of family life, and perhaps the film's box-office failure explains why Roth, who claimed Ingmar Bergman among the filmmakers who influenced him, hasn't attempted to direct again. Which is a pity because every frame of *The War Zone*, confronting as it is, is indicative of a filmmaker of talent.

98

Warm Nights on a Slow Moving Train

(AUSTRALIA, 1987)

Western Pacific Films. DIRECTOR: Bob Ellis. SCRIPT: Bob Ellis, Denny Lawrence. ACTORS: Wendy Hughes, Colin Friels, Norman Kaye, John Clayton, Rod Zuanic, Lewis Fitz-Gerald, Steve J. Spears, Grant Tilly, Peter Whitford, Chris Haywood, John Flaus, Peter Carmody. 91 MINS.

A young woman (Wendy Hughes), who is never named, teaches art at a Catholic school in Melbourne and cares for her crippled brother Brian, (Lewis Fitz-Gerald), a former athlete. She also has a secret life. Every weekend she travels to Sydney on the *Southern Aurora* train, and has arranged with a steward (Peter Whitford) to allow her to occupy the Judy Garland suite. On each journey she solicits one of the male passengers, adapting her style and personality—and a variety of wigs—so as to attract the type of man she targets. The first client we see her with is a football coach and famous sports writer, who has recently been sacked (John Clayton). On the next journey she meets a young soldier (Rod Zuanic). Then there is a retired travelling salesman (Norman Kaye), recently widowed, and also a recent convert to Christianity. Each of these men have to pay for the woman's services ($250 is the top price), and all of them have to leave her bed at 3 a.m., with the woman threatening to call the guard if they refuse. One night she is approached by a man (Colin Friels) who apparently works for the government. She falls in love with him, and he persuades her to solicit a visiting politician (Grant Tilly) and then to assassinate him.

Bob Ellis (1942–2016) was an Australian original—a witty, waspish gadfly who gained fame, and notoriety, as a political speechwriter, satirist, playwright, screenwriter and the director of three fascinating feature films, the other two being *Unfinished Business* (1985) and *The Nostradamus Kid* (1992). The wonderfully titled *Warm Nights on a Slow Moving Train*, which he scripted in

194

collaboration with Denny Lawrence, was a troubled production with which Ellis was not entirely happy. He quarrelled with one of his producers, Ross Dimsey, who, he claimed, reduced his 130-minute running time by almost 40 minutes, and he wasn't entirely happy with the casting of Wendy Hughes ('She was a joy to work with, but she wasn't right for the role,' he complained soon after the film was released).

Setting all this aside, however, there's a vast amount to enjoy in this cheeky, very original film. Hughes, despite the director's misgivings, gives a magnificent performance, one of her best, as the chameleon-like protagonist. There are wonderful performances, too, from one of Paul Cox's favourite actors, Norman Kaye, as the weary retired commercial traveller, and from the always impressive John Clayton as the broken-down sports writer. ('There's a Dostoyevskian novel to be written about football politics,' he tells her, solemnly.)

It's intriguing to see the ways in which the woman reacts to the very different men who become her clients on these long journeys through the night ('If you listen and look you know what they want,' she says), and most of the film is wittily written and immensely enjoyable. It becomes more serious with the intriguing final section involving Colin Friels as an ASIO agent, and Grant Tilly as a politician who might well have been based on the then-Prime Minister of New Zealand, David Lange.

It's a sad fact that few Australian films return the cost of production at the box office, and *Warm Nights* was no exception. Despite the efforts made by Dimsey to make the film more obviously exploitable, it quickly dropped out of sight and it was a struggle for Ellis to raise the money to make his third and, as it transpired, final film.

99

We Don't Live Here Anymore

(USA, 2004)

Front Street Pictures. DIRECTOR: John Curran. SCRIPT: Larry Gross, from stories by Andre Dubus. ACTORS: Mark Ruffalo, Laura Dern, Naomi Watts, Peter Krause, Sam Charles, Haili Page, Jennifer Bishop, Marc Baur. 99 MINS.

A small town in New England, America. The Lindens and the Evans are close friends. Jack Linden (Mark Ruffalo) and Hank Evans (Peter Krause) both teach at the local college, while their wives, Terry Linden (Laura Dern) and Edith Evans (Naomi Watts), care for their children. Jack and Edith are having a secret affair. While he claims to be at work and she says she's out shopping, they meet in a forest or in a motel to have sex. Terry becomes suspicious that Jack is being unfaithful to her and starts an affair with Hank. The truth comes out in a series of confrontations.

This low-budget project was co-produced by Naomi Watts and Mark Ruffalo, and directed by John Curran who, six years earlier, had made the remarkably intense *Praise* in Australia (with Sacha Horler, Joel Edgerton and Marta Dusseldorp). The screenplay by Larry Gross is based on two short stories—'Adultery' and 'We Don't Live Here Anymore', written by Andre Dubus in the 1970s, and in form the movie is a cross between *Who's Afraid of Virginia Woolf?* and *Bob & Carol & Ted & Alice*, though it lacks the humour of the latter. Curran has said that he wanted this drama of infidelity to unfold in a timeless period, which explains why there are no mobile phones in evidence—though Hank works on a laptop computer.

'Even adultery has morality to it,' says Terry at one point; Hank remarks that 'it's much easier living with a woman who feels loved', in reference to his wife's apparent contentment with the status quo, living with him and at the same time having regular, very satisfying, sex with his best friend. The challenge here is to make these affluent but irresponsible people sympathetic, and this Curran achieves through the casting. Watts, an actor of exceptional sensitivity, has rarely been better than she is here, playing a woman who is able to keep her trysts a secret with apparent success—at least until the end. On the other hand Laura Dern's flaky, uncertain Terry is Edith's opposite; her feelings are not to be concealed. And Mark Ruffalo's Jack is also a complex character, barely able to control his lust for Edith, while at the same time attempting to keep his family together ('It's a sublimely happy marriage,' he remarks at one point).

The children—played by Sam Charles and Haili Page as Sean and Natasha Linden, and by Jennifer Bishop as Sharon Evans—are all around the same age, ten or thereabouts. When the film begins we're barely aware they exist, apart from some distant voices drowned out by the quarrels and confrontations of their parents. But soon they make their presences felt and we realise that they're probably more aware of what's happening than their parents are willing to admit. In two tense sequences it seems that one of the parents—a different parent on each occasion—will seek to end the impasse in murder/suicide; in the first such scene nothing happens, but the second is left open for audience interpretation.

We Don't Live Here Anymore is beautifully realised by Curran, with some creative editing that cuts back and forth between the families, and a firm appreciation that the character of the women is reflected in their homes—the Linden house is cluttered and panelled with dark wood, while the Evans home is bright and clean with white walls and everything in its place.

But despite the superb performances and the honest approach to its subject matter, this intense domestic drama failed to spark much interest in audiences.

. . . a drama of infidelity

The Well

(AUSTRALIA, 1997)

Southern Star Xanadu. DIRECTOR: Samantha Lang. SCRIPT: Laura Jones, from the novel by Elizabeth Jolley. ACTORS: Pamela Rabe, Miranda Otto, Paul Chubb, Frank Wilson, Steve Jacobs, Geneviève Lemon. 98 MINS.

The Snowy Mountains region of New South Wales. Hester (Pamela Rabe), who lives in a grand house on an isolated, rundown property with her elderly father, Francis (Frank Wilson), hires Katherine (Miranda Otto), a rather wild young woman, as a live-in servant. Finding the work too hard, Katherine soon announces she's leaving, but Hester begs her to stay and promises to give her much less work to do. They begin to share an increasingly warm relationship. Francis dies suddenly, and Hester, spurred on by Katherine, decides to sell the house—for cash—and move into a small cottage elsewhere on the property. The women plan to visit Europe and America but, one night after a dance in town, Katherine is driving home recklessly when she hits a man walking on the road. Frightened of the repercussions (Katherine was drunk), Hester decides to conceal the body at the bottom of the abandoned well near the cottage. Only after the body has been disposed of do the women discover they've been robbed, and all their cash stolen—was the dead man the thief, and, if so, is all their money at the bottom of the well?

Samantha Lang's first feature, made when she was 29, is essentially a two-hander in which a pair of accomplished actors play out a creepy tale of loneliness, frustration, mutual dependence, suppressed sexual longing, and madness. After a sedate opening, in which the characters are vividly introduced ('She's for me,' proclaims Hester, when her father queries the presence of Katherine), the film then delves into this strange relationship in which the repressed Hester and the wild, hedonistic Katherine become closer and closer. After the disposal of the body of the unknown man in the well, the film edges towards the horror genre without quite going that far: Katherine hears the man speak and is convinced he's in love with her, while Hester becomes increasingly distraught.

Cinematographer Mandy Walker films this intense drama in drab colours—blues, greys, greens—that emphasise the isolation and loneliness of these women, and the beautiful but bleak landscape in which they live (the film was shot around Nimmitabel near the Snowy Mountains). Lang emphasises the duality of the drama. Apart from the presence of these two contrasted women, some scenes unfold twice. One example of this is the sequence that takes place at the town dance, where Katherine gyrates wildly while Hester watches her; also repeated is the fateful drive home after the dance, and there are also two versions of the scene in which Katherine leaves the property and walks out onto the road, heading nowhere.

Rabe brilliantly conveys a lifetime's inhibition and isolation as Hester's narrow world is literally rocked by the presence of the beautiful, energetic, wilful Katherine. Otto as the thoughtless, selfish young girl matches her all the way. Paul Chubb has a small but important role as the family's business manager who becomes frustrated with Hester's strange behaviour.

The film was selected to compete at the Cannes Film Festival in 1997, a singular honour for a movie by an unknown, first-time director. Sadly it was not as well received as had been hoped, and nor did it perform very well at the Australian box office. It disappeared from view until a restored copy screened at the 2017 Sydney Film Festival. Lang has only made two films since: *The Monkey's Mask* (2000) and, in France, *L'idole* (2002).

Wrong is Right

(USA, 1982)

Columbia Pictures-Rastar Productions. DIRECTOR/SCRIPT: Richard Brooks, from a novel by Charles McCarry. ACTORS: Sean Connery, George Grizzard, Katharine Ross, Robert Conrad, Leslie Nielsen, G.D. Spradlin, John Saxon, Henry Silva, Robert Webber, Rosalind Cash, Hardy Krüger, Dean Stockwell, Ron Moody, Cherie Michan, Jennifer Jason Leigh. 118 MINS.

Patrick Hale (Sean Connery) is a top news reporter for WTN, currently on assignment in the Middle East, where his mission is to interview King Awad (Ron Moody) about an oil deal. Meanwhile, freelance journalist Sally Blake (Katharine Ross) is following a story involving a shady arms dealer, Helmut Unger (Hardy Krüger), who is offering to sell two nuclear bombs to radical Arab leader Rafeeq (Henry Silva). Sally is killed by a bomb while talking to an Israeli agent, and King Awad dies suddenly, an apparent suicide, but actually at the hands of the CIA on direct orders from President Lockwood (George Grizzard), who is in the middle of a presidential campaign against Mallory (Leslie Nielsen), a strong opponent. A series of suicide bombings on American streets rock the nation and Rafeeq, who claims to have acquired the nuclear bombs, threatens to destroy New York unless President Lockwood resigns.

Charles McCarry's 1979 book, *The Better Angels*, and Richard Brooks' startling screen adaptation of it, were attacked and ridiculed in 1982, but now seem incredibly prescient. *Wrong is Right* predicts not only the presence of suicide bombers, including women, causing death and destruction on the streets of Western cities, but also the invasion of Iraq. Newspaper headlines reading 'War at Last' and 'Peace Through War' are not as fanciful today as they were 36 years ago, and nor is the scene in which the boss of a TV network tells a military officer, 'Before you take the oil wells, remember there's a three-minute commercial break'; 'If it's good for America it can't be wrong,' intones the CIA Chief (G.D. Spradlin), as the cowardly president orders the assassination of an Arab leader while worrying that his office is being bugged (it is). The film is extremely ambitious, setting up a truly disturbing situation in the first half and then undercutting it with brutal satire in the second. It's not quite *Dr. Strangelove*, but it's in the same ballpark.

The film's targets are many, including the entire political system (nobody can be trusted) and the media. Brooks was a journalist before he became a film director, and his distinguished career includes the films *Blackboard Jungle* (1955), *Elmer Gantry* (1960), *In Cold Blood* (1967) and *Deadline—U.S.A.* (1952). The military also comes in for some savage criticism, via the character of General Wombat (Robert Conrad), the President's chief military adviser. And then there's the generation gap: a very young Jennifer Jason Leigh appears as a girl who hates her parents so much she would happily pay to have them eliminated.

In the midst of all this is Sean Connery's TV journalist, Hale, a public figure so popular he can sit at the table with the President and his aides ('Call this journalism? We're in show business!'). While his boss (Robert Webber) is thrilled that he's getting $300,000 for each commercial break, Hale blithely uses his TV program to influence the country's foreign policy, only to find he himself has been used by the CIA and was unwittingly responsible for the death of the Arab King.

Brooks took plenty of risks with this film, not least killing off the popular Katharine Ross early in the movie. But his bitter view of contemporary America is filled with home truths: the leader of the terrorists queries the meaning of the word 'terrorism'—does it, he demands, describe the French in Algeria? Hitler against the Jews? The Jews against us? It was a bitter pill for audiences to swallow under the guise of entertainment. The situations don't seem so improbable and ridiculous now, and *Wrong is Right* is another forgotten and overlooked film worthy of serious reconsideration.

Note to readers

Most of the movies listed in this book are available from mainstream subscription streaming sites like Netflix, iTunes, Amazon Prime Video, Google Play and Stan. Some are only available in VHS or DVD format, and some may only be available second hand or from libraries. Below are details of where each movie can be obtained at the time the book went to print, but this can change, and you may find you need to search online. Useful websites are listed below for different countries.

Note that if you intend to purchase a DVD from an international retailer, you need to check first whether you can play it on your own device. Key regions are:

Region 1: United States, US Territories, Canada and Bermuda
Region 2: Japan, Europe, South Africa and the Middle East, including Egypt
Region 3: Southeast Asia and East Asia, including Hong Kong
Region 4: Australia, New Zealand, Pacific Islands, Central America, South America and the Caribbean

A Region 0 DVD should be playable worldwide. A 'universal' DVD player should be able to play a DVD from any region. If you do not have a universal DVD player, be sure to check the region code of the DVD you plan to purchase.

Useful websites

For Australian readers
www.justwatch.com/au—index of movies available from a large number of streaming sites in Australia

arovideo.co.nz—a New Zealand-based movie retailer and rental service that ships within New Zealand and to Australia

www.thedvdhut.com

www.dvdland.com.au

filmclub.com.au—a Sydney-based rental service and DVD store that will mail DVDs within Australia and supply specialist orders from overseas

fishpond.com.au—an online store with extensive DVD listings, though not all are for region 4

www.jbhifi.com.au

raremovies.biz

www.sanity.com.au

trove.nla.gov.au—a National Library of Australia catalogue which lists movies in libraries around Australia that can be borrowed through interlibrary loan

---

For New Zealand readers

www.justwatch.com/nz—index of movies available from a large number of streaming sites in New Zealand

arovideo.co.nz—a New Zealand based movie retailer and rental service

fishpond.co.nz—an online store with extensive DVD listings, though not all are for region 4

For United States readers

www.justwatch.com—index of movies available from a large number of streaming sites in the United States

---

For United Kingdom readers

www.justwatch.com/uk—index of movies available from a large number of streaming sites in the United Kingdom

Where you can find the movies

Details of some of the streaming sites, online DVD retailers, DVD rental services and libraries from which the movies in this book can be obtained. The information was correct at the time this book went to print.

1. **Affliction (1997)** — DIRECTOR: Paul Schrader
   AVAILABLE FROM: Amazon Australia, DVDLand (region 4)

2. **After Dark, My Sweet (1990)** — DIRECTOR: James Foley
   AVAILABLE FROM: Amazon Australia, iTunes

3. **Agora (2009)** — DIRECTOR: Alejandro Amenábar
   AVAILABLE FROM: Amazon Australia, iTunes, JB Hi-Fi, Sanity

4. **Apartment Zero (1988)** — DIRECTOR: Martin Donovan
   AVAILABLE FROM: arovideo.co.nz

5. **At Close Range (1985)** — DIRECTOR: James Foley
   AVAILABLE FROM: iTunes, Stan, Google Play

6. **An Awfully Big Adventure (1994)** — DIRECTOR: Mike Newell
   AVAILABLE FROM: Film Club (region 4), Fishpond (Hugh Grant box set collection, region 1), raremovies.biz

7. **Bad Blood (1981)** — DIRECTOR: Mike Newell
   AVAILABLE FROM: arovideo.co.nz, Film Club (region 4), Trove (https://trove.nla.gov.au/version/220405391)

8. **Bad Influence (1990)** — DIRECTOR: Curtis Hanson
   AVAILABLE FROM: Amazon Australia, Stan

9. **Beyond Rangoon (1995)** — DIRECTOR: John Boorman
   AVAILABLE FROM: iTunes

10. **Beyond the Sea (2004)** — DIRECTOR: Kevin Spacey
    AVAILABLE FROM: Amazon Australia, arovideo.co.nz, Film Club (region 4), Fishpond (regions 1 and 2), Trove (https://trove.nla.gov.au/version/191666699)

11. **Billy Lynn's Long Halftime Walk (2016)** — DIRECTOR: Ang Lee
    AVAILABLE FROM: Amazon Australia, Foxtel, iTunes, JB Hi-Fi

12. **The Birth of a Nation (2016)** — DIRECTOR: Nate Parker
    AVAILABLE FROM: Amazon Australia, Foxtel, iTunes, JB Hi-Fi

13. **Blessed (2009)** DIRECTOR: Ana Kokkinos
    AVAILABLE FROM: Amazon Australia, iTunes, JB Hi-Fi

14. **Bobby (2006)** DIRECTOR: Emilio Estevez
    AVAILABLE FROM: arovideo.co.nz, Film Club (region 4), Fishpond
    (region 4), Trove (https://trove.nla.gov.au/work/32584863)

15. **Broken (2012)** DIRECTOR: Rufus Norris
    AVAILABLE FROM: Amazon Australia, iTunes

16. **A Bronx Tale (1993)** DIRECTOR: Robert De Niro
    AVAILABLE FROM: Amazon, JB Hi-Fi

17. **Buffalo Soldiers (2001)** DIRECTOR: Gregor Jordan
    AVAILABLE FROM: Amazon Australia, JB Hi-Fi

18. **Bullseye (1986)** DIRECTOR: Carl Schultz
    AVAILABLE FROM: arovideo.co.nz

19. **Bulworth (1998)** DIRECTOR: Warren Beatty
    AVAILABLE FROM: Amazon Australia, iTunes, JB Hi-Fi

20. **Burke & Wills (1985)** DIRECTOR: Graeme Clifford
    AVAILABLE FROM: Angus & Robertson ebay store, arovideo.co.nz, Film Club (region 4)

21. **Citizen Ruth (1996)** DIRECTOR: Alexander Payne
    AVAILABLE FROM: arovideo.co.nz (VHS), Film Club

22. **The Clinic (1982)** DIRECTOR: David Stevens
    Available to view at the National Film and Sound Archive access centre
    in each Australian state: access@nfsa.gov.au (NFSA reference # 8892)

23. **Close My Eyes (1990)** DIRECTOR: Stephen Poliakoff
    AVAILABLE FROM: Amazon Australia

24. **Cradle Will Rock (1999)** DIRECTOR: Tim Robbins
    AVAILABLE FROM: arovideo.co.nz (VHS), Film Club

25. **The Crossing Guard (1995)** DIRECTOR: Sean Penn
    AVAILABLE FROM: Amazon Australia, Fishpond (region 4)

26. **The Custodian (1993)** DIRECTOR: John Dingwall
    AVAILABLE FROM: Film Club (region 4)

27. **Daniel (1983)** DIRECTOR: Sidney Lumet
    AVAILABLE FROM: Film Club

28. **The Deep Blue Sea (2011)** DIRECTOR: Terence Davies
    AVAILABLE FROM: Amazon Australia, iTunes

29. **Devil in the Flesh (1985)** DIRECTOR: Scott Murray
    Available to view at the National Film and Sound Archive access centre
    in each Australian state: access@nfsa.gov.au (NFSA reference # 266894)

30. Enemy (2013)   DIRECTOR: Denis Villeneuve
    AVAILABLE FROM: Amazon Australia, Google Play, iTunes, Netflix

31. Everybody Wins (1990)   DIRECTOR: Karel Reisz
    AVAILABLE FROM: Film Club (takes 2–3 months to import)

32. Family Business (1989)   DIRECTOR: Sidney Lumet
    AVAILABLE FROM: iTunes

33. Father (1990)   DIRECTOR: John Power
    Available to view at the National Film and Sound Archive access centre
    in each Australian state: access@nfsa.gov.au (NFSA reference # 57142)

34. The Favour, the Watch and the Very Big Fish (1991)   DIRECTOR: Ben Lewin
    AVAILABLE FROM: arovideo.co.nz

35. Finders Keepers (1984)   DIRECTOR: Richard Lester
    AVAILABLE FROM: Amazon Australia, arovideo.co.nz (region 1),
    Film Club (takes 2–3 months to import)

36. Following (1999)   DIRECTOR: Christopher Nolan
    AVAILABLE FROM: DVD Hut, Film Club (takes 2–3 months to import),
    Fishpond (region 2)

37. Force of Destiny (2014)   DIRECTOR: Paul Cox
    AVAILABLE FROM: Amazon Australia, Google Play, iTunes, JB Hi-Fi, Stan

38. Garage Days (2002)   DIRECTOR: Alex Proyas
    AVAILABLE FROM: Amazon Australia, iTunes

39. Ginger & Rosa (2012)   DIRECTOR: Sally Potter
    AVAILABLE FROM: Amazon Australia, Google Play, iTunes, JB Hi-Fi

40. The Glass Shield (1994)   DIRECTOR: Charles Burnett
    AVAILABLE FROM: Amazon Australia

41. Goya's Ghosts (2006)   DIRECTOR: Miloš Forman
    AVAILABLE FROM: Amazon Australia

42. Grace is Gone (2007)   DIRECTOR: James C. Strouse
    AVAILABLE FROM: Amazon Australia, JB Hi-Fi

43. Hero (1992)   DIRECTOR: Stephen Frears
    AVAILABLE FROM: JB Hi-Fi, Netflix

44. Honkytonk Man (1982)   DIRECTOR: Clint Eastwood
    AVAILABLE FROM: iTunes

45. Housekeeping (1987)   DIRECTOR: Bill Forsyth
    AVAILABLE FROM: Amazon Australia, Google Play, iTunes

46. How I Live Now (2013)   DIRECTOR: Kevin Macdonald
    AVAILABLE FROM: Amazon Australia, JB Hi-Fi, Stan

47. **Impulse (1989)**
DIRECTOR: Sondra Locke
AVAILABLE FROM: Film Club (takes 2–3 months to import)

48. **In the Bleak Midwinter (1995)**
DIRECTOR: Kenneth Branagh
Alternative title: *A Midwinter's Tale*
AVAILABLE FROM: arovideo.co.nz, Film Club (region 4)

49. **In the Electric Mist (2008)**
DIRECTOR: Bertrand Tavernier
AVAILABLE FROM: Amazon Australia, iTunes

50. **In the Land of Blood and Honey** (*U zemlji krvi i meda*) **(2011)**
DIRECTOR: Angelina Jolie
AVAILABLE FROM: Amazon Australia, Film Club (region 4)

51. **In This World (2002)**
DIRECTOR: Michael Winterbottom
AVAILABLE FROM: iTunes

52. **The Journey (2016)**
DIRECTOR: Nick Hamm
AVAILABLE FROM: Amazon Australia, arovideo.co.nz, Film Club (region 4),
Fishpond (regions 1 and 2)

53. **King of the Hill (1993)**
DIRECTOR: Steven Soderbergh
AVAILABLE FROM: arovideo.co.nz, Film Club (region 4)

54. **Little Dorrit (1987)**
DIRECTOR: Christine Edzard
AVAILABLE FROM: arovideo.co.nz, Film Club (takes 2–3 months to import)

55. **Love at Large (1990)**
DIRECTOR: Alan Rudolph
AVAILABLE FROM: Amazon Australia, Fishpond (region 4)

56. **Love's Labour's Lost (1999)**
DIRECTOR: Kenneth Branagh
AVAILABLE FROM: arovideo.co.nz

57. **Mad City (1997)**
DIRECTOR: Costa-Gavras
AVAILABLE FROM: iTunes

58. **The Meyerowitz Stories (New and Selected) (2017)**
DIRECTOR: Noah Baumbach
AVAILABLE FROM: Netflix

59. **Mike's Murder (1984)**
DIRECTOR: James Bridges
AVAILABLE FROM: Film Club (takes 2–3 months to import), Fishpond (region 1)

60. **Mississippi Grind (2014)**
Directors: Anna Boden, Ryan Fleck
AVAILABLE FROM: iTunes, Stan

61. **Molokai: The story of Father Damien (1999)**
DIRECTOR: Paul Cox
AVAILABLE FROM: Film Club (takes 2–3 months to import), Fishpond (regions 1 and 2)

62. **Moonlight Mile (2002)**
DIRECTOR: Brad Silberling
AVAILABLE FROM: iTunes

63. **The More Things Change . . . (1985)**
DIRECTOR: Robyn Nevin
AVAILABLE FROM: Film Club (region 4)

64. **Mullet (2000)**
DIRECTOR: David Caesar
AVAILABLE FROM: arovideo.co.nz, Film Club (region 4), Fishpond (regions 1 and 2)

65. **Ned Kelly (2003)**   DIRECTOR: Gregor Jordan
    AVAILABLE FROM: DVDLand, Foxtel, Fishpond, iTunes

66. **Nobody's Fool (1994)**   DIRECTOR: Robert Benton
    AVAILABLE FROM: Film Club (region 4)

67. **The Old Man Who Read Love Stories (2000)** DIRECTOR: Rolf de Heer
    AVAILABLE FROM: arovideo.co.nz (region 4), Film Club (region 4), Fishpond

68. **Open Range (2003)**   DIRECTOR: Kevin Costner
    AVAILABLE FROM: Stan

69. **Out of the Blue (1980)**   DIRECTOR: Dennis Hopper
    AVAILABLE FROM: arovideo.co.nz, Film Club (region 4)

70. **Pawno (2015)**   DIRECTOR: Paul Ireland
    AVAILABLE FROM: iTunes, Stan

71. **The Pledge (2000)**   DIRECTOR: Sean Penn
    AVAILABLE FROM: Stan

72. **Power (1986)**   DIRECTOR: Sidney Lumet
    AVAILABLE FROM: iTunes

73. **Queen & Country (2014)**   DIRECTOR: John Boorman
    AVAILABLE FROM: iTunes

74. **Rendition (2007)**   DIRECTOR: Gavin Hood
    AVAILABLE FROM: Google Play, JB Hi-Fi, Stan

75. **Return Home (1989)**   DIRECTOR: Ray Argall
    AVAILABLE FROM: arovideo.co.nz, Film Club (region 4)

76. **Reunion (1989)**   DIRECTOR: Jerry Schatzberg
    AVAILABLE FROM: Amazon UK (regions 1 and 2)

77. **Ride with the Devil (1999)**   DIRECTOR: Ang Lee
    AVAILABLE FROM: Film Club (region 4), Fishpond (regions 1 and 2)

78. **River of Grass (1995)**   DIRECTOR: Kelly Reichardt
    AVAILABLE FROM: Film Club (rent only, region 4)

79. **Road to Nhill (1997)**   DIRECTOR: Sue Brooks
    AVAILABLE FROM: Film Club (region 4)

80. **Romance & Cigarettes (2005)**   DIRECTOR: John Turturro
    AVAILABLE FROM: iTunes, Stan

81. **Running on Empty (1988)**   DIRECTOR: Sidney Lumet
    AVAILABLE FROM: iTunes

82. **The Search (2014)**   DIRECTOR: Michel Hazanavicius
    AVAILABLE FROM: Trove (https://trove.nla.gov.au/version/253230917)

83. **The Sessions (2012)**   DIRECTOR: Ben Lewin
    AVAILABLE FROM: iTunes, JB Hi-Fi

84. **She's Funny That Way (2014)**
    DIRECTOR: Peter Bogdanovich
    AVAILABLE FROM: arovideo.co.nz, Film Club (region 4)

85. **S1m0ne (2002)**
    DIRECTOR: Andrew Niccol
    AVAILABLE FROM: arovideo.co.nz, Film Club (region 4)

86. **The Straight Story (1999)**
    DIRECTOR: David Lynch
    AVAILABLE FROM: arovideo.co.nz, Film Club (region 4)

87. **Sunshine on Leith (2013)**
    DIRECTOR: Dexter Fletcher
    AVAILABLE FROM: iTunes, JB Hi-Fi

88. **Taking Sides (2001)**
    DIRECTOR: István Szabó
    AVAILABLE FROM: arovideo.co.nz, Film Club (region 4)

89. **The Three Burials of Melquiades Estrada (2005)**
    DIRECTOR: Tommy Lee Jones
    AVAILABLE FROM: Google Play, iTunes

90. **Timecode (2000)**
    DIRECTOR: Mike Figgis
    AVAILABLE FROM: iTunes

91. **Truth (2015)**
    DIRECTOR: James Vanderbilt
    AVAILABLE FROM: iTunes, Stan

92. **25th Hour (2002)**
    DIRECTOR: Spike Lee
    AVAILABLE FROM: iTunes, Google Play, Stan

93. **Until the End of the World (*Bis ans Ende der Welt*) (1991)**
    DIRECTOR: Wim Wenders
    AVAILABLE FROM: Netflix

94. **Valmont (1989)**
    DIRECTOR: Miloš Forman
    AVAILABLE FROM: arovideo.co.nz, Film Club (region 4), Fishpond

95. **Waiting (1990)**
    DIRECTOR: Jackie McKimmie
    AVAILABLE FROM: arovideo.co.nz

96. **Walk the Talk (2000)**
    DIRECTOR: Shirley Barrett
    AVAILABLE FROM: arovideo.co.nz

97. **The War Zone (1999)**
    DIRECTOR: Tim Roth
    AVAILABLE FROM: Film Club (region 4)

98. **Warm Nights on a Slow Moving Train (1987)**
    DIRECTOR: Bob Ellis
    AVAILABLE FROM: Film Club (region 4), Umbrella Entertainment
    (www.umbrellaent.com.au)

99. **We Don't Live Here Anymore (2004)**
    DIRECTOR: John Curran
    AVAILABLE FROM: Film Club (region 4)

100. **The Well (1997)**
    DIRECTOR: Samantha Lang
    AVAILABLE FROM: arovideo.co.nz

101. **Wrong is Right (1982)**
    DIRECTOR: Richard Brooks
    AVAILABLE FROM: iTunes

Index